MEMOIRS
MUSEUM OF ANTHROPOLOGY, UNIVERSITY OF MICHIGAN
NO. 25

The Leavitt Site

A Parkhill Phase Paleo-Indian Occupation in Central Michigan

by
Michael J. Shott

with a foreword by Henry T. Wright

ANN ARBOR, MICHIGAN
1993

Printed in the United States of America

ISBN 0-915703-32-7

Cover design by Katherine Clahassey

The University of Michigan Museum of Anthropology currently publishes three monograph series: Anthropological Papers, Memoirs, and Technical Reports. We have over seventy titles in print. For a complete catalog, write to Museum of Anthropology Publications, 4009 Museums Building, Ann Arbor, MI 48109-1079, or call (313) 764-0485

Library of Congress Cataloging-in-Publication Data

Shott, Michael.
The Leavitt site : a Parkhill phase paleo-Indian occupation in central Michigan / Michael J. Shott ; with a foreword by Henry T. Wright.
p. cm.—(Memoirs / Museum of Anthropology, University of Michigan ; no. 25)
Includes bibliographical references.
ISBN 0-915703-32-7 (alk. paper)
1. Leavitt Site (Mich.) 2. Paleo-Indians—Michigan—Clinton County. 3. Stone implements—Michigan—Clinton County. 4. Clinton County (Mich.)—Antiquities. I. Title. II. Series: Memoirs of the Museum of Anthropology, University of Michigan ; no. 25.
GN2.M5s no. 25
[E78.M6]
306 s—dc20 92-42187
[977.4'24] CIP

The paper used in this publication meets the requirements of ANSI Standard Z39.48-1984 (Permanence of Paper)

Contents

Tables

Figures

Foreword

Henry T. Wright
University of Michigan

Recently, the Museum of Anthropology has made two major contributions to the study of the first colonists in the Great Lakes region. In 1992 we published as our Memoir No. 24 a monograph entitled *Thedford II: A Paleo-Indian Site in the Ausable Watershed of Southwestern Ontario,* by D. Brian Deller and Christopher J. Ellis. This was the first full site report on a campsite of the Parkhill phase, the material manifestation of a people who established themselves in what is now southwestern Ontario and southern Michigan about 11,000 years ago. We now present a second monograph on a related site in lower Michigan, by Michael Shott.

What we term the Leavitt site was long known to members of the Leavitt family as one of the places on their farm where chipped stone tools could be found. Unbeknownst to other members of the family, Mildred Leavitt Malkin had found several Paleo-Indian tools on the site decades ago. In 1973, her sister, Elsie Leavitt Moore, went out with her grandson Peter Sanford "to find a fluted point." Imagine the surprise of Peter's mother, Donna Hebert, when he returned with a magnificent complete fluted biface (Fig. 6.4c). The site came to my attention in 1977 when Mrs. Hebert brought their collection to the Museum of Anthropology. The subsequent events and the narrative of his own exemplary excavation and analysis are recounted by Michael Shott in the following pages.

Throughout the successive years of fieldwork and analysis, the Leavitt project has profited from frequent contact with our Canadian colleagues working on manifestations of the same culture in nearby Ontario. Originally, it was intended that we publish the two monographs in a single volume, but circumstances prevented that. Nonetheless, the reader will note frequent cross-referencing between the two volumes, a testimony to the close communication which has stimulated all of us in our efforts to understand the earliest occupants of the Great Lakes region.

This monograph has a number of strengths, some of them innovations in the area of forager archaeology in general, and Paleo-Indian studies in particular.

—Every well-preserved retouched tool, rather than merely a selected sample, is described, and detailed measurements are presented. Most are illustrated at life size. Unit by unit, aggregate statistics are given for the debitage. The reader should be able to use these data to evaluate a wide range of propositions other than those considered here.

—Rather than forcing all the chipped stone items into a single unified reduction sequence, or *chaine operatoire,* Shott argues conservatively for three discrete reduction sequences for Bayport chert—nodule/block core reduction, biface core reduction, and biface reduction per se—and leaves their integration to a future time when samples are available from sites where the primary working of nodules was common.

—The analysis of tools made on unifacial flakes factors the variability into three classes: (1) that resulting from the original removal of the blank from its core; (2) that resulting from hafting the tool with a handle; and (3) that resulting from use and resharpening. The system of measurement he proposes is one that has evolved from principles first introduced by Wilmsen in the 1960s to meet the demands of our increasingly dynamic view of the tool-using process. Each class of measurement is targeted to answer questions about different aspects of technological organization.

—The analysis of tools made from bifaces also factors the variability resulting from (1) the production of the fluted form from its blank; (2) hafting; and (3) use and resharpening. The system of measurements he proposes is based on McCary's work in the 1950s.

—Shott has complemented conventional visual and refitting approaches to internal site structure with formal cluster analyses to demonstrate the existence of, and variability in, concentrations of stone tools. In surprising contrast to Thedford and other Great Lakes Paleo-Indian sites, the excavated Leavitt site clusters are relatively homogenous. This condition cannot be explained in terms of greater recent disturbance such as cultivation, and is therefore a likely result of activities of the early occupants during what seems to have been a relatively long stay.

As Shott emphasizes, this monograph does not exhaust the potential of the Leavitt samples and records, even for questions generated by current theoretical perspectives and available analytical techniques. For example, a microwear study that might answer questions about changing tool uses has not yet been attempted. Fortunately, through the generosity of members of the extended Leavitt family, most of the collections reside permanently in the Museum of Anthropology and will be available for reexamination.

Acknowledgments

A project of even modest scale like the Leavitt excavation and analysis owes a great debt to many individuals. It is a pleasant task upon completion to acknowledge the many colleagues who assisted along the way.

The Leavitt site was collected for a number of years by Elsie Moore and her daughter Donna Sanford. Moore and her sister, Mildred Malkin, who also has a collection from Leavitt, were born into the family whose name the site bears. By the mid-1970s, the scope of the collection made it clear to Sanford that Leavitt was an important Paleo-Indian site deserving of lengthy study. She called its attention to the University of Michigan Museum of Anthropology and encouraged the Museum to further its study of Michigan Paleo-Indian cultures by excavating the site. Museum archaeologists Doreen Ozker and Henry Wright were quick to realize the research value that Leavitt possessed. In 1978, Wright organized a brief surface collection of the site. By then, Moore and Sanford had donated their collections from Leavitt to the Museum, donations which formed an important part of the assemblage described in this report. Without Sanford's active encouragement and interest—in the long tradition of research activity and support that characterizes the Michigan Archaeological Society—there would have been no Leavitt project. Our greatest debt of thanks, therefore, is owed to her.

Thanks are due as well to John Szarka, the owner of the Leavitt site, who was a gracious host during the 1978 visit and the longer excavation in 1984. We were fortunate in having so congenial and understanding a host, and his many kindnesses are greatly appreciated.

Jerome Voss, then and now of Michigan State University, originally contemplated work at Leavitt. He cheerfully relinquished to me any claims to research at the site and offered his support during the project.

Henry Wright took the first active Museum of Anthropology role in the Leavitt project by leading the 1978 expedition to the site. He subsequently encouraged me to continue the work begun there, and offered support and guidance at all stages of analysis. Wright also prepared most of the artifact drawings that grace this report.

The 1984 excavation was funded by a grant from the National Science Foundation (BNS-8314076), support which is gratefully acknowledged. Fieldwork was carried out by an able crew consisting of Michael Adler, Margaret Danowsky, Kenichi Sasaki and Miriam Stark. Adler deserves special praise for his cheerful and unfailing efforts. George Schwartz also worked on the crew for several weeks. I owe a tremendous debt to Michael Hambacher of Michigan State University, who offered invaluable assistance on nearly a daily basis at all stages of fieldwork. We would have accomplished much less in the field without his contribution. Further assistance in excavation was rendered by a cadre of MSU archaeologists that included Philip Franz, George Galasso, Margaret Holman, Max Houk, Francis Ike, Peter Kotila, William Lovis, Dale McCririe, Virgil Noble, James Robertson and Beverly Smith. Lovis also made MSU Museum facilities available for project use. Others who volunteered their time and efforts at Leavitt include Scott Beld, C. Wesley Cowan, James Krakker and Clare McHale of the University of Michigan; Thomas Austin, Paul Foster, Eric Hellman, Robert Langdon, Donald Simons and Daniel Wymer of the Michigan Archaeological Society; and Brian Deller, Christopher Ellis and James Payne. Simons also lent us his motor home for temporary use. Keith King of Mott Community College in Flint, Michigan, laid out the site grid. My sincere thanks to all.

Selected data from Leavitt were used in my dissertation (Shott 1986a), but the detailed report that the site and its assemblage deserve was beyond the scope of that study. Preparation of this report spanned five years, positions in Michigan, Kentucky, and Iowa, and a major research and excavation project in the Ohio Valley. The manuscript was finished during a visit to Michigan in the summer of 1991, bringing the project full circle in a literal geographic sense. I would not recommend such a course of events to others seeking to finish such work in a timely manner. Nevertheless, the report would have been completed sooner had I attacked it more diligently. My original aim was to publish it jointly with Brian Deller and Christopher Ellis's monograph on the Thedford II site (1992). Their manuscript was finished by 1986 and was inexcusably delayed in publication by my failure to complete this report sooner. Deller and Ellis suffered the delay cheerfully and deserve my thanks not only for their patience and forbearance, but for their wise counsel on Paleo-Indian matters as well.

Kathryn Egan of MSU applied her considerable expertise to the analysis of Feature 4 charcoal, and contributed a report on its results that appears in this volume. Leavitt charcoal samples were dated at the University of Arizona's Laboratory of Isotope Geochemistry; thanks are due to C. Vance Haynes for facilitating that analysis. Joachim Hahn of the University of Tubingen, Germany, drafted Figure 5.12c and Kay Clahassey of the University of Michigan Museum of Anthropology produced the maps and other non-artifact figures that appear in the report. Jill Morrison, also of the Museum of Anthropology, aided the project in many ways, for which I thank her gratefully. Able editing and guidance in the production process were provided by Museum editor Sally Horvath.

Much of the analysis and writing took place at the universities of Kentucky and Northern Iowa. Thanks are due to my colleagues in both Lexington and Cedar Falls, and to the universities themselves for providing a congenial atmosphere in which to pursue my research.

Finally, I owe a great debt of gratitude to my wife, Elisabeth Bacus, for her constant support of my efforts.

CHAPTER 1

Introduction and Narrative of Investigation

Introduction

Paleo-Indian studies in the Great Lakes region have enjoyed two periods of popularity. The first occurred in the late 1950s and early 1960s, and was characterized by preliminary distributional studies concerned with chronological placement and the reconstruction of settlement patterns (Mason 1958, 1962; Quimby 1958; Roosa 1965). Then-recent geological work (Hough 1958) had erected a framework within which to establish the antiquity of humans in the Great Lakes region and to chart changing patterns of settlement. These pioneering studies provided a solid foundation for progress in subsequent years. This was realized in a modest flurry of data collection in Michigan, which culminated in landmark reports on the Barnes site in Midland County (Wright and Roosa 1966) and the Holcombe site in southeastern Michigan (Fitting et al. 1966).

The broad chronological outlines of Paleo-Indian occupation and the technological character of Paleo-Indian industries were established in this initial period. Evidence concerning subsistence practices, heretofore elusive in eastern North America, also was recovered with the discovery of caribou remains at Holcombe (Cleland 1965). But a hiatus of nearly a decade followed these efforts, until new work at Barnes (Voss 1977) signaled a renewal of interest in Great Lakes Paleo-Indian studies. A flood of studies has ensued, mostly from Ontario (summarized in Ellis and Deller 1990). In combination with important typological analyses (Wright 1981), these provide a firm grounding in data for advanced studies of Paleo-Indian cultures.

This report describes the nature and distribution of stone tools and features found at the Leavitt site (20CL81) in Clinton County, Michigan (Fig. 1.1). Leavitt is a Parkhill phase Paleo-Indian site excavated by the University of Michigan Museum of Anthropology (UMMA) in 1984 as part of its Paleo-Indian research program (Simons et al. 1984a, 1984b, 1987). One focus of that program concerned the relationship between mobility practices and the organization of technologies in Paleo-Indian forager societies (Shott 1986a).

Great Lakes Paleo-Indian Systematics

As elsewhere in eastern North America, Paleo-Indian systematics in the Great Lakes are based on typological studies of fluted bifaces. Fortunately, work here is relatively advanced (Deller and Ellis 1988; Ellis and Deller 1988; Roosa 1965; Storck 1983; Wright 1981), defining at least three major biface types: Gainey, Barnes and Crowfield. The typology is firmly established by the consistent co-occurrence of certain technological, morphological, and metrical characteristics (Deller and Ellis 1988:255). In turn, it defines three successive Paleo-Indian complexes and chronological phases, two of which—Gainey and Crowfield—take the name of their diagnostic fluted biface types. Barnes bifaces characterize the Parkhill phase, which lies between the earlier Gainey and later Crowfield phase occupations of the region. (A possibly earlier Enterline phase is tentatively identified at only one site, and a later Holcombe phase marks terminal or post-Paleo-Indian occupation.)

Regional systematics are fairly consistent (Deller and Ellis 1988; Roosa and Deller 1982; Storck 1983; Shott 1986a; Shott and Wright in press; Wright 1981). Sites of each complex and phase are widely distributed, although Crowfield sites are somewhat less common and no major Crowfield site has yet been identified in Michigan. Importantly, most sites are single-component occupations, yielding bifaces and associated tool types of one complex only (Deller and Ellis 1988; Shott 1986a). Gainey is the type site for the Gainey phase, which is thought to date to around 11,000-10,600 B.P. Barnes in Michigan and numerous Ontario sites—Parkhill, Fisher

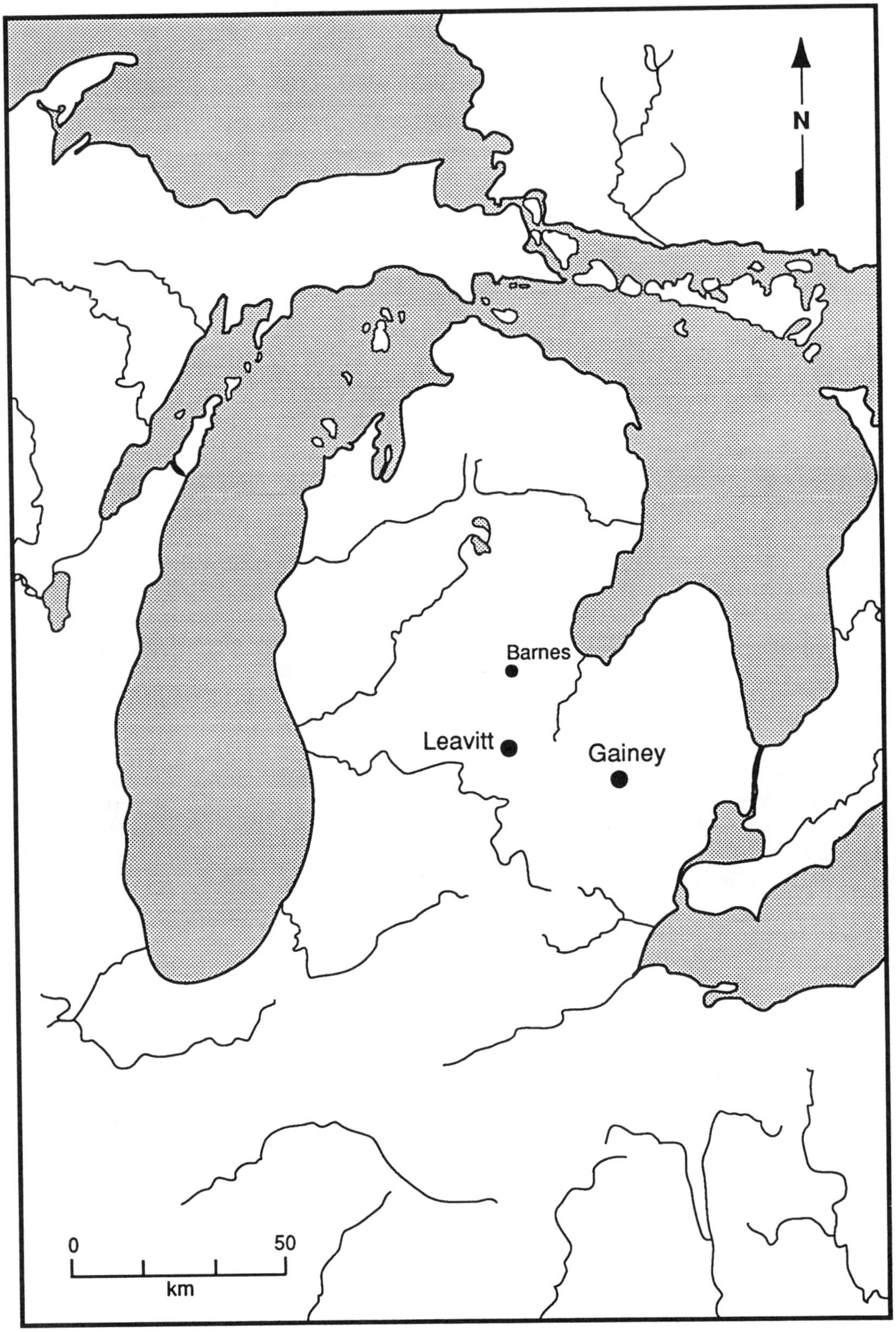

Figure 1.1. Location of the Leavitt site in Clinton County, Michigan. The Barnes site is located in Midland County.

and Thedford to name only the most prominent examples—represent the Parkhill phase, dated to around 10,600 B.P. and of unknown length. The eponymous Crowfield-Willaeys site is the best example of Crowfield occupation, thought to post-date 10,600 B.P. It bears emphasizing that the upper Great Lakes Paleo-Indian chronology is largely inferred, resting principally on site distributions associated with geological deposits of known age. No Paleo-Indian site in the region has been satisfactorily dated by radiocarbon. Summarizing Paleo-Indian systematics in the upper Great Lakes, Deller and Ellis (1988:255) view the phases as "arbitrary segments in a continually changing system, each of which is sufficiently differentiated in time to be recognized as a separate type." This view nicely emphasizes the dynamic quality of regional Paleo-Indian cultural practices necessary for survival in difficult and constantly changing environments.

Although the renewal of activity in the past fifteen years has significantly increased our knowledge of Paleo-Indian cultures in the upper Great Lakes region, the current state of research is far from ideal. Paleo-Indian groups covered vast areas over a considerable span of time; without a doubt, they left behind dozens if not hundreds of major sites in Michigan alone. Indeed, Barnes and other Paleo-Indian biface types actually are widely distributed in the state (Mason 1958, 1962; Quimby 1958). In the absence of systematic survey of the sites, however, the size and nature of associated assemblages, if any, remains unknown. The Sanford collection, described below and from which several diagnostic Parkhill phase bifaces were found at Leavitt, also includes Barnes bifaces from two Shiawassee County sites. The Mead site, also located in Shiawassee County, has yielded two Barnes bifaces and a cache of possible Paleo-Indian affinity (D.B. Simons, pers. comm.). Shiawassee County, which is east of the Leavitt site, deserves close attention in future Paleo-Indian studies in Michigan. Barnes bifaces also have been found in Otsego, Missaukee (Brunett 1966), Grand Traverse (Dekin 1966), and Macomb (Boylan 1977) Counties. Peru (1965, 1967) documents their considerable frequencies in the southwestern part of the state as well. Near Ann Arbor in Washtenaw County, the Four Mile Lake site probably includes a significant Parkhill phase occupation, although the provenience of collected specimens is not secure. Other specimens also have been documented (H.T. Wright, pers. comm.), most from the southern half of the Lower Peninsula and none from the Upper Peninsula.

The material record of eastern North American Paleo-Indian occupation is surprisingly extensive (Brennan 1982; Mason 1962), and recent work strongly supports this proposition (Jackson and McKillop 1990; Munson 1990). Even today, however, only a handful of sites is adequately documented. The uncertain provenience and inadequate documentation of discoveries has suggested to some that much Paleo-Indian occupation in the East was ephemeral, consisting of many brief occupations sparsely scattered over the landscape. Until well-controlled surveys are conducted and many more sites are excavated, however, reliable conclusions cannot be expected. What distinguishes the Paleo-Indian archaeological record in eastern North America is not its ephemeral nature but its comparative neglect in favor of more obtrusive and spectacular remains of later cultures.

Federally funded and state-administered survey programs blossomed in the 1970s, and many archaeological sites have been documented through field survey, inspection of private collections, or a combination of the two. Systematic gleaning of these data for Paleo-Indian diagnostics, followed by more intensive and focused field studies, doubtlessly would improve the state of documentation of the Paleo-Indian record as well as fulfill the potential of the original surveys.

In the meantime, Barnes and—with this report—Leavitt stand as the only reasonably well-documented Parkhill phase localities in Michigan, a situation which contrasts sharply with the state of the field in neighboring Ontario. Although Parkhill phase land-use practices and assemblage formation processes probably were not as complex and diverse as those of the preceding Gainey phase (Shott 1986a, 1989a, 1989b), they certainly were more diverse than the record from two sites can reveal. The current sample is not merely small, but completely inadequate to gauge the full range and magnitude of variability in Parkhill phase adaptations.

Site Setting

The Leavitt site is located in Clinton County, Michigan, a short distance north of Lansing (Fig. 1.1). Because the site is intact and therefore vulnerable to unauthorized and uncontrolled actions, its exact location cannot be disclosed. The location is on record at the Michigan Bureau of History and the UMMA. Elevation is approximately 259 m (850 ft) above mean sea level, in an area of moderate relief and relatively poor drainage (Fig. 1.2). The site falls in the Ionia District, Lansing Subdistrict, in Albert et al.'s (1986:16) regional landscape scheme.

Leavitt is situated in a broad belt of Wisconsin-age

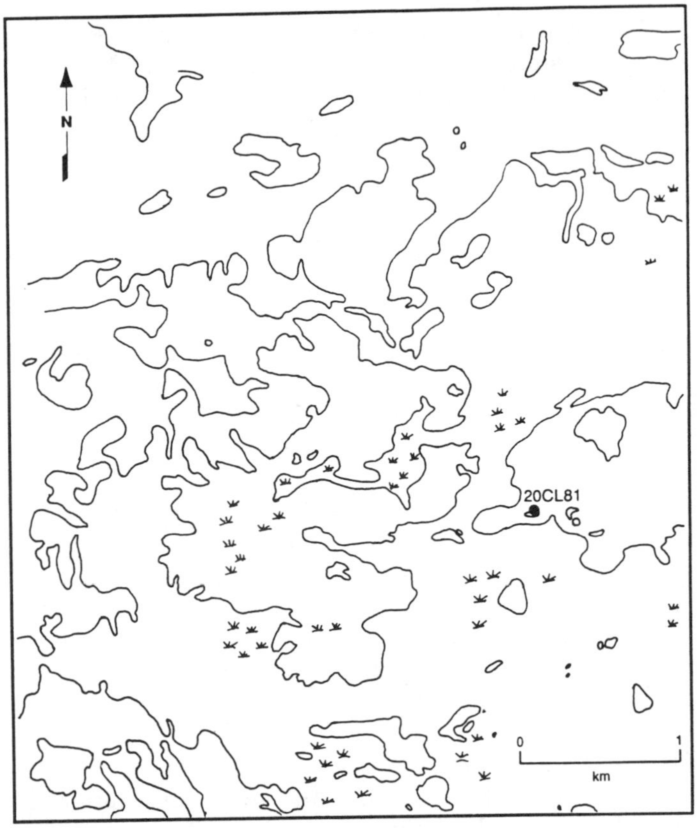

Figure 1.2. Local relief in the Leavitt site vicinity. Modern cultural features are omitted to impede unauthorized access. The contour interval is 5 feet (or approximately 1.5 meters) and the site lies on the 850 ft line. SOURCE: U.S. Geological Survey.

end moraines and till plains. These are heterogeneous deposits that include "medium-textured glacial till—gray, grayish brown or reddish brown, non-sorted glacial debris; matrix is dominantly loam and silt loam texture, [with] variable amounts of cobbles and boulders" (Farrand and Bell 1982) and that occur in plains of moderate relief as well as "narrow linear belts of hummocky relief" (ibid.). Leavitt occupies the crest and part of the north-facing backslope of an east-west trending ridge in this till–moraine complex. The northern and southeastern slopes are relatively gentle but the ground surface falls off steeply to the southwest (Fig. 1.3).

Soils at the site consist principally of Marlette loams of 12-18% slope. According to Pregitzer (1978:22-23), these soils form in "calcareous loamy glacial till" and narrow ridges. They are described as "moderately well drained" (1978:22) loams, an observation somewhat at odds with field experience; excavation units exposed to rain often required several days to dry out sufficiently to resume work.

History of Investigation

Leavitt was chosen for excavation for several important reasons. First, knowledge of Parkhill phase sites in Michigan was largely confined to the Barnes site itself. Although a considerable amount of research has been carried out on Parkhill affinity sites in adjacent southwestern Ontario, no other assemblages of this period were well documented in Michigan. Barnes itself appeared to be a hunting camp (Voss 1977) while Leavitt, on admittedly limited grounds, more closely resembled a base camp. The radiocarbon age of Parkhill phase occupation, in both Ontario and Michigan, was unknown, and one quite simple hope was that datable carbonized material might be found at the site. Accurate dating was and is considered critical to our understanding of the environmental context of Parkhill phase occupation because of the rapidly changing character of early postglacial habitats in Michigan. Parkhill phase occupation had previously been fixed by inference to a time after the Main Algonquin retreat of 10,400 B.P. (Wright 1981).

The Leavitt site was discovered and collected for a number of years by members of the Leavitt family. Mildred (Leavitt) Malkin was the first to collect artifacts from the site shortly after her family purchased the property. Mrs. Malkin's sister, Elsie Moore, and Mrs. Moore's daughter, Donna Sanford, amassed one of the most important collections from the site, and called it to the attention of the UMMA. In response to Ms. Sanford's approach, Henry T. Wright made a controlled surface collection from the site in 1978. As the Paleo-Indian research program unfolded, Leavitt's unique status as a Parkhill phase residential camp called for renewed efforts there, which culminated in the 1984 excavation.

Collections from the Leavitt Site

The Leavitt site collection is a true amalgam, consisting of four main components, as described below.

The Malkin Collection. Mildred Malkin began her collection when her family purchased the property in the early 1930s. In fact, she also retains two artifacts found by the owner from whom the Leavitt family acquired the farm. Mrs. Malkin collected artifacts from all parts of the property. She is able to recall the exact or approximate locations of some specimens, but most can be provenienced only to the property as a unit. She is certain that most artifacts in her collection were not found in the area of 20CL81 and, in fact, most of her specimens are not diagnostic Paleo-Indian tools. Nevertheless, Mrs. Malkin's collection includes at least five tools of

Figure 1.3. View of the Leavitt site from the southwest. The site occupies a narrow, east-west trending ridge that falls off steeply to the south and southwest.

apparent Paleo-Indian affinity. Because they lack exact provenience, it is impossible to determine if these specimens were found at 20CL81. Two of them, however, are unmistakeable fluted bifaces and a third is a probable Paleo-Indian end scraper. Therefore, the three specimens are assumed to be from 20CL81. Conversely, nondiagnostic tools or later-period diagnostics in Mrs. Malkin's collection may be from the site as well. Malkin specimens were examined but not measured; in this report, they are described but omitted from all data analysis.

Moore and Sanford Collections. Elsie Moore and Donna Sanford compiled surface collections based on repeated visits to the site. Material in this collection is recorded by site provenience only. Although these collections include some chert debris and tool fragments, they are selective to some degree. Ms. Moore and Ms. Sanford both donated their collection to the UMMA in 1979.

UMMA Surface Collection. The third collection is from a visit made by a UMMA party in 1978. A controlled surface collection was made, and one 2 ft by 2 ft excavation unit was excavated.

UMMA Excavation (Accession 85-27, catalog numbers 85-27-1 through 85-27-335). The largest collection from Leavitt was obtained in the 1984 excavation. Most of the collection consists of material recovered from one-meter-square excavation units. In addition, however, several collections were made of the site surface; in some, artifacts including chert debris were piece-plotted by transit, in others they were collected by 10 m by 10 m units keyed to the excavation grid. Furthermore, some items were discovered incidentally during field operations as they were exposed by foot traffic or wind.

Collections made before the 1984 UMMA expedition often applied a single catalog number to several specimens. In some cases, specimens were assigned unofficial individual numbers when the collection was illustrated and examined between 1978 and 1984. In such cases, the unofficial number is attached to the official UMMA catalog number to aid the reader in distinguishing specimens as they are described and illustrated. However, not all pre-1984 specimens received such treatment, and some specimens share a single catalog number as, in fact, do specimens recovered from the same provenience in the 1984 UMMA investigation.

Methodology of Investigations

The 1978 UMMA collection was a limited but extremely useful effort. In that visit, Leavitt was gridded into 24 units measuring 20 by 20 ft each; the entire grid measured 120 by 80 ft (36.6 by 24.4 m), for a total of 9600 ft^2 (892.2 m^2)(Fig. 1.4). All artifacts were collected by unit provenience. Although single inspections can be unreliable in revealing spatial patterning at archaeological sites, the results of that survey at least suggest that the densest distribution of both tools and debris tapered off toward the southeast (Fig. 1.4). This suggestion was strengthened by 1984 work at Leavitt. Specimen 88216, the proximal fragment of a quartzite fluted biface (Fig. 6.4e), was found in Unit 500N 580E at the southern edge of the grid, well south of the main artifact distribution. A second fluted biface, specimen 90072, was found near the southeastern margin of the main distribution in unit 580N 600E (Fig. 1.4).

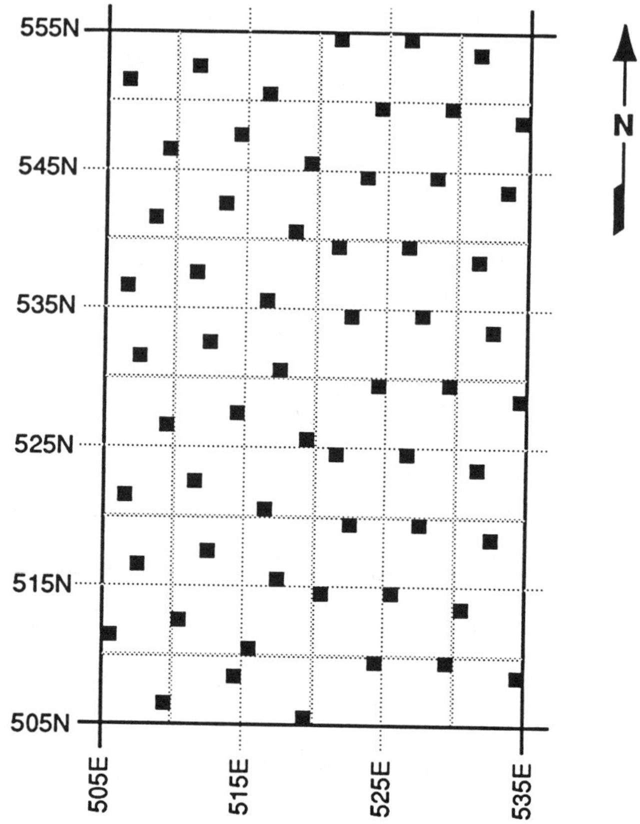

Figure 1.5. 1984 UMMA collection grid showing the location of Stage 1 units in the stratified systematic unaligned sample.

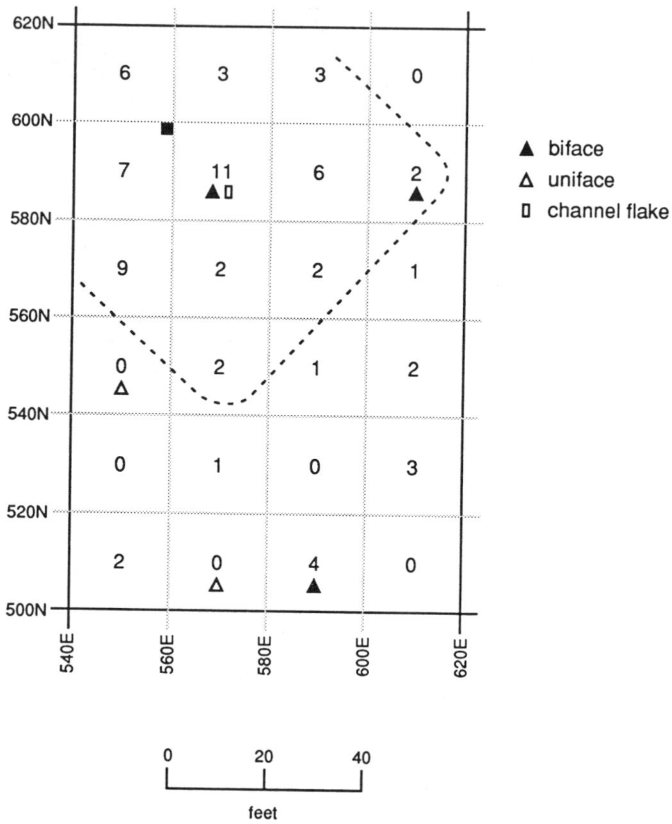

Figure 1.4. 1978 UMMA collection grid and summary of results.

The first stage of excavation in 1984 involved the establishment of an excavation grid encompassing most of the 1978 collection grid and the main areas of the site collected by Moore and Sanford. The grid measured 50 m north-south by 30 m east-west, for a total of 1500 m^2 (Fig. 1.5). An initial surface collection was conducted and then a stratified systematic unaligned sample (Redman 1974) of 43 one-meter-square units (2.9% of the excavation grid) was excavated. These are termed "Stage 1" units in this report. Inspection of the density and distribution of artifacts found in Stage 1 identified the area of highest artifact density at the site. Figure 1.6 shows the distribution of flake debris across Stage 1 units at the site. (Although systematic controlled surface collection was confined to the grid, the steeply sloping field surface to south and southwest also was closely inspected. Downslope movement of artifacts may be considerable in some cases, but the few items found suggest that such movement was slight at Leavitt.)

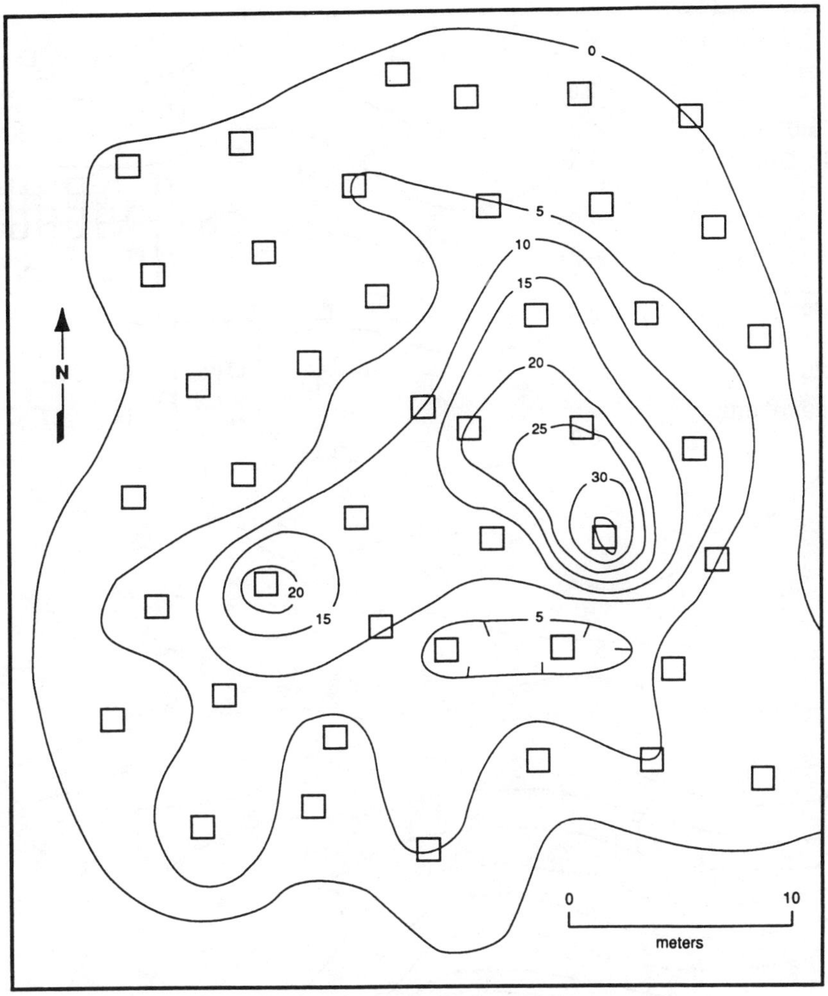

Figure 1.6. Flake debris distribution across Stage 1 units.

Excavation efforts then were concentrated in areas of high artifact density, resulting in the excavation of 206 m^2 distributed in two excavation blocks. The larger, Block 1, measured 163 m^2 including Stage 1 units, and the smaller, Block 2, measured 43 m^2 including Stage 1 units (Fig. 1.7). Units also were excavated southeast of the main excavation blocks, in the vicinity of the quartzite fluted biface fragment found in the 1978 surface collection. Figure 1.8 shows the excavation areas and the Stage 1 units located in and around them in relation to the Stage 1 flake debris distribution. It shows that the density peaks in the latter were largely excavated. In addition, several units were excavated between 500N and 535-539E, near the quartzite fluted biface, specimen 88216/88255 found in the 1978 collection. Unfortunately, no tools and few flakes were recovered from those units. No excavations were carried out in the vicinity of the other fluted biface found in the 1978 collection (Fig. 1.4). Including the first stage excavation, a total of 244 m^2 of the Leavitt site was excavated, constituting 16.3% of the area covered by the collection grid. Correspondence of the 1978 collection grid and the 1984 excavations is shown in Figure 1.9. In effect, much of the northern half of the former was excavated, as well as a considerable area to the west.

Since the site is located in a cultivated field, original provenience of all material within approximately 20 cm of the ground surface has been destroyed. Piece-plotting of artifacts was not attempted, therefore, and all material was collected from unit provenience. Matrix was removed by shovel and processed through quarter-inch (.63 cm) hardware mesh. Following established practice in recent excavations of Paleo-Indian sites (e.g. Deller and Ellis 1992; Simons et al. 1984), the base of

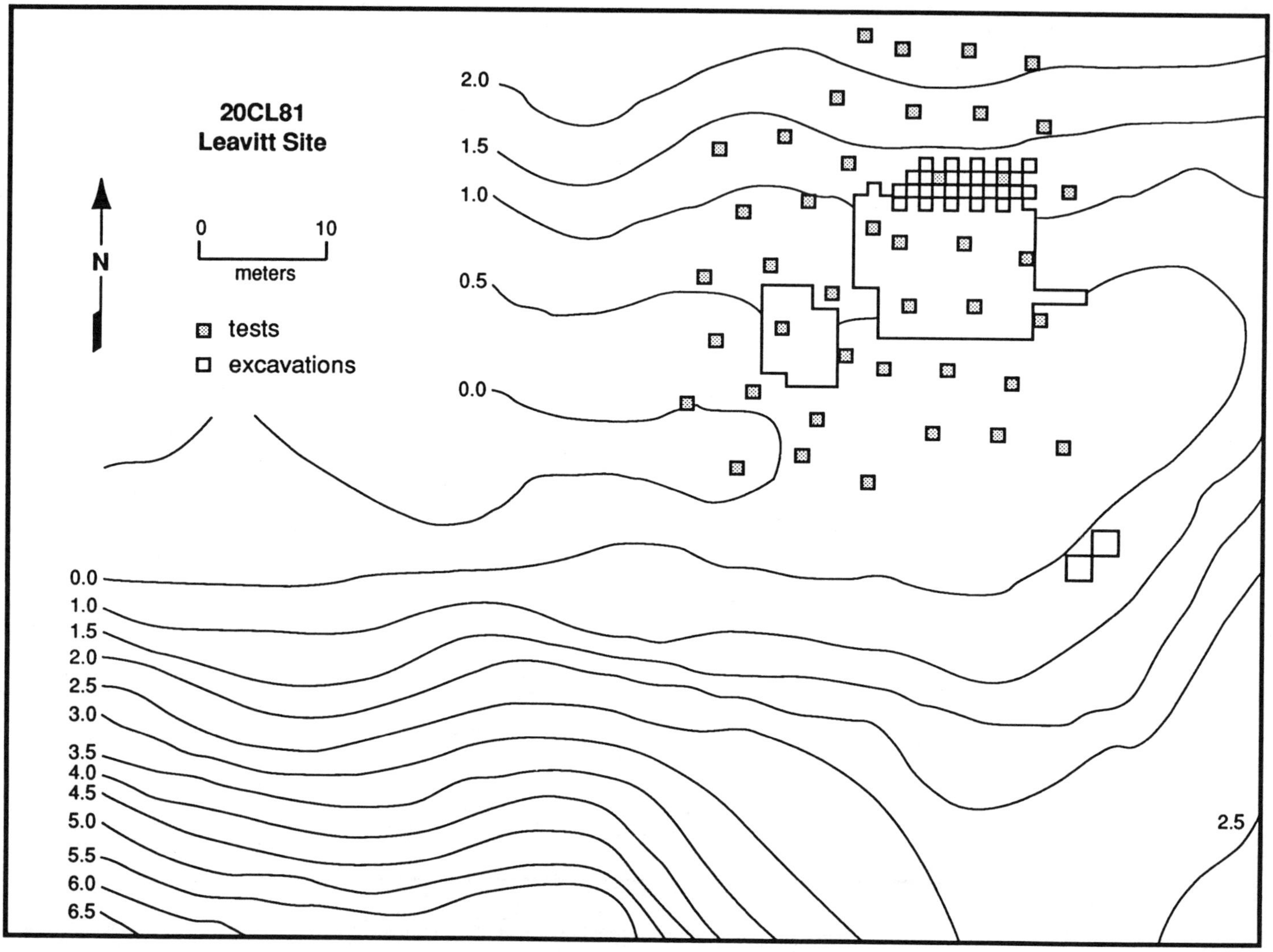

Figure 1.7. Plan of 1984 excavations at Leavitt.

each unit was shoveled or troweled clean and inspected for the presence of features. Excavation then continued 5 cm into the sub-plow zone matrix, both to recover artifacts removed from original context by natural agents and to search for traces of features or other occupational deposits. The only feature found at Leavitt was not visible at the plow zone base, and was discovered only because of this measure.

Overview of Report

Chapter 2 of this report presents the environmental context of human occupation at Leavitt, including a discussion of paleoclimate, biota, and chert resources. Although gross environmental characterizations are insufficient to describe the parameters and conditions relevant to Paleo-Indian adaptation, available data are inadequate for the more detailed and relevant characterization necessary. Leavitt's setting and stratigraphy are briefly described in Chapter 3, which also discusses at length the single cultural feature found at the site. Although finished tools are the chief focus of study, the lithic production process begins with cores, and it generates debris or flakes at all stages. Chapter 4 therefore describes and discusses first the cores recovered at Leavitt and then the character of its debris assemblage. Unifaces and bifaces are described and analyzed in Chapters 5 and 6, respectively. Chapter 7 views the assemblage from the perspective of its characteristic for-

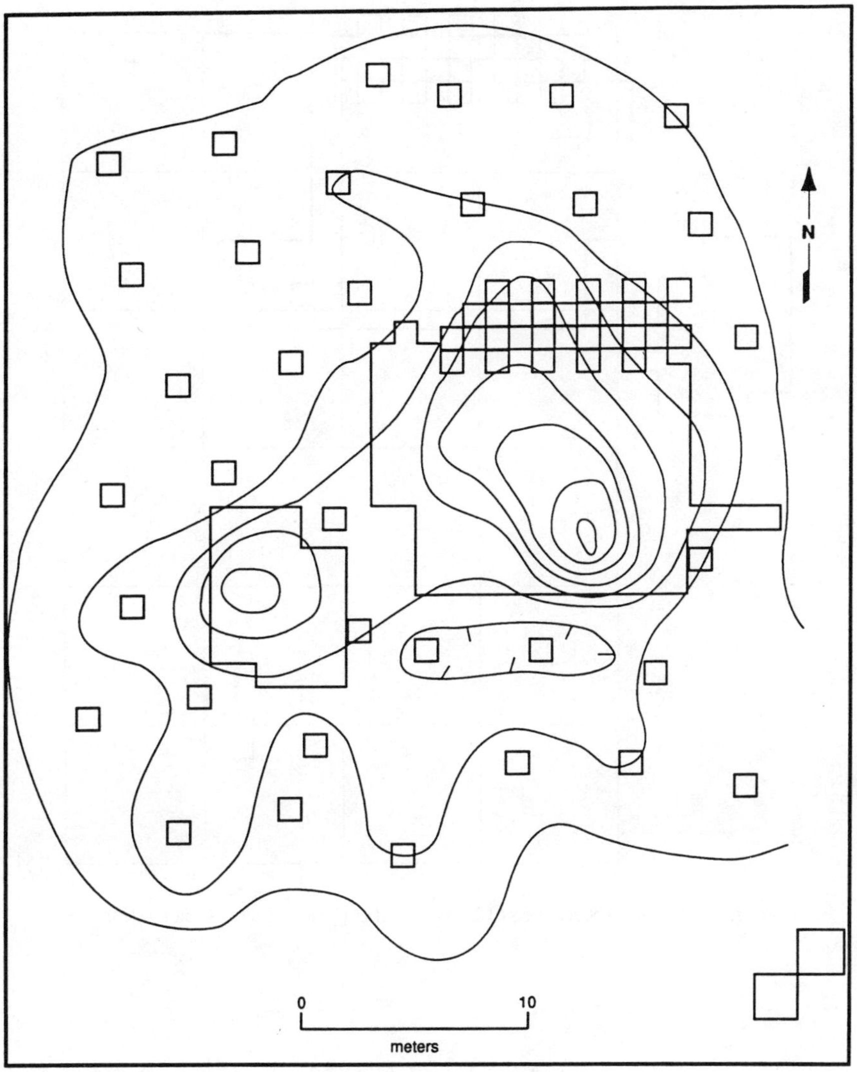

Figure 1.8. Correspondence of Stage 1 flake debris distribution and block excavations. Contour intervals as in Figure 1.4.

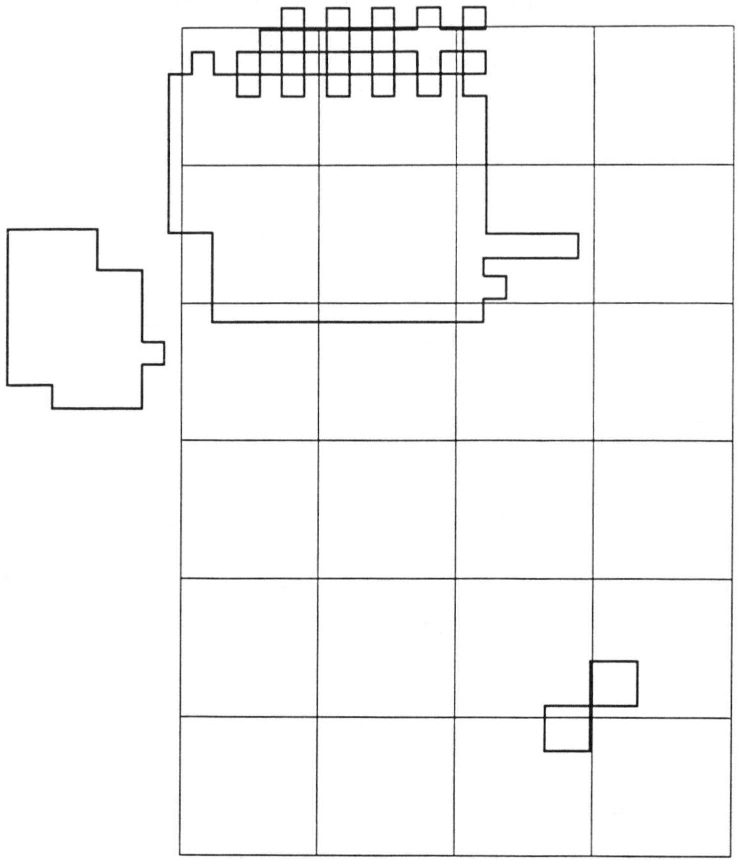

Figure 1.9. Correspondence of 1978 collection grid and 1984 excavations.

mation processes—how it came to be deposited in the archaeological record—complementing the earlier treatment which emphasized how tools were made and used. Chapter 8 considers the spatial distribution of remains, analysis which is complicated by the several collections with varying degrees and kinds of provenience control that form the aggregate Leavitt assemblage. A brief conclusion in Chapter 9 discusses some of Leavitt's significance as a Paleo-Indian occupation and closes with suggestions for future research directions.

CHAPTER 2

The Environmental Context of Occupation at Leavitt

Introduction

Paleo-Indian foragers of eastern North America occupied diverse, unstable and unforgiving habitats. Their ability to adapt to these conditions is attested eloquently by the 11,000-year legacy of their descendants. Yet the relevant parameters of the paleoenvironment and the adaptive properties by which Paleo-Indians dealt with them remain poorly understood.

Prevailing views of Paleo-Indian adaptations emphasize gross environmental distinctions and the culture types thought to correspond to them. Archaeologists often speak of two habitats—tundra/parkland and boreal forest—and associate with them two distinct types of modal adaptations—specialized and generalized, respectively. This view rests on limited environmental synthesis and extremely broad surveys of site distributions, the data for which vary widely in quality and context. Useful to a degree, the tundra vs. boreal forest model is nevertheless unsatisfactory. Early Holocene habitats differed in important respects from modern analogues (Dincauze 1986). Thus, modern tundras and boreal forests are inaccurate models for any Paleo-Indian habitats and their use limits our understanding of Paleo-Indian adaptations. Also, the model contrasts two modal types of habitat and, by implication, two modal types of adaptation. This places undue emphasis on the central tendencies of cultural systems, which can mask important adaptive properties and dynamic potentials (Winterhalder 1980). Diversity in adaptive systems—their range of behavioral variation—is an equally important property (Shott 1989b).

To reach these goals, we require not only revised views of Paleo-Indian cultures and adaptations (Shott 1990) but more detailed and informed reconstructions of Paleo-Indian habitats. Our needs far outpace the available data, however, and the following summary of the paleoenvironmental context of Parkhill phase occupation at Leavitt reflects this shortcoming at the same time that it, I hope, suggests the direction that future studies should take.

The Paleoenvironment, 11,000-10,000 B.P.

The time span under consideration encompasses most if not all the Paleo-Indian occupation of the Great Lakes region (Deller and Ellis 1988). At the risk of belaboring a point of which Paleo-Indian specialists are acutely aware, we lack at present a firm radiometric basis for determining the absolute age and time span of that occupation. Thus, the selected interval is deliberately wide, much wider than the postulated time span of Parkhill phase occupation.

Paleoclimatic and biotic data identify this period as the most dynamic interval since the retreat of Wisconsin ice from the region (Jacobson and Grimm 1987:32-35). Any consideration of paleoenvironmental conditions at the time of Paleo-Indian occupation must keep in mind that those conditions changed continuously. Because specific occupations cannot be fixed precisely in time, it is virtually impossible to identify those occupations with particular environmental conditions. Paleo-Indians probably faced essentially static conditions only for extremely short periods, a situation which might have favored resourcefulness and adaptability over closely calibrated adaptation to particular conditions. Nevertheless, at least the general character of early Holocene habitats in the region may be assayed.

Flora

The region was covered primarily by spruce (*Picea* spp.) forest during most of the study period. This forest type is documented in pollen cores from southwestern Ontario (Karrow et al. 1975; Mott and Farley-Gill 1978), southeastern Michigan (Kerfoot 1974; Benninghoff and Southworth 1963), southwestern Michigan (Manny et al. 1978) and from Michigan's Thumb area (Ahearn and Bailey 1980). In these pollen spectra, *Picea* usually accounts for more than half of the pollen grains identified. However, this strong percentage dominance is somewhat misleading because, although *Picea* is the most common pollen by far, there is relatively little pollen in general (Mott and Farley-Gill 1978:1108, Fig. 4; Manny et al. 1978:252-253; Kerfoot 1974:54). Thus, the spruce community is thought to be more closed than the herbaceous woodland, but not a closed, homogeneous spruce stand like those found in many high-latitude habitats today. Well drained, sandy soils would have supported some hardwoods (e.g., *Quercus, Betula, Carpinus-Ostrya, Fraxinus*), a few pines (e.g., *Pinus banksiana*), and a ground cover of herbs and grasses (e.g., *Artemisia, Cyperaceae, Gramineae*).

Useful data remain sparse, but recent study of the Rappuhn mastodont locality in Lapeer County, Michigan, and reanalysis of existing data from that site show considerable biotic diversity among both pollen and macrofossil assemblages dating to 10,750±400 B.P. (Holman et al. 1985), well before the spruce retreat from the region.

Amundsen and Wright (1979) note that the spruce retreat was quite abrupt across eastern North America. In pollen profiles they studied, the transition to the succeeding pine community is marked by a comparatively short-lived but distinct community dominated by birch and other cold-tolerant hardwoods (1979:14). Until more detailed studies are carried out in Michigan, the nature of the comparable transition there will remain poorly understood, but it is no longer valid to assume that the spruce maximum is followed immediately by a pine-dominated community. Instead, if the sequence documented in Minnesota is found in Michigan as well, a brief hardwood maximum must have occurred around 10,400 B.P. Relatively high percentage values for hardwoods in regional pollen spectra support this scenario (Holman et al. 1986:438, Tables I and III), establishing that cold-tolerant hardwoods including not only birch but also oak, elm and ash existed in significant quantities. This possibility will affect our reconstructions of Paleo-Indian subsistence practices and our interpretation of plant charcoal from Paleo-Indian deposits. Because this community was not as climate-controlled as was the succeeding pine community, it was probably at once more dynamic and more diverse than any modern hardwood communities in the region.

As noted above, the dominant spruce community ultimately was replaced by jack pine (*Pinus banksiana*). The replacement is unusually well dated, occurring in southwestern Ontario immediately prior to 10,400 B.P. (Karrow et al. 1975), perhaps the time when Main Lake Algonquin drained in the Michigan-Huron basin. In the Michigan Thumb, the replacement occurred within several centuries of that date (Davis 1983; Bernabo and Webb 1977). The replacement of spruce by pine is thought to have been caused by the arrival of northward-migrating pine communities in an area already well suited to them climatically (Davis 1983). Thus, the rapidity of the replacement is not necessarily due to sudden and drastic climatic change. That is, not only climate but migration rates, refugia locations, and edaphic conditions determined the composition of early Holocene biotic communities (Amundsen and Wright 1979; Shott and Welch 1984). Consequently, analogies to modern communities controlled much more strongly by climate tend to exaggerate the stability of those communities. Davis (1983:175) and Webb et al. (1983:160-61) both stress the role of these other factors and concur that no strict modern analogues to early Holocene communities exist. It is clear, moreover, from the numerous analyzed pollen cores from the region that these plant communities were substantially more diverse than are modern counterparts. Finally, the apparently rapid shift from spruce to pine dominance may be due in part to nothing more than differences in interpretation (Watt 1973). Faunal communities may have been as diverse as the reconstructed flora, but the evidence in this respect is sparse.

In summary, a spruce parkland or taiga habitat characterized central Michigan at the start of the study interval. It retreated at an unknown rate, possibly abruptly, to be replaced first by a mixed community with substantial hardwood representation and no modern analog and then, by 10,400 B.P., by a pine-dominated community roughly comparable to modern boreal forests.

Fauna

Previous discussion of the early Holocene habitat has been concerned primarily with plant species of little direct importance to human foragers. Instead, they are indicators of climatic conditions prevalent at the time of initial human occupation of the Great Lakes region. Information on the abundance and distribution of those species, however, is common. Vertebrate fauna, in contrast, are more directly relevant to the Paleo-Indian economy; ironically, however, early Holocene faunal remains are comparatively rare.

Graham and Lundelius (1984) summarize the direct evidence, most of which is derived from rockshelters, caves, bogs and other unusual depositional environments. Although Paleo-Indian foragers may have exploited the small game species common in these deposits, it is likely that larger mammals were more important components of their diet. These, alas, are largely absent from fossil assemblages.

One of Graham and Lundelius's (1984:224) specific conclusions is relevant to the issue: species currently confined to boreal habitats were widely distributed in eastern North America at the Pleistocene-Holocene transition, and their occurrence at lower latitudes probably produced faunal communities of considerably greater diversity than in any modern habitat. It is doubtful that a simple combination of modern temperate, boreal and tundra assemblages characterized the early Holocene faunal community in the Great Lakes region, since competition as well as environment can limit the distribution and abundance of species. Nevertheless, early Holocene habitats in the region almost certainly were more diverse than their modern tundra and boreal forest counterparts.

Available evidence does not permit definitive reconstruction of the early Holocene faunal community. Large cervids such as moose, elk and caribou probably were common. Caribou were widely distributed across eastern North America in Pleistocene and early Holocene deposits, but their occurrence in archaeological context is much more limited (Cleland 1965; Spiess et al. 1985; Storck 1988; perhaps Funk et al. 1969; Kopper et al. 1980; Savage 1981). Moreover, their behavior may have differed from modern caribou in important respects, owing to differences in climate and the spatial and temporal patterns of abundance in resources they consumed (Dincauze 1986:128). Species now extinct also may have persisted in significant numbers when humans arrived. Paleo-Indian subsistence diversity has been underemphasized, and a surprising variety of resources actually have been identified, from fish and berries (Dent and Kauffman 1985: Tables 5.1, 5.2) to fox and hare (Storck 1988:24). Shoshani et al. (1990:14) report caribou, elk, moose, deer and several other mammal species from early Holocene deposits at 20OK394, a southeastern Michigan site. The age, stylistic affinity and association with the fauna of cultural remains from the site remain to be determined. While eastern North American Paleo-Indian specialists have been acutely and rightly aware of harsh preservation conditions in their reconstructions of material culture, there remains the tendency, based on negative evidence, to minimize the presumed diversity of faunal resources.

In this connection, the advent of human occupation in North America broadly corresponds to the extinction of a number of Pleistocene species, mastodons and other megafauna being the most notable. These species may have been important components of the Paleo-Indian diet, but evidence establishing a direct association between humans and megafauna is sparse. This may be a recognition problem in part, since Fisher (1987) presents a strong argument that humans butchered mastodons in the Great Lakes region. Stone tools have not yet been recovered in association with these remains, but this too may prove to be a recognition or sampling problem; rare stone tools composed of dark cherts like Upper Mercer and Bayport do not stand out in bog deposits. The role of human predators in the extinction of such Pleistocene megafauna is hotly contested and beyond the scope of this study. In eastern North America, at least, the sparse evidence argues against a major role for humans in this process, although hunting pressure may have made some contribution to the demise.

Estimating Habitat Parameters

Concluding that caribou probably were an economic staple of the economy is neither original nor satisfactory as a characterization of the Paleo-Indian adaptation. Paleo-Indians probably ate few plant species, so any more advanced study of the environmental conditions in which they lived must focus on faunal resources.

Modern cultural ecology demands far more than a simple list of major prey species, but more sophisticated and detailed reconstructions of the biotic parameters of unstable early Holocene habitats is daunting. Using data from modern habitats despite the limited nature of the analogy they provide, studies by Coe et al. (1976) and Belovsky (1987) offer at least the prospect of predicting the abundance of animal resources. Both define regressions of secondary biomass (SB), a gross measure of the abundance of animal species, against net primary productivity (NPP). An accurate estimate of regional SB at the time of Leavitt occupation would overestimate the quantity of food available to Paleo-Indian occupants, unless they literally ate everything that moved, including voles and other very small mammals. Nevertheless, even a reliable estimate of SB is problematic.

In theory, NPP in ancient habitats can be estimated as a relatively simple product of climatic parameters like mean annual temperature and precipitation, but the relationship apparently is complicated at the margins of the ranges of climatic parameters such that meaningful estimates of early Holocene Great Lakes NPP cannot be made (Shott 1986a:104-6). Making the perilous assumption (see above) that modern high-latitude habitats faithfully represent early Holocene Great Lakes ones, NPP values for the former can be applied to the regressions in order to predict SB.

Unfortunately, other uncontrolled factors complicate the exercise. There are considerable differences between the regressions linking NPP and SB that Coe et al. (1976) and Belovsky (1987) define. The former is drawn from semi-arid habitat data and perhaps its use should be confined to similar habitats. Belovsky's (1987: Fig. 4) model, however, is intended for global application. Estimates of high-latitude habitat NPP also vary considerably (McDonald 1984: Table 18.1). One can, using a combination of particular regression and input NPP data, produce SB estimates ranging from 0.3 to 5,248.1 g/m^2. Until we know much more about the biotic properties of many local habitats in the Great Lakes region during the 11,000-10,000 B.P. interval, any such estimates of available faunal resources are questionable.

Structural Properties of Early Holocene Habitats

Even were there reliable estimates of faunal abundance, it would be somewhat problematic to infer Paleo-Indian subsistence practices from gross environmental data. Equally important as the composition of the regional biota were its structural properties (Shott 1990), which can produce inherent subsistence variability even under stable climatic conditions. Forager subsistence economies, for example, may be influenced by stable limit cycles. Belovsky (1987:353-58, Fig. 10) proposes three stages in a hypothetical early Holocene limit cycle that may be relevant to the upper Great Lakes region. Some accounts of prey availability in modern boreal forest habitats provide empirical support for the notion of considerable inherent, possibly cyclical, variability in prey abundance (Dunning 1959:27; Gronnow et al. 1983:13-16; Winterhalder 1977:175-99; Yesner 1989:98-99).

Under equilibrium environmental conditions, stable limit cycles ultimately dissipate, producing stability. But early Holocene habitats probably included two additional dimensions of inherent instability. First, random year-to-year fluctuations in resource availability probably occurred; such habitats doubtless were unpredictable in the short term. Second, long term or directional change as a corollary of postglacial global amelioration is well documented. In effect, early Holocene habitats occupied by Paleo-Indian cultures were characterized by three types of inherent variation, each with its characteristic frequency and scale. Random, annual fluctuations were superimposed on structural fluctuations occurring at perhaps 50 to 100 year cycles (Gronnow et al. 1983:13; Winterhalder 1977:175-99) which, in turn, may have been displaced along directional vectors of change.

It is merely a truism to say that Paleo-Indians adapted to unique environmental conditions, but this discussion establishes a framework for inferring those conditions. Paleo-Indians probably were resourceful and quick to change their economic practices in the face of daunting and almost constant instability, but the variability expressed in their adaptive practices can be gauged only through careful, detailed study and appropriate theory that links substantive variability (Shott 1989a) to properties of the archaeological record.

Chert Sources

Stone tool raw material can only be regarded as an indirect subsistence resource. Obviously, it cannot be eaten, but its importance in the subsistence quest and other activities (Ellis 1989) can scarcely be exaggerated. Therefore, chert source used by inhabitants of Leavitt are discussed in this chapter, in order of abundance.

Identification of chert raw materials is important in virtually all archaeological analyses. Accurate raw material identification is especially important, however, in Paleo-Indian studies, both because eastern North American Paleo-Indians typically exhibited strong and specific preferences in stone (Ellis 1984:38-51, 1989; Goodyear 1989) and because distances between natural and archaeological occurrences provide a minimum measure of distance traveled by groups in their annual rounds (Binford 1979; Hester and Grady 1977; Storck 1983; Tankersley 1990). These measures should not be identified with territory size, however, since forager mobility practices are sufficiently complex and organized to seriously complicate the equation (Shott 1986a:141), and chert procurement can be "embedded" (Binford 1979:259) in other activities and movements.

Until recently, raw material source ascription was based primarily on simple inspection of archaeological specimens. The considerable variability in visible properties within and between chert sources, however (Luedtke 1976; Tankersley 1990) raises serious doubts about the validity of these simple practices. Many archaeologists, this writer included, are guilty of employing such nonrigorous and potentially misleading practices. Several common Great Lakes Paleo-Indian raw materials, Upper Mercer and Flint Ridge cherts in particular, are extremely variable in appearance (Tankersley 1990; D.B. Simons, pers. comm.; M. Seeman, pers. comm.), which casts even greater doubt on the validity of simple visual methods applied to Paleo-Indian assemblages.

Fortunately, rigorous source ascription techniques have been applied by archaeologists in recent years. Luedtke (1976) determined diagnostic trace element constituents of common archaeological cherts in the Great Lakes region using neutron activation methods. Tankersley (1990) identifies diagnostic fossil and other inclusions in Ohio Valley and Great Lakes cherts using petrographic methods at low magnification. W.A. Fox (pers. comm.) has used similar techniques on Great Lakes cherts.

Most artifacts in the Leavitt assemblage are thought to be composed of Bayport chert. In large measure, this judgment rests on the imperfect visual methods criticized above, a fact mitigated very little by Bayport's distinctive properties. Visual identification, after all, can be misleading (Tankersley 1990). Although rigorous source ascription of any large number of archaeological specimens is impractical, a total of 75 flakes visually identified as Bayport were taken from four excavation units at Leavitt—515N 511E, 515N 513E, 515N 515E and 517N 515E—and submitted to L. Pavlish at the University of Toronto in 1985 for neutron activation analysis. A Bayport sample obtained from an outcrop on Charity Island in Saginaw Bay (Luedtke 1976: Fig. 10; Shott 1986a: Fig. 6.5) was submitted with the archaeological samples. Unfortunately, the samples were accidentally combined in the laboratory with Upper Mercer source samples and archaeological specimens, and the results of the subsequent analysis are meaningless for purposes of source ascription.

Bayport

Bayport chert occurs in the Upper Mississippian Bayport Limestone Formation. It is found chiefly as nodules embedded in the formation's limestone matrix (Luedtke 1976:200). Typically, nodules are circular to oval spheres whose surface is occupied by a coarse, grainy cortex of grey to buff in color. Luedtke (1976:200-201) describes the internal matrix of Bayport chert as follows:

> Bayport chert in general is concentrically banded, with bands usually 1 cm or less in width. There are occasional mottles and specks of darker and lighter colors. The material is blue-grey, N5/ to N6/ to N7/ with creamy white cortex, N8/. The chert sometimes has a brown tinge, 10YR6/1 to 10YR7/1, and sometimes weathers chocolate brown, 10YR5/4. The texture is coarse to medium, luster is dull to medium, and the material is opaque. Chalcedony and quartz-filled cavities are found as inclusions, along with calcite and sphalerite crystals . . . the most common inclusions are fossils of many sorts and sizes.

Although nodular Bayport chert is somewhat variable in visible properties, variability compounded by cultural selection, treatment and differential weathering in archaeological deposits, Luedtke (1976:203) describes it in general as "remarkably homogeneous visually." Moreover, it is reasonably distinctive in trace element composition when compared to other regional cherts commonly found in Paleo-Indian assemblages, although it is internally variable to some degree (Luedtke 1976: Tables 8, 23).

Bayport Limestone Formation chert also occurs in tabular form in at least two sources: the Bayport quarry in Huron County (Ozker 1982) and on Charity Island in Saginaw Bay (Shott 1986a:Fig. 6.5; D.B. Simons, pers. comm.). Ozker (1982:86) describes tabular Bayport chert from the former location as "dark lustrous gray to black (Munsell N3-N5); its texture is waxy." She also describes it as superior in flaking properties to nodular Bayport chert. Charity Island tabular specimens differ somewhat in appearance, being neutral light grey (Munsell N7) in color with fine, diffuse, irregular laminae and subparallel zones of darker grey (Munsell N5), finer-grained chert. Crystalline and cryptocrystalline quartz and/or calcite inclusions are common, often in laminar form. Fossil and chalk inclusions also are common. Archaeological specimens closely resembling Charity Island raw material are fairly common in adjacent Arenac County (Krakker et al. 1982).

The Bayport Limestone Formation is distributed in a wide arc across the lower peninsula of Michigan (Martin 1936). Modern chert-bearing limestone quarries are common in the Saginaw Bay region, and there is no doubt that aboriginal quarries also were common there. Most known Bayport quarries lie at elevations below the 184 m elevation of the Early and Main Lake Algonquin Stage in the Huron basin (Luedtke 1976:200; Shott 1986a:124-25; Wright 1981a:3-4), which is fixed by conventional geomorphological interpretation (Eschmann 1985:87; cf. Kaszicki 1985).

The possibility that chert-bearing outcrops existed elsewhere in the parent formation is difficult to gauge. Detailed survey and bedrock mapping have not been undertaken on a scale sufficient to identify chert-bearing outcrops accessible to prehistoric artisans, but it is at least possible that the formation outcrops or outcropped widely in Michigan. Ozker (1982:84) discusses the maximum distribution of outcrops. However, outcrop size, accessibility and chert abundance have been gauged only in scattered accounts. For instance, Ehlers and Humphrey (1944) record a Bayport Limestone outcrop in Grand Rapids, over 160 km southwest of Saginaw Bay and considerably southwest of the Leavitt site. Their account, however, does not mention nodular chert inclusions in the bedrock matrix. Unfortunately, the Grand Rapids outcrop was destroyed by quarrying operations (Ehlers and Humphrey 1944:117), so it can no longer be studied. Douglass (1928 [1849]) reports an outcrop of chert-bearing Bayport Limestone in Eaton County, roughly 50 km southwest of Leavitt. Lane (1900, cited in Luedtke 1976:203) also reports an Eaton County source near Bellevue, possibly the same one noted by Douglass. A third source is identified by Dustin (1935:472), who cites earlier reports of a limestone outcrop exposed by the Cass River in Township 13 North, Range 11 East in Tuscola County. Elevation there exceeds 700 ft (213.4 m), well above the level of Main Lake Algonquin.

However, several possible outcrops exist in Arenac County, west of Saginaw Bay, at elevations above the Main Lake Algonquin level (Shott 1986a:125). Such sources, if known and accessible to Paleo-Indians, could have supplied them with the raw material from which known Paleo-Indian assemblages in Michigan were produced. Furthermore, it is conceivable that geologically brief fluctuations in the surface elevation of Main Lake Algonquin occurred, which may have exposed Bayport outcrops on the shoreline. Larsen (1984) postulates such climatically controlled oscillations for the later Nipissing stage, and presents evidence suggesting that fluctuations during that lake stage may have exceeded 4 m (1984:97). Clearly, Algonquin and Nipissing stage climates differed substantially, and it remains for detailed field studies to determine the magnitude of possible Main Lake Algonquin fluctuations, if any in fact occurred. If they did, Bayport outcrops may have been exposed in the Saginaw Bay area, even during the Main Lake Algonquin stage in the Huron basin.

In summary, numerous Bayport chert outcrops were available in the Saginaw Bay region to Paleo-Indian inhabitants of Michigan. Outcrops may have existed elsewhere in the state, west, south and northeast of Leavitt (Fig. 2.1), although the amount and quality of chert occurring at such sources are unknown. Finally, it is possible that Bayport nodules were found in drift deposits west and south of the Saginaw Bay source area. If they existed, however, drift sources probably were sparse and unpredictable in occurrence. For Paleo-Indian foragers concerned in part with the logistics of chert procurement (Ellis 1984, 1989), the importance of such sources probably was limited at best. The possibility that they were exploited, at least in opportunistic fashion, is discussed in Chapter 4.

Ten Mile Creek

A series of outcrops in northwestern Ohio and adjacent southeastern Michigan are grouped under the heading of Ten Mile Creek chert. Provenience is reported as the Traverse Formation of the Devonian System (Stout and Schoenlaub 1945:24; Tankersley 1990:277) or the Tenmile Creek Formation of the same system (Luedtke 1976:283). Ten Mile Creek chert is variable but generally buff-colored (N1, N3, N9; Tankersley 1990:277) with considerable bioclast inclusions. Luedtke describes it as follows:

> Colors range from pale bluish grey, 10YR7/1, to yellowish, 7.5YR8/4 or 7.5YR7/4, and material weathers reddish, 5YR5/3. The texture is coarse to fine, the luster is dull to medium, and the chert is opaque. [1976:283]

The formation outcrops from central Ohio to Monroe County, Michigan. The sources closest to the Leavitt site lie approximately 200 km to the southeast. Stout and Schoenlaub (1945:32) describe an outcrop section along Ten Mile Creek in northwestern Ohio, and report dense exposures of chert-bearing limestone in the region.

Ten Mile Creek chert is a distant second to Bayport as a raw material source for Leavitt site artifacts. Specimens were assigned to this chert type strictly by visual inspection.

Upper Mercer chert

Upper Mercer chert is a variable but usually fine-grained and lustrous chert that outcrops in the eponymous formation of the Lower Pennsylvanian System. Luedtke describes it as

> homogeneous to mottled and streaked, with color ranging from dark black, N2/ through bluish grey, N3/, N4/, N5/, N6/, to light bluish grey N7/, and N8/. The texture is medium to fine, luster is medium to shiny, and the chert is opaque. Veins of white and blue chalcedony are common inclusions, and fossils also occur. [1976:288]

Upper Mercer distribution is described at length by Stout and Schoenlaub (1945:39-60; see also Luedtke

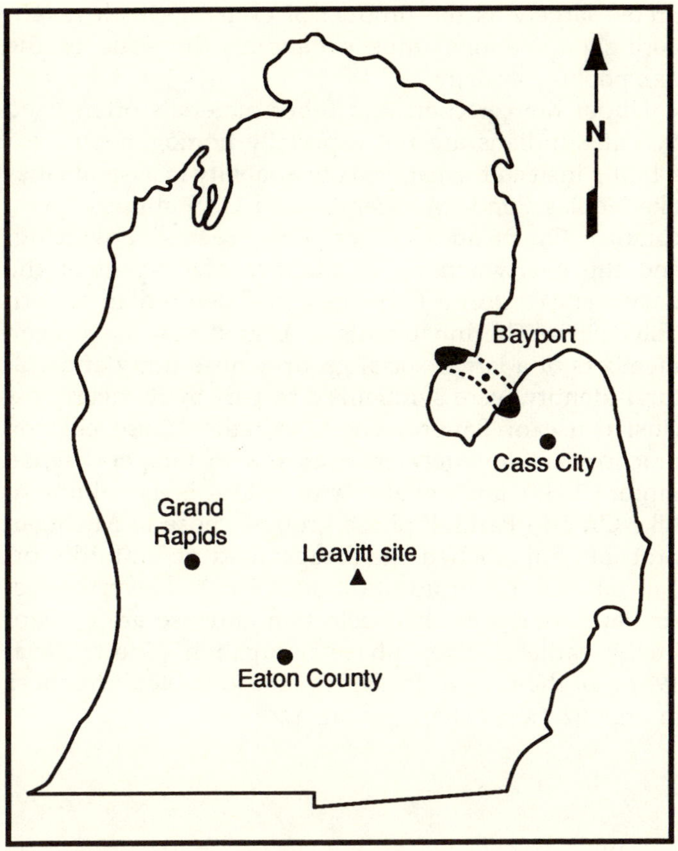

Figure 2.1. Location of Bayport chert sources in Michigan.

1976: 285-288 and Tankersley 1990:289). It is found in restricted outcrops, chiefly in Coshocton County of east-central Ohio, roughly 400 km southeast of the Leavitt site. Like many cherts, Upper Mercer has its look-alikes (Tankersley 1990:289), but it is not easily confused with Pipe Creek chert or other cherts of northwest Ohio. Upper Mercer chert often is found in dark blue (Munsell 5B), homogeneous beds, and is usually tabular in form (Luedtke 1976:288).

Upper Mercer chert is the chief constituent of the Gainey site assemblage (Simons et al. 1984; Shott 1986a) and other Gainey phase Paleo-Indian sites in Michigan and Ohio (Prufer and Wright 1970). It also forms the majority of the important Nobles Pond assemblage (Gramly and Summers 1986; M. Seeman, pers. comm.), where it assumes a bewildering variety of appearances from buff to dark blue.

Three artifacts from Leavitt are identified as Upper Mercer on the strength of visual inspection only. Admittedly, this is a somewhat questionable practice; Luedtke (1976:288, Table 66) describes the material as both "variable" and "distinctive," although its trace element composition is highly distinctive (1976: Table 65). Ideally, neutron activation analysis or some other form of rigorous source ascription should be performed. The small number of apparent Upper Mercer specimens in the Leavitt assemblage makes it impractical to seek such measures there. Significantly, Upper Mercer has low tolerance for heat stress, and is prone to potlid fracture (Purdy 1975:135-36) upon exposure to moderately intense heat. The only two Leavitt site specimens bearing potlid fractures are composed of Upper Mercer chert.

Quartzite

Several artifacts in the Leavitt assemblage, including one conjoined fluted biface, are composed of a buff crystalline quartzite. Tankersley (1990:290) broadly defines such material as "any rock whose composition is coarse-grained quartz resulting from a sedimentary, igneous, or metamorphic process." Hixton silicified sandstone and other crystalline quartzites are common, if usually secondary, constituents in eastern North American Paleo-Indian assemblages (Tankersley 1990:290-92). Such material probably occurs in drift deposits dislodged from Canadian Shield sources. Therefore, its distribution and abundance are difficult to gauge. Quartzite is a difficult material to work under the best of circumstances. Quartzite specimens from Leavitt are coarse grained and probably were refractory.

Collingwood

Collingwood or Fossil Hill chert is the chief constituent of Parkhill phase sites in Ontario (Deller and Ellis 1992:11-12; Roosa 1977a, 1977b; Storck, pers. comm.). Found in the Fossil Hill Formation, this chert is variable but chiefly buff, N/7-N/8; it is fine grained, but is not lustrous. Its distinct banding is a source of immensely useful information on the aboriginal reduction of tabular cores of the material (Ellis 1984).

Collingwood's provenience, stratigraphic context, and composition have been discussed at length by Eley and von Bitter (1989). Although it occurs in the Fossil Hill Formation, archaeologists have traditionally identified this chert as Collingwood because major sources are found near the town of that name in Ontario. Since Fossil Hill Formation chert can be somewhat variable, "Collingwood" remains the preferred term for the distinctively banded raw material found south of Georgian Bay (Fox 1989:26). The Collingwood source lies approximately 400 km northeast of Leavitt, on the opposite side of the Huron basin.

Although Bayport chert has been recovered in secondary but significant quantities at Ontario Parkhill sites, the occurrence and abundance of Fossil Hill chert in contemporaneous Michigan sites is unassayed. Ontario scholars generally regard the presence of Bayport chert there as evidence of exchange between interacting social groups, not the product of direct procurement. If correct, this interpretation implies that Fossil Hill chert should be found in roughly similar quantities and forms in Michigan Parkhill sites.

Discussion

Ellis (1989; see also Deller and Ellis 1992:135) argues that raw material selection and use in Great Lakes Paleo-Indian cultures was governed by social as well as material factors. Specifically, he views the preference for a single material—usually abundant, capable of standardized reduction and easy transport, relatively homogeneous and visually distinctive—as part of a culturally determined strategy that unifies members of the group and distributes risk among them. Small amounts of other raw materials—typically one or two—are interpreted largely as the product of exchange with neighboring populations, thus expanding the scale of the risk-pooling strategy.

Upper Mercer chert and other materials often used by Paleo-Indians are not especially homogeneous, exhibiting instead a great deal of variability in assemblages like Nobles Pond (M. Seeman and G. Summers, pers. comm.). On balance, Ellis's thesis seems convincing, and the overwhelming dominance of Bayport at the Leavitt site conforms to the general Paleo-Indian pattern (Ellis 1989). The inhabitants of Leavitt may have been members of a larger social group whose unity and cultural identity were symbolized in part by its nearly exclusive use of Bayport chert. Whether these cultural practices are uniquely associated with foragers (sensu Binford 1980), and not also with collectors, is unknown. Like Ontario Parkhill phase groups, those in Michigan probably approached the forager end of Binford's organizational continuum (Shott 1986a). Nevertheless, similar patterns of chert selection and use are evident in the earlier Gainey phase occupation (Shott 1986a, 1989b) of the region, for which considerable differences in organizational character are adduced.

Chapter 3

Site Stratigraphy

The physiographic setting and pedological character of the Leavitt site were discussed in Chapter 1. In this chapter, site stratigraphy or, more aptly, its absence, is described, and the single intact cultural deposit found at the site documented.

Virtually all Paleo-Indian sites in eastern North America were disturbed in some manner before excavation. Leavitt, as a plow zone site, is no exception to this generalization. Thus, no intact cultural deposits were encountered between the surface and the base of the plow zone.

Although plow zone depth varies to some degree across Leavitt, that variability is neither great nor systematic. Mean depth is 23.90 cm (s.d. = 3.97). As Figure 3.1 shows, there is no tendency for plow zone depth to rise near the bottom of the backslope nor, for that matter, at any other point on the site. The figure was compiled using plow zone depths in Stage 1 units. Observation points are accurately placed along the north-south axis, but all eastings between 505 and 509 were collapsed onto the line labeled 505E, all between 510 and 514 onto the 510E line, and so forth.

Feature Discovery at Leavitt

Features have been found at a number of Parkhill phase sites (Deller and Ellis 1992:93ff; Stewart 1984:50; Storck 1979:22, 35-38; Voss 1977:256-57). Many share certain characteristics worth summarizing before describing the single cultural feature found at Leavitt (Table 3.1).

First and perhaps foremost, Paleo-Indian features are usually ill-defined and difficult to detect. As the oldest cultural deposits in the Great Lakes region, they have been subject to leaching for considerably longer than later-period features. It is possible too that little organic material was deposited in Paleo-Indian features; organics stain feature sediments, distinguishing them from sterile soil. Whether or not this was true, it is clear that fire-cracked rock and other large debris is rarely found in Paleo-Indian features, which tends to reduce their visibility or obtrusiveness even further. Finally, poor definition is partly the result of postoccupational natural disturbances, which also are common in Great Lakes Paleo-Indian features. At least four of the ten Parkhill phase features from other sites listed in Table 3.1 were disturbed in some manner, including three of the four definite Paleo-Indian features at Thedford (Deller and Ellis 1992:93-98).

Second, and probably related to the prevalence of natural disturbance just noted, many features contain charcoal of hardwood species not thought to have existed in the region at the time of Paleo-Indian occupation. Maple and beech, for instance, consistently occur in features at Thedford. Uncarbonized botanics, usually an indication of disturbance, were found in Feature 1 at Barnes (Voss 1977:255) and Feature 8 at Thedford (Deller and Ellis 1992:94-95). Conversely, charcoal of species found in early Holocene forest communities is not especially abundant. Spruce, the most abundant such species, is not positively reported from any features at Barnes, Thedford, Zander or Banting, although Feature 2 at Zander contained unidentifiable conifer charcoal (Stewart 1984:50). Voss (1977:257) believes that charcoal of Paleo-Indian age would not have preserved in the sandy soil at Barnes. Not surprisingly, then, charcoal from Parkhill phase features has failed to yield satisfactory Paleo-Indian dates. Zander's Feature 1 yielded a date of 3380 ± 470 B.P. (Stewart 1984:50), and compound Feature 13 at Thedford produced a date of 2120 ± 230 B.P. (Deller and Ellis 1992:98).

Finally, Parkhill phase features often are defined more as concentrations of debris and tools than as discolored areas. The Crowfield site (Deller and Ellis 1984) is the most spectacular, but not the sole, example of this

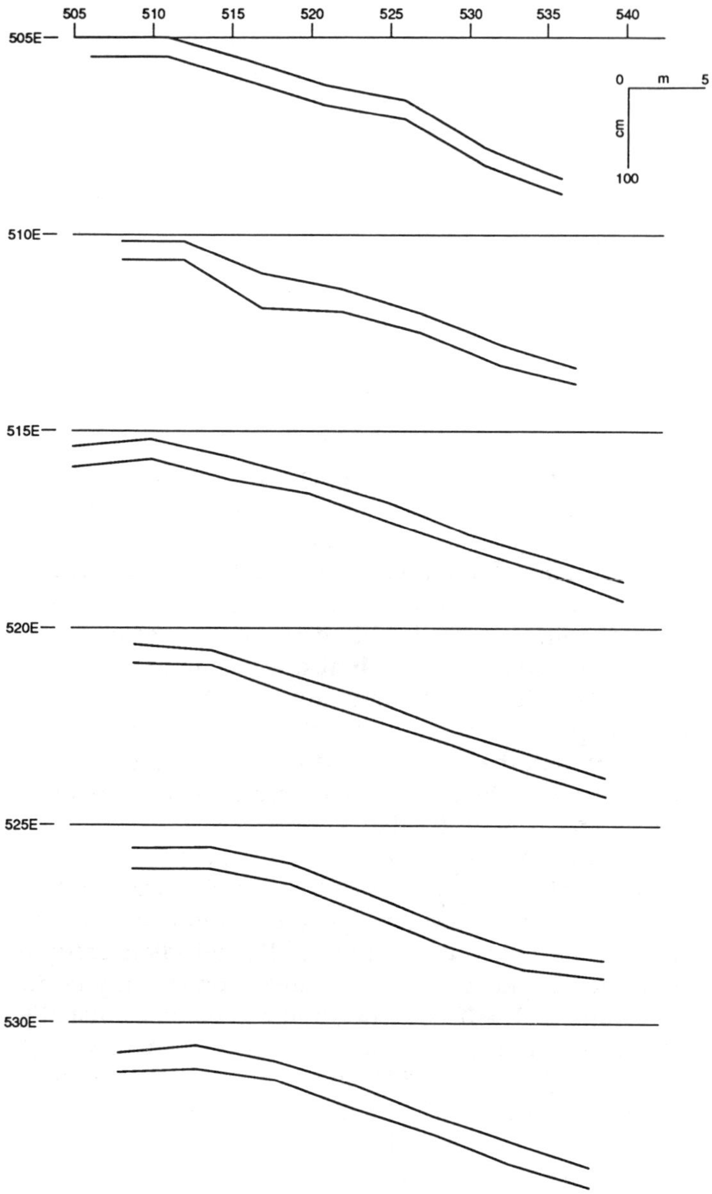

Figure 3.1. Surface elevations and plow zone depth across the site. North-south transects from Stage 1 excavation units. Horizontal lines represent site elevation datum.

characteristic. Typically, the plow zone near features, especially those with artifact concentrations, also contains high densities of artifacts (Deller and Ellis 1992: 93, 100). It is probable that many of those artifacts originally were deposited in the features, and were subsequently disturbed and dispersed by plowing. In fact, it is possible—though impossible to prove—that much of the contents of a typical Parkhill phase site originally was deposited in features. Those features shallow enough to be completely penetrated by the plow would disperse their contents but leave no trace of their existence.

Deeper ones would be truncated, with some of their contents dispersed and the rest preserved in the sub-plow zone remnant. Artifact dispersal at Crowfield is considerable but not tremendous (Deller and Ellis 1984: Fig. 10, cf. 44). Recent experiments suggest that dispersal in general is considerable and has cumulative effects (Odell and Cowan 1987:466-67), and any site plowed many times is apt to have somewhat, if not extensively, dispersed contents.

To some degree, defining features as artifact concentrations is a default judgment; anomalies difficult to recognize by soil color or texture can only be recognized in some other way. Yet it has an unpleasant implication also noted by Deller and Ellis (1992:93): when artifact concentrations are produced by burrowing rodents or other natural agents, features are recognized by their disturbed nature, not their intrinsic properties. Moreover, Paleo-Indian features that contain few artifacts are less likely to be recognized and excavated than are those with dense contents.

Feature 4

Although several sub–plow zone anomalies were recorded in the field, only one was considered an occupational feature. All such anomalies were numbered and excavated. Feature 4 is the only cultural feature found at Leavitt ("Features" 1 through 3 were later interpreted as natural disturbances). Located in the southeast corner of the main excavation block (Fig. 3.2), Feature 4 appeared as a dense concentration of flakes at the plow zone base in Units 520N 528E and 520N 530E.

In plan, Feature 4 has an irregular oval form (Fig. 3.2). The exact boundaries of walls and floor could not be determined; the vertical distribution of flakes in transverse section (Fig. 3.2b) suggests the original cross-section was basin shaped. In general, the feature boundaries were difficult to detect, probably the result of leaching over many millennia and perhaps due to low organic content of the original fill. That fill was relatively homogeneous, and nothing was found to indicate distinct episodes of filling. Although no obvious evidence of disturbance to the feature was found, the irregularity formed by the lobe or spur on Feature 4's south wall suggests a disturbance of some kind.

All flakes found in Feature 4 were piece-plotted. No diagnostic artifacts—in fact, no tools of any kind—were found in the feature. The flake debris assemblage, discussed in Chapter 4, numbered 48 specimens. Flake de-

TABLE 3.1
Summary Data on Parkhill Phase Features

Site	Feature	Plan X-sec.	Dimensions (cm)	Vol (m^3)	Flakes	Flakes/ m^3
Barnes	1	oval —	130 × 60 × 14	0.11	123	1118.2
Barnes	2	oval basin	105 × 20 × 12	0.02	0	0.0
Zander	1	oval —	<100 × <100 × ?	—	10	—
Zander	2	oval irr.	150 × ? × ?	—	126	—
Thedford	3	rec. basin	250 × 64 × 20	0.32	28	87.5
Thedford	8	oval basin	180 × 134 × 42	1.01	35	34.6
Thedford	10	——	150 × 150 × 29	0.65	8	12.3
Thedford	13	irr. rec.	85 × 64 × 50	0.27	85	314.8
Banting	—	oval basin	60 × 32 × 17	0.03	0	0.0
Banting	—	circ. —	45 × 45 × 7	0.01	11	1100.0
Leavitt	4	oval basin	120 × 65 × 14	0.11	48	436.4

irr. = irregular, rec. = rectangular, circ. = circular

bris appears dispersed in longitudinal section, but somewhat aggregated in transverse section (Fig. 3.2). The meaning of this distribution is far from clear; although natural agents like tree falls and burrowing rodents can produce such aggregation, so could dumping of debris *en masse* by Paleo-Indians along one wall of the feature.

Wood charcoal also was found in considerable amounts. Several pieces were collected by hand for ethnobotanical analysis, which is described in Appendix A by Kathryn Egan. *Picea, Tilia* and *Quercus* are the only genera positively identified in the Feature 4 charcoal assemblage. Although hardwoods were not abundant in early Holocene communities, certain genera, including *Tilia* and *Quercus,* did occur in considerable number. On balance, all identified genera are consistent with an early Holocene cultural deposit, especially if Paleo-Indians preferred hardwoods like *Tilia* and *Quercus* as fuel sources.

Nothing in the matrix of Feature 4 suggests its use or function. Neither fill nor margins are noticeably oxidized by heat, as though the feature were used as a hearth. However, its maximum depth of 42 cm below surface is not especially deep for a Paleo-Indian or later feature (Table 3.1), so use for storage cannot be assumed either. Until more sites are excavated and Paleo-Indian features studied in detail, Feature 4's function will remain unknown.

Dating Feature 4

Because it was the only intact cultural deposit at the Leavitt site, an attempt was made to date charcoal recovered from Feature 4. After ethnobotanical analysis (Appendix A), two individual specimens—one identified as spruce, the other as probable spruce—were sent to the University of Arizona's Laboratory of Isotope Geochemistry for assay by tandem accelerator mass spectometry. This procedure is suitable for dating specimens, such as those from Leavitt, which are too small for conventional methods (Haynes et al. 1984). Consultation with the Arizona laboratory was undertaken before submitting samples; its judgment was that the samples, although small, were sufficiently large to produce accurate and reliable results.

Unfortunately, results of analysis were unsatisfactory. A sample of spruce charcoal weighing 0.016 g yielded a date of 7886 ± 115 B.P. (AA-1223). A second probable spruce specimen, weighing only 0.010 g, yielded a date of 1100 ± 600 B.P. (AA-1222). The latter's sigma makes the result virtually meaningless. Even sample AA-1223, with an acceptably small sigma, is difficult to reconcile with accumulated Paleo-Indian systematics and paleoenvironmental reconstructions. Very simply, it is unlikely for spruce to be present in southern lower Michigan after approximately 11,000 B.P. *Quercus, Tilia* and other hardwood genera found in modern communities in the area could be introduced into a feature after cultural occupation, but that possibility is remote for spruce. On balance, there is no obvious explanation for the dating results. At any rate, they fail to accurately establish the age of the Leavitt site occupation.

Although a number of Early Archaic bifaces were found at the site (see Chapter 6), it is extremely unlikely that the 7886 ± 115 B.P. assay documents Early Archaic occupation. Like the great majority of the Paleo-Indian debris and tool assemblages, Feature 4 contents were composed of Bayport chert; in contrast, most diagnostic

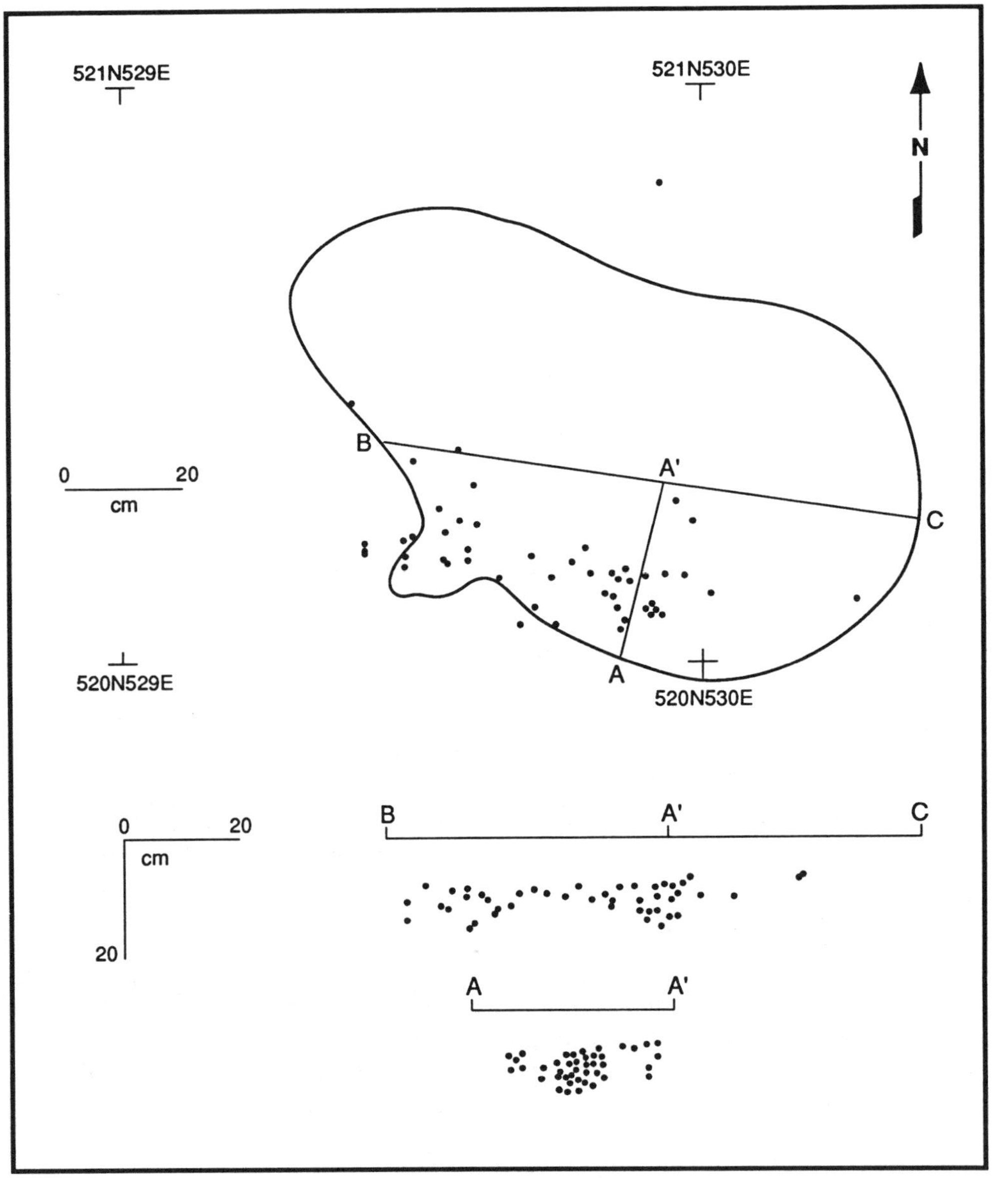

Figure 3.2. Feature 4. Piece-plotted flakes are represented by dots. *a*. Plan showing feature boundaries. Letters denote termini of section lines. *b*. Vertical distribution of flakes. Horizontal lines represent section lines at 25 cm below surface. Flake locations are reduced to the two dimensions of depth and horizontal location along section line; that is, flakes are plotted without regard to distance from section line. For transverse section A-A', two flakes are reduced to the same point in several cases.

Early Archaic bifaces found at Leavitt are composed of other chert types. Also, the feature lies in a fairly dense concentration of debris, as well as tools of demonstrable Paleo-Indian affinity. In fact, the closest diagnostic specimen of any kind is the unfinished proximal fluted biface fragment (85-27-100) found in unit 518N 528E. Early Archaic bifaces, in contrast, are found primarily on the margin of the Paleo-Indian concentration in the main excavation block.

Discussion

Feature 4's plan and profile resemble that of most Parkhill phase features (Table 3.1). Features vary con-

TABLE 3.2
Feature-Provenience Flake Debris from Leavitt and Thedford

Site	Feat.	Broken	BR	UR	CF	Fac	Flat
COUNTS							
Leavitt	4	22	13	6	0	4	3
Thedford	3	12	14	0	1	1	0
Thedford	8	14[a]	0	18	0	3	0
Thedford	10	1	6	1	0	0	0
Thedford	13[b]	53[a]	31	0	1	0	0
PERCENTS							
Leavitt	4	45.8	27.1	12.5	0.0	8.3	6.2
Thedford	3	42.8	50.0	0.0	3.6	3.6	0.0
Thedford	8	40.0	0.0	51.4	0.0	8.6	0.0
Thedford	10	12.5	75.0	12.5	0.0	0.0	0.0
Thedford	13	62.3	36.5	0.0	1.2	0.0	0.0
POOLED FREQUENCIES							
Leavitt		45.8	27.1	12.5	0.0	8.3	6.2
Thedford		51.3	32.7	12.2	1.3	2.6	0.0

BR = biface retouch, UR = uniface retouch, CF = channel flakes, Fac = large faceted platform flakes, flat = large flat platform flakes
[a]Includes "other" flakes.
[b]Includes sub-plow zone flakes both in and near feature.

TABLE 3.3
Feature Density at Parkhill Phase Sites

Site	No. Feat.	Area m^2	Feat/ m^2
Barnes	3[a]	256	0.012
Thedford	4[b]	500	0.008
Zander	2	96	0.021
Banting	2	490	0.004
Hussey	0	127	0.000
Leavitt	1	247	0.004

[a]Features 1–3, although the latter may not be Paleo-Indian (Voss 1977:256–57).
[b]Features 3, 8, 10, 13 (Deller and Ellis 1992:94–98, Fig. 68).

siderably in dimensions, however, and Feature 4 is somewhat smaller than most others. A rough measure of the volume of feature remnants (i.e., not estimated volume of the original, unplowed feature) is found as the product of reported feature dimensions. By this measure, Leavitt's Feature 4 again appears somewhat small. Its flake debris density, however, is considerable (Table 3.1), but it lacks the finished tools that several other Parkhill phase features contain.

Virtually no ethnographic data are sufficiently detailed to compare to feature debris density listed in Table 3.1. Although secondary disposal of debris in pits or other receptacles is well documented ethnographically (Clark 1986; Clark and Kurashina 1981; Gallagher 1977), the kinds and amounts deposited are unknown. Nevertheless, it is plausible to suggest that abandoned features were used as dumps for trash, including lithic debris. Accepting this suggestion, each discard episode probably represents the debris accumulated in one or several distinct episodes of tool production or maintenance. Feature debris contents, then, may be the nearest thing we have to the remains of single reduction episodes.

Flake debris platform classes are defined in Chapter 4, but are briefly considered here. Table 3.2 shows debris by platform class from Feature 4 and from Paleo-Indian features at Thedford. Since assemblage size varies, relative frequencies are the best means of comparison. Considerable variability in percentage-composition is seen among Thedford features, reflecting the varying nature of distinct reduction and discard episodes there. Biface retouch flakes are common, although none were found in Thedford's Feature 8. Conversely, uniface retouch flakes are abundant only in that feature. When all feature debris assemblages from Thedford are pooled, the two sites yield similar values; in that sense, the Leavitt Feature 4 assemblage might be considered typical of the general pattern at Thedford, but not the contents of particular features. The only significant difference is slightly lower values at Leavitt for broken and biface retouch flakes and, correspondingly, higher values for large flake classes. For what it is worth, assuming that all feature debris are from a single reduction episode, both tool finishing and maintenance apparently took place in the same episode at Leavitt.

Only a single cultural feature was found at Leavitt, giving the site a considerably lower feature density than most other Parkhill phase sites (Table 3.3). The observed density at Leavitt is half that of Thedford and one-third that of Barnes. Of course, one or more Barnes and Thedford features may be natural or, if cultural, from more recent occupations, as the authors of both reports are careful to note. Zander, at any rate, stands out for its high density, while only Banting and Hussey—the latter with no features at all—display lower densities than does Leavitt.

Chapter 4

Cores and Flake Debris

All stone tool production begins with cores, and flake debris is a necessary by-product. In this chapter, cores are described and flake debris from the 1984 excavations are analyzed for their assemblage characteristics and spatial distribution.

Cores

Metric attributes of Leavitt site cores are listed in Table 4.1. Specimens are briefly described by general class in this section. Unless otherwise noted, all specimens are composed of Bayport chert.

Tabular and Irregular Cores

85-27-292. This specimen has a complicated history. It is the spent remnant of a core probably formed by splitting a Bayport cobble in half and using the exposed flat surface of each as a platform for flake removal. This origin is deduced from the specimen's flat ventral surface, which bears a single large facet. The core is triangular; flakes were struck from two of the margins but the third is formed by the hinge termination of a large flake. No attempt is evident to rework this third margin or use it as a platform for flake removal, so the core probably was abandoned when detached from the larger piece.

85-27-139. The specimen is a snapped or split fragment of a small nodular or tabular core and is spherical to oblong in form. Numerous long, narrow, bladelike flakes were struck, principally from one pole, from the convex face of the core. No facets originate on the lateral margin, although there is crushing and possible abrasion along it. The opposite face bears a single large facet perpendicular to the direction from which flakes were struck on the obverse face. It also bears several smaller facets. The fracture surface is not reworked, suggesting that the core was abandoned when it fractured.

85-27-86. Like specimen 85-27-139, this item is a snapped or hinged fragment of a polyhedral core of an unknown material. It too is heavily faceted on the convex surface, although the facets are expanding and form a radial pattern. Thus, they probably were struck along the entire margin, unlike the previous specimen, and with a soft hammer. The convex surface is more nearly circular than oblong. The margins exhibit no crushing or abrasion. The reverse face has been largely removed by the hinge or snap fracture, but also bears several facets. Since the fracture surface is not reworked, the specimen probably was abandoned following fracture.

88252. A fragment of a Bayport nodule, this core retains cortex along one margin. It may be the remnant exposed face of a split and quartered nodule that has been extensively reduced for flake production.

Several large Bayport flakes (cat. no. 88229) bear three mutually perpendicular dorsal facets, and thus may be fragments or corners of tabular Bayport blocks. Ridges separating the facets are rounded, and clearly indicate that the facets are not the product of intentional reduction. Rather, these are Bayport blocks or cores that were tabular in form when obtained by Leavitt's inhabitants. It is unlikely that Bayport chert occurs in this form at bedrock sources. Together these specimens demonstrate that at least some reduction of prepared cores took place at Leavitt. Such cores appeared to be polyhedral, circular or discoidal in form. All are small and fractured, indicating that core failure was not uncommon and that cores were reduced heavily. It is unknown, however, whether they were imported to Leavitt in partly reduced form or were completely reduced at the site.

This general form of reduction is not surprising; the majority, at least, of available Bayport chert is nodular

TABLE 4.1
Metric Attributes for Cores

Spec.	Length (mm)	Width (mm)	Thickness (mm)	Weight (g)
TABULAR/IRREGULAR				
85–27–292	58.3	42.7	17.3	29.5
85–27–139	50.3	27.2	12.7	18.8
85–27–86	42.9	24.7	15.4	14.3
88252	65.6	38.6	15.4	42.3
BIPOLAR				
85–27–89	29.0	18.9	8.1	5.1
85–27–1–41	34.3	14.0	7.7	3.2
85–27–8	32.9	24.8	5.4	4.8
88246	39.3	21.8	9.1	7.3
88280	28.3	25.6	6.5	.
85–27–1–6	22.6	19.1	11.4	3.9
85–27–1–34	17.1	17.1	7.9	2.1
RAW MATERIAL				
88275	44.3	33.3	21.0	44.4
88233	51.8	27.5	30.6	91.5
88252	89.8	57.3	43.0	256.3

in form. Clearly, core reduction and flake blank production at Leavitt at least, and probably elsewhere in Michigan Parkhill phase assemblages, differed considerably from that found in adjacent Ontario. Ellis (1984) and Deller and Ellis (1992) have meticulously documented the standardized reduction of tabular Fossil Hill chert cores at Thedford II and other Parkhill phase sites in Ontario. They link these practices to the highly standardized flake blanks and tool forms also found in Ontario Parkhill assemblages. Although the evidence from Leavitt is limited, it strongly suggests that a similar degree of standardization was not found in Michigan Parkhill industries.

Bipolar Cores

Since the Debert site report appeared (MacDonald 1968), Paleo-Indian scholars have debated the merits of the bipolar core/*pièce ésquillée* controversy. The former school holds that these items are spent products of bipolar reduction, the latter they are a distinct tool form used as wedges for slotting and especially dislodging lengths of bone and antler. This is not the place to discuss the issues at length. In this report, bipolar objects are considered cores, the product of poorly controlled reduction techniques used on an expedient basis (Goodyear 1993; Shott 1989c). Significantly, MacDonald himself may now share this general view (Hayden 1980:2).

Bipolar cores are common on Paleo-Indian sites in eastern North America. Crabtree defines bipolar reducation as follows:

> Technique of resting core, or lithic implement, on anvil and striking the core with a percussor. Contrary to popular belief, bulbs of force are not present on both ends of bipolar flakes or blades. This technique causes the cone of force to be shattered or severed. Cone confined to one end and is sometimes sheared. [1972:42]

Several Leavitt site bipolar specimens are exhausted or abandoned tools reworked as cores. This practice was apparently common at eastern Paleo-Indian sites (e.g., MacDonald 1968; Gramly 1982), although Goodyear (1993) argues that it may not reflect expedient reduction as much as depletion of the raw material supply. For the purposes of this discussion, these artifacts are treated both as finished tools and as bipolar cores.

85-27-89. A small, broken specimen, this core is roughly rectangular in form. Flakes were detached from three margins on both faces, but none was removed using the edges formed by the fracture. Thus, the core probably was abandoned upon fracture. All worked margins are irregular and sinuous when viewed on edge. Although most facets are broad, expanding and short, there are few snap fracture terminations and virtually no crushing or abrasion along the worked margins. If this item was a reworked tool, the fracture and extensive reduction have removed all traces of its original form.

85-27-1-41. This item also is broken, but it bears two perpendicular fracture surfaces. One of the fracture planes actually is a facet formed by the splitting of the core, but the second is irregular and may be heat-induced or crenelated. This latter intersects and truncates the first plane. Thus, the specimen was split and then probably shattered by heat. However, there are no potlid fractures on either remaining faceted face. Most flakes struck from this specimen originate on a single ridge, opposite and running toward the crenelated fracture plane. Both worked margins bear crushing and slight abrasion. Although the core is too small to be certain of this point, it is possible that before the fracture no flakes were struck from the ridge opposite the main worked margin, as no facets originate from that direction. The specimen is extensively reworked, but it may have been a large biface or biface core which was further reduced in bipolar fashion when no longer large enough to continue reducing in the original manner.

85-27-8. This specimen is a broken biface extensively reworked as a bipolar core. The specimen still retains its biface outline form and thinness, but both faces are occupied by bipolar flake facets. Flakes were struck from all margins, especially the fracture plane. One or more blows delivered on that plane have removed roughly one third of the original broken half of the biface. Crushing and abrasion are confined to a distinct length of the core, along one margin of one face only.

88246. This specimen is a fragment of a classic bipolar core, or a large flake removed from one. It bears extensive, massive step-fracture damage at one pole and finer crushing and stepping at the other. The central ring of a Bayport nodule is found on the specimen, suggesting that bipolar reduction formed the final stage of nodular core use.

88280. Like 85-27-8, this specimen was apparently formed on a recycled biface. Reworking is not as heavy as on 85-27-8. One face bears only two large facets and several very small ones; the large ones were formed when flakes were detached from one margin. The other face bears facets of flakes struck from all margins, and a remnant crown of the original biface surface exists in the center of the face. Therefore, this item was not reworked over its entire face. Margins are sinuous and there is little visible crushing or abrasion. Two burin blows were delivered from the fracture plane along one margin. Although they bear no visible trace of wear, burin edges rarely do. They could be deliberate or merely incidental.

85-27-1-6. This specimen is a bipolar flake, strictly speaking, not a bipolar core. It was struck from what must have been a broken biface. The specimen is trihedral in form, and two of its planes are the faceted surfaces of the biface; they meet to form the sinuous edge of the original tool. Flaking from this edge is small, fine and well controlled. The flake bears crushing at its poles, but is not otherwise faceted.

85-27-1-34. This specimen is a marginal fragment of what probably was a large uniface. It is reworked slightly in bipolar fashion on an axis perpendicular to the margin.

Discussion. Neither prepared nor bipolar cores are numerous at Leavitt, a finding consistent with other Paleo-Indian sites in eastern North America. Typically, cores form a smaller percentage of Paleo-Indian assemblages than later ones, suggesting that most primary reduction occurred at or near quarries (Ellis 1989), and that only preforms and finished tools were carried to sites.

Two of the three prepared cores are variants of a single type, the large biface core. Ellis suggests (1984:120-26; Deller and Ellis 1992) that such cores were gradually reduced and then finished themselves as bifaces. This practice could have produced many bifaces found at Leavitt, although most were probably fashioned from flake blanks; these two cores demonstrate that some biface cores were reduced to an irretrievable point of exhaustion and then discarded. The third core probably represents a distinct reduction practice involving the splitting of Bayport nodules and the reduction of each resulting half using the split face as a platform. This practice could have produced a number of the unifaces found at the site.

Some bipolar cores are probably expedient in nature, and occur in varying proportions on eastern Paleo-Indian sites. Several are found at Leavitt, including reworked tools. Bipolar reworking of finished tools also is common at Paleo-Indian sites (MacDonald 1968; Gramly 1982), although the preference demonstrated for bifaces is somewhat unusual.

Raw Material Nodules

Several Bayport nodules were found at Leavitt that are technically not cores, since they bear no evidence of reduction. Their significance lies in the fact that they probably were not obtained at bedrock sources, and thus suggests that at least small amounts of chert were collected from scattered sources in the glacial drift. Data are presented in Table 4.1.

88275. This specimen is one half of a small spherical cobble. Measuring 44.3 mm in diameter, it probably was too small to be utilized. The convex surface of the specimen is cortex. Its edges are heavily rounded, although no evidence of use is apparent and no flakes were removed from it. Such rounding is not likely to be the result of weathering at the site, since few other artifacts found at Leavitt were weathered. Instead, it may have occurred through mechanical abrasion in glacial drift deposits. Why an apparently unusable chert cobble would be carried to the site is unknown.

88233. This irregular cobble lacks cortex, but has a single crenelated fracture plane similar to fire-cracked rocks (Taggart 1981). It measures 51.8 mm in longest dimension. Apart from the crenelated fracture, no other signs of use are evident.

88252. Measuring 89.8 mm in longest dimension, this specimen is a fragment of a chert nodule. It retains part of the original cortex as well as the central ring marking the first stage of formation of the nodule. The single noncortical face is heavily weathered, and the specimen bears no evidence of use.

Discussion. These specimens demonstrate that irregular, possibly naturally fractured, pieces of Bayport chert were collected and transported to the Leavitt site. Their form and appearance is consistent with a drift rather than a bedrock origin. Nevertheless, the great majority of lithic material at Leavitt probably was obtained from bedrock sources.

No systematic attempt was made to reconstruct cores from flakes. Although a worthwhile goal (e.g., Payne 1987), this measure is extremely time-consuming. Bayport, by far the most common chert found at Leavitt, is rather dull, grainy and variable both between and within nodules. Thus, flakes from the same core need not resemble each other, and many which do can be from different cores. In the face of such difficulties, core reconstruction was not a practical goal. Parenthetically, machine-vision equipment may hold great promise for core reconstruction in lithic studies. Although many such instruments are programmed to extremely close specifications, it should not be impossible to code them to observe and store the shape of individual flakes and to identify matching specimens.

Cores in Perspective. The tabular or nodular specimens described above—857-27-292, -139, and -86—are spent remnants of reduction. As subsequently discussed in Chapters 5 and 6, tabular core reduction is one major type of lithic reduction practiced by Parkhill phase knappers. The other major type, biface reduction, is inferred from the flake-blank form of a number of specimens, especially unifaces. No spent biface cores, however, were recovered at Leavitt, suggesting either that biface-core blanks were imported to the site from workshops elsewhere or that bipolar cores were preferentially fashioned from depleted biface cores. The latter alternative is questionable *a priori*—biface cores are no more suitable for bipolar reduction than is any other core or, for that matter, artifact type—and the former is left as the only apparent explanation for this pattern. Interestingly, workshop reduction as inferred at Barnes (Wright and Roosa 1966:859), the only other Parkhill phase site in Michigan that has been studied closely, starts with tabular cores that eventually were reduced to bifacial form. The admittedly limited core assemblage from Leavitt suggests that some tabular cores were reduced to depletion without passing through an intervening biface form.

Flake Debris Analysis

Introduction

Flake debris is easily the most abundant material found at Paleo-Indian sites, in spite of its comparative analytical neglect. Flakes are not considered diagnostic (although in some respects they may be), especially informative, or photogenic. But recent advances in the analysis of flake debris, inspired in part by Wilmsen's (1970) and Frison's (1968) pioneering work, have demonstrated the considerable value of this class of remains (Bamforth 1985; Deller and Ellis 1992:79-92; Voss 1977).

Analysis of flake debris can identify stages or paths of chert reduction and tool production and maintenance at sites. It also can reveal what types of tools were brought to and used at those sites. Spatial patterning might be revealed in debris distributions but not in other artifact classes (Henry et al. 1976:61). The highly organized nature of Great Lakes Paleo-Indian tool production and use (Deller and Ellis 1992; Ellis 1984; Shott 1986a) makes flake debris an especially important class of Paleo-Indian remains, since tools often are carried to and then removed from sites when their inhabitants depart. In such circumstances, only flake debris registers the presence of the tools.

Archaeologists already have discovered general patterns in the occurrence of flake debris at Paleo-Indian sites. The relatively few sites found at or near quarries typically contain a great deal of debris, representing virtually all stages or points of reduction except perhaps for the finishing and maintenance of tools (Funk et al. 1969; Gardner 1983; Payne 1987; Prufer and Wright 1970; Ritchie and Funk 1973; Sanders 1983; Storck 1978). More numerous habitation sites contain debris produced by intermediate and especially advanced stages of reduction, and also by maintenance or resharpening. As Ellis (1984; see also Deller and Ellis 1992) stresses, variability in debris need not be gradual or continuous. Organization in Paleo-Indian technologies can resist entropy in patterns of material use and discard. Quantities of material worked and used do not necessarily fall off smoothly and continuously from source areas, and critical shortages in material supplies can be avoided with due foresight. Since planning cannot be flawless, of course, shortages may nevertheless occur at times (Goodyear 1993), and significant patterning may exist in the rates of reduction and quantity of material used. Despite this, Ellis's construct is an extremely useful device for the analysis and comparison of Parkhill phase Paleo-Indian assemblages. In Ontario at least, many Parkhill phase sites apparently fall into one of two classes as a consequence of organization: quarry/workshops, and other, presumably habitation, sites. Relatively advanced blanks probably were made at and taken from the former, and finished and used as circumstances demanded at other sites. Nevertheless, comparatively slight or subtle variability may exist within the latter class of sites, which has not been thoroughly tapped by Paleo-Indian archaeologists.

Debris Platform Classes

Lithic reduction is a continuous process, and both stone tools and flake debris are best analyzed with respect to their continuous properties (Magne and Pokotylo 1981; Sullivan and Rozen 1985). For flake debris, this requires either the measurement of individual specimens or the use of mass analysis techniques. This study does not approach the thoroughness and virtuosity of those (Deller and Ellis 1992:80-87, Lothrop 1988; Voss 1977) who chose the former option. Nor were mass analysis techniques used. Instead, all specimens were inspected and assigned to one of a set of discrete flake debris classes defined by platform type. Aggregate weight of flake debris by provenience unit also was calculated, but neither individual flake weights nor aggregate weight by raw material or platform type were calculated.

Faceted-platform flakes. The platforms of these flakes bear scars from prior flake removals. Two classes of faceted-platform flakes were recognized in the analysis. The first, *large faceted-platform flakes* (n = 267), is defined chiefly by size, and comprises all faceted-platform flakes that are not retouch or resharpening flakes. Instead, they were struck at earlier stages or points in the biface production process, either from bifacial cores or large biface blanks. Platform angles are variable but generally low and platforms sometimes are abraded. Marginal use-wear at the platform:dorsal surface juncture is extremely rare. Although flake size is relatively large, platforms also are large. Lateral margins are convex to straight in most cases. Many large faceted-platform flakes are excurvate in longitudinal section. Dorsal flake scar frequency and patterns are extremely variable; they include parallel to convergent patterns but some specimens bear few scars and others have complex patterns. Especially on highly excurvate flakes, scars originating from the opposite bifacial margin are found at the distal end. Terminations are variable, and many specimens are broken. The size, excurvate section and variable dorsal scar patterning of these flakes strongly suggest that they represent bifacial core reduction or biface production rather than finishing or retouch. Thus, the class is generally equivalent to Deller and Ellis's (1992:80-81) "normal biface thinning flakes," although it also includes their relatively specific classes of end biface thinning, biface thinning in retouch and biface reduction errors. It may also represent the reduction of bifacial cores.

Biface retouch flakes (n = 636) bear faceted platforms, which often are abraded and lenticular in plan. Marginal use-wear is evident at the platform:dorsal surface juncture on many specimens. Platform angle generally is low. Lateral margins are convex to straight, giving specimens a lamellar to circular plan. These flakes generally are small and thin, and platforms tend to be large relative to overall flake size. Specimens are flat to slightly excurvate in longitudinal section. Dorsal scar patterns are variable; as at Thedford (Deller and Ellis 1992:84-86), some are parallel, from collateral flaking. Others, however, are more variable. Despite their small size, most specimens bear a number of scars on their dorsal surfaces. Terminations are by feathering in most cases, although step fractures and hinging are not rare. Biface retouch flakes probably are equivalent, at least generally, to Deller and Ellis's biface finishing flakes. However, many if not most specimens from Leavitt are retouch, not finishing, flakes as attested by the use-wear found on them.

Flat-platform flakes. These have smoothed, unfaceted platforms. Again, two size classes were recognized in the analysis. *Large flat-platform flakes* (n = 393), consist unsurprisingly of large flakes with relatively large platforms. Platform abrasion is rare, and platform angle is extremely variable but generally high. Marginal use-wear at the platform:dorsal surface juncture was observed on no specimens. Platforms are variable in plan, from lenticular to crescentic to irregular. Although platforms are unfaceted, many are curved or concave rather than flat. Lateral margins are expanding to parallel, with most tending toward the latter. Some specimens are excurvate in longitudinal section, but most are flat. Dorsal scar properties are difficult to summarize, both for their low frequency and variable patterning. Flake terminations are variable as well, but hinging is not uncommon and many specimens are broken. Large flat-platform flakes are difficult to interpret. Although some may represent the finishing of uniface blanks, many are too large to account for in this way. Instead, they may represent stages or points of core reduction of various kinds or even relatively early stages of the reduction of large flake blanks.

Uniface retouch flakes (n = 340) have small, flat platforms, and overall flake size is small. Platform abrasion is rare, platform angle is high and not especially variable, and platform plan is lenticular to circular. Platform size generally is small, especially platform thickness. This may reflect a desire to minimize attrition to tools during resharpening, a practice documented in ethnoarchaeological studies (Clark and Kurashina 1981:308; Gallagher 1977:411). As at Thedford (Deller and Ellis 1992:86), many specimens have pronounced bulbs on their ventral surfaces. Marginal use-wear is extensive, lying entirely on the dorsal surface at the platform juncture. Lateral margins are parallel to convex, and longitudinal section is flat to excurvate. Curvature is found especially near the distal end of many specimens, which terminated by traversing the entire bit of the uniface and feathering out on its dorsal face. Terminations other than feathering are extremely rare. Uniface retouch flakes clearly are the product of the maintenance of unifacial tools and are equivalent to Deller and Ellis's (1992:86-87) class of the same name. No distinction was made between end scraper and side scraper retouch flakes (Frison 1968:150-52, Figs. 1 and 3).

Channel flakes. These (n = 10) are a special diagnostic class of faceted-platform flake, produced in the fluting of bifaces. Platforms almost always are abraded, lenticular in plan and isolated. The platform angle is higher than in biface retouch flakes. Channel flakes are thin, and lateral margins are parallel. Intact channel flakes generally are rectangular in plan and flat in longitudinal section, but no intact specimens were found at Leavitt. Most channel flake fragments are square to rectangular medial fragments bearing the distinct dorsal scar patterning of facets originating from opposite margins. Although channel flakes or flake fragments can be curated for use as tools (Payne 1987:114), none from Leavitt bore any visible signs of use.

Broken flakes. This describes all specimens that lack platforms (n = 2,780); that is, medial and distal fragments. Although proximal fragments also are broken, they retain their platforms and therefore can be assigned to specific flake classes. Broken flakes are a residual category analogous to Deller and Ellis's (1992:87) "flat flake and other classes," although Deller and Ellis consider most of their specimens to be broken retouch flakes, especially bifacial ones, and not broken specimens from all flake classes.

The research design employed in this study, as described above, shares the defects of many other studies. It uses one or, more often, several properties as diagnostic of a type of reduction, thereby implicitly making inferences about flake-producing practices at the coding stage, before analysis (Sullivan and Rozen 1985). Some properties may be inadequately defined, and comparison with other studies cannot be determined. No matter how well defined, some properties simply are not diagnostic of a particular point, stage or type of reduction. These defects are acknowledged with the somewhat lame justification that they are common elsewhere. Future analyses of Paleo-Indian flake debris assemblages should apply more clearly defined properties so they can be more easily compared and results replicated. This, combined with mass analysis techniques, will facilitate more efficient analysis of large debris assemblages.

Results

Flake debris from Leavitt was tabulated by the raw material types discussed in Chapter 2, as well as by platform type (Tables 4.2-4.4). Bayport is by far the most common raw material type, forming 93.4% of the assemblage. At Thedford, Collingwood chert forms 94.5% of the flake debris assemblage (Deller and Ellis 1992:80), a nearly identical figure. This pattern of overwhelming predominance by a single material is virtually a diagnostic property of Paleo-Indian assemblages in the midcontinent (Ellis 1989). Where Leavitt perhaps departs from the general pattern is in the relative diversity of minor raw material sources; many upper Great Lakes Paleo-Indian assemblages contain only one or two minor sources, but at least five are found at Leavitt.

TABLE 4.2
Flake Debris by Class and Material

	Platform Class						
Material	Bkn	BR	UR	CF	Fac	Flat	Total
Ten Mile	31	5	6	0	1	4	47
Upper Mercer	17	7	12	0	0	0	36
Quartzite	62	1	1	0	1	1	66
Greywacke	10	1	0	0	0	1	12
Collingwood	1	0	1	0	0	0	2
Unknown	92	4	5	0	4	22	127
NON-BP TOTAL	213	18	25	0	6	28	290
Bayport	2567	608	315	10	261	365	4126
TOTAL	2780	626	340	10	267	393	4416

Bkn = broken; BR = biface retouch; UR = uniface retouch; CF = channel flake; Fac = faceted

Over half of the Bayport flake debris is broken. As expected, large faceted- and flat-platform flakes are not common. Most Paleo-Indian industries emphasized reduction to relatively advanced tool blanks at or near quarry sources, with final stages of reduction occurring at residential sites. Biface retouch flakes are the most numerous diagnostic flake class found at Leavitt, indicating that biface finishing and maintenance was common there. Moreover, their true frequency may be higher; many of the broken flakes probably are fragments of biface retouch flakes, since this class is thinner and somewhat more susceptible to breakage than most others. If a considerable number of the broken flakes are indeed from biface retouch, and if the platform-bearing proximal fragments were not also recovered, then even more biface retouch flakes were deposited at Leavitt than Tables 4.2-4.4 record. Uniface retouch flakes occur in lesser but considerable amounts, and channel flake fragments are rare.

Ventral uniface retouch flakes are a distinctive but rare debris class (Frison 1968:150, Fig. 1), no examples of which were found at the Leavitt site.

Cherts other than Bayport make up less than 10% of the flake debris assemblage (Tables 4.2, 4.4). A residual category of unidentifiable materials is the most common. Among recognizable materials, quartzite is most numerous, and the great majority of quartzite flakes are broken (Table 4.4). Ten Mile Creek chert also is dominated by broken specimens, but biface and uniface retouch flakes are not uncommon. Upper Mercer chert is distinguished by the number of uniface retouch flakes in the class. Although absolute frequencies are extremely low, uniface retouch flakes are more common than biface ones, a clear difference from the pattern observed in Bayport chert. It is possible that Upper Mercer was used preferentially for unifaces, although only a single possible Upper Mercer uniface was found in the tool assemblage at Leavitt (Chap. 5). Few greywacke flakes were found, and most of these are broken. Two specimens document the presence of Collingwood chert, but say little about its pattern of use.

Flakes of other materials are somewhat more likely to be broken than are Bayport ones. Conversely, faceted-platform flakes are less common in the former, while frequencies of flat-platform flakes do not differ substantially between the groups. Although somewhat different reduction practices may have characterized Bayport and non-Bayport cherts, it is likely that most tools, regardless of composition, were imported to Leavitt in partly finished form.

Despite careful inspection of the debris assemblage from Leavitt, only ten channel flakes were identified. All are composed of Bayport chert. This figure is surprisingly low for a Parkhill phase site, even considering Leavitt's occupational context. Biface fluting traditionally is thought to have occurred most often at or near chert sources, a finding supported to some degree in Great Lakes Paleo-Indian industries. Thus, the Fisher site yielded at least 153 channel flakes (Storck 1983:84) and probably more, and Voss (1977:258) reports 102 channel flakes from Barnes. Although MacDonald (1983:99) questions the latter figure, there are no grounds for dismissing it and the figure is valid. The channel flake:fluted biface ratio at Barnes is 5.37, indicating a high rate of fluted biface production but subsequent curation or at least removal from the site. The high absolute figure for Fisher is mitigated to some degree, since the similar ratio there is 0.98 (based on the channel flake count of 153, which may be a minimum value). Nevertheless, a high rate of fluted biface production is indicated at both sites, consistent with traditional interpretations.

However, Ellis's (1984) concept of staged biface production suggests that fluting should occur at least at modest rates at sites located far from quarries, since it is to some extent a response to situational factors. Channel flake frequencies at Parkhill (Roosa 1977b) and Thedford (Deller and Ellis 1986:93) support this inference. Data from all relevant sites are compiled in Table 4.5, which shows that the absolute and relative frequency of channel flakes is exceptionally low at Leavitt.

Excavation-Block Debris Assemblages. The behavioral

TABLE 4.3
Bayport Debris by Class and Provenience

	Bkn	BR	UR	CF	Fac	Flat	Total
Main Block	1884	442	212	8	180	249	2975
Small Block	634	157	96	2	73	98	1060
Stage 1[a]	49	9	7	0	8	18	91
Total	2567	608	315	10	261	365	4126

[a]Stage 1 excavation units that do not fall in either excavation block.

TABLE 4.4
Non-Bayport Chert by Class and Provenience[a]

	Bkn	BR	UR	Fac	Flat
TEN MILE CREEK					
Main Block	21	0	3	1	3
Small Block	7	3	2	0	0
Other	3	2	1	0	1
UPPER MERCER					
Main Block	11	3	8	0	0
Small Block	3	3	3	0	0
Other	3	1	1	0	0
COLLINGWOOD					
Main Block	0	0	0	0	0
Small Block	1	0	1	0	0
Other	0	0	0	0	0
QUARTZITE					
Main Block	45	1	0	1	1
Small Block	14	0	0	0	0
Other	3	0	1	0	0
GREYWACKE					
Main Block	7	0	0	0	1
Small Block	2	1	0	0	0
Other	1	0	0	0	0

Bkn = broken; BR = biface retouch; UR = uniface retouch; Fac = faceted

[a]Only identifiable specimens are listed.

TABLE 4.6
Flake Debris Assemblages by Excavation Block

	Bayport							
	Bkn	BR	UR	CF	Fac	Flat	Non-Bayport	Total
Main Block								
#	1884	442	212	8	180	249	189	3164
%	(63.3)	(14.9)	(7.1)	(0.3)	(6.0)	(8.4)	(6.0)	
Small Block								
#	634	157	96	2	73	98	86	1146
%	(59.8)	(14.8)	(9.1)	(0.2)	(6.9)	(9.2)	(7.5)	

Bkn = broken, BR = biface retouch, UR = uniface retouch, CF = channel flake, Fac = faceted-platform, flat = flat-platform

TABLE 4.5
Channel Flake and Fluted Biface Frequencies at Selected Parkhill Phase Sites

Site	CF	Fluted Bifaces	Ratio	Source
Barnes	102	19[a]	5.37	Voss; Wright & Roosa
Fisher	153[b]	156	0.98	Storck 1983
Parkhill[c]	192	113	1.70	Roosa & Deller 1982
Zander	49	25	1.96	Stewart 1984
Thedford	41	32	1.28	Deller & Ellis 1992
Leavitt	10	8	1.25	this report

[a]Three are reported by Voss (1977), 16 by Wright and Roosa(1966).
[b]Minimum figure.
[c]All values are minimum figures from totals for Grids B, C and D only.

TABLE 4.7
Feature 4 Flake Debris Assemblage

	Broken	BR	UR	CF	Fac	Flat	Total
#	22	13	6	0	4	3	48
%	(45.8)	(27.1)	(12.5)	(0.0)	(8.3)	(6.2)	

BR = biface retouch, UR = uniface retouch, CF = channel flake, Fac = faceted-platform, flat = flat-platform

TABLE 4.8
Metric Attributes of Feature 4 Flake Debris

Debris Class	Length $\bar{x}$	s.d.	Width $\bar{x}$	s.d.	Thickness $\bar{x}$	s.d.	Weight $\bar{x}$	s.d.
Broken	40.0	(—)	12.9	(4.7)	2.4	(1.2)	0.7	(1.0)
Bif. ret.	10.3	(3.4)	9.7	(2.9)	1.7	(0.4)	0.2	(0.1)
Unif. ret.	17.0	(—)	12.0	(5.6)	2.0	(1.0)	0.3	(0.3)
Faceted	24.0	(8.7)	18.9	(5.2)	3.1	(0.9)	1.7	(1.0)
Flat	22.0	(9.9)	18.2	(4.6)	4.5	(1.0)	1.2	(0.7)

Measurements in millimeters and grams.

TABLE 4.9
Platform Metric Attributes of Measured Flake Debris

Debris Class	Width $\bar{x}$	s.d.	Thickness $\bar{x}$	s.d.	Angle degree	s.d.
Broken	6.5	(3.5)	2.0	(1.4)	70.0	(0.0)
Bif. ret.	5.3	(2.6)	1.7	(0.7)	55.0	(13.2)
Unif. ret.	5.3	(4.2)	1.7	(1.2)	50.0	(—)
Faceted	9.1	(5.0)	2.4	(1.3)	60.0	(11.1)
Flat	5.5	(1.3)	2.7	(1.5)	67.5	(11.9)

Width and thickness measurements in millimeters

significance of the two chief excavation blocks is discussed in Chapter 8, but a brief inspection of their flake debris assemblages is in order. The two areas display virtually identical relative frequencies of all Bayport debris classes and similar relative frequencies of other cherts (Table 4.6). However else they differ, the excavation blocks are very similar in their flake debris assemblages.

Feature 4 flake debris. Forty-eight flakes were recovered from sub–plow zone excavation in Feature 4, all but two of them composed of Bayport chert. As Table 4.7 shows, broken flakes are less common there than in the overall assemblage, suggesting, not surprisingly, that plowing has caused some of the breakage of flakes at Leavitt. Conversely, biface and uniface retouch flakes are more common in the undisturbed Feature 4 debris assemblage. The cumulative relative frequencies of broken, biface retouch and uniface retouch flakes are nearly identical in the overall and Feature 4 assemblages, suggesting by extension that the small and thin retouch flakes apparently are more susceptible to breakage than are other flake classes.

Although most flakes from Leavitt were not individually measured, piece-plotted specimens found in sub–plow zone context in and near Feature 4 were measured (Tables 4.8-4.9). Comparison with the Thedford debris assemblage (Deller and Ellis 1992:Tables 42-43) shows that, with few exceptions, metric attributes at Leavitt are greater. No direct comparison can be made to broken or "flat" flakes at Thedford, but Leavitt biface retouch flakes, uniface retouch flakes and faceted-platform flakes generally exceed their Thedford equivalents in metric attributes. In flake weight, typically a good overall measure of size (Magne and Pokotylo 1981), Leavitt specimens exceed Thedford ones by factors of 1.7 in faceted-platform flakes to 3.0 in uniface retouch flakes.

In addition, Leavitt flake debris is more variable, having higher coefficients of variation for most attributes in most debris classes. Interestingly, platform attributes of Leavitt specimens are especially more variable than their Thedford counterparts. The standard Collingwood tabular form and highly standardized reduction practices at Thedford (Ellis 1984; Deller and Ellis 1992) suggest that platform attributes should be relatively standardized as well. Greater coefficients of variation at Leavitt suggest, by extension, that reduction practices there and at related Michigan Parkhill phase sites were less standardized and more variable.

Mean weight of all measured flake debris at Leavitt is 0.74 g, substantially lower than the 0.92 g mean figure calculated for all Leavitt debris. These flakes, in short, are lighter and probably smaller than the average flake debris at the site. Because sub-plow zone debris is not subject to breakage in plowing, it might be expected, all else equal, to consist of larger and hence heavier specimens. The smaller value suggests that the sub-plow zone flakes are not representative of the entire debris assemblage, perhaps because they were deposited after an unusual or unique reduction episode. Nevertheless, even if the measured specimens are unusually small for Leavitt, they remain larger than the average values at Thedford.

Comparative Analysis

Relative frequencies of debris classes at Leavitt and Thedford are compared in Table 4.10. Equivalence of debris classes has been discussed; although strict equivalence cannot be guaranteed, the classes defined here and in Deller and Ellis (1992) are essentially comparable, and only slight differences in results can be ascribed to flake classification. A class of large, flat-platform flakes not produced by uniface retouch is the only class used here that does not appear in Deller and Ellis's analysis.

Leavitt and Thedford both are Parkhill phase habitation sites located some distance from raw material sources. Their flake debris assemblages differ substantially, however, and illustrate the degree of interassemblage variability to be found in Great Lakes Paleo-Indian industries. Large faceted-platform flakes occur in greater frequency at Leavitt, especially in the dominant Bayport chert class. Conversely, retouch flakes of both platform types and channel flakes are more common at Thedford. In general, a lower incidence of biface retouch and maintenance is seen at Leavitt than at Thedford. The combined percentage of the two flat-platform classes at Leavitt compares closely to the figure for uniface retouch flakes alone at Thedford. Apparently, somewhat less advanced stages or points of reduction were carried out at Leavitt. The range of variability in Paleo-Indian assemblages from habitation sites is considerable, belying the view that Paleo-Indian cultural practices and assemblage formation processes were simple.

TABLE 4.10
Relative Frequencies of Flake Debris Classes at Leavitt and Thedford

	LEAVITT			THEDFORD[a]		
	Bp	Other	All	Cw	Bp	All
Faceted-platform	6.3	2.1	6.0	3.8	3.6	2.8
Flat-platform	8.8	9.6	8.9	N/A	N/A	N/A
Biface retouch	14.7	6.2	14.2	32.2	21.8	31.6
Uniface retouch	7.6	8.6	7.7	15.3	41.8	16.8
Channel flakes	0.2	0.0	0.2	4.1	3.6	4.1
Broken	62.2	73.4	62.9	42.4	27.3	41.6

Bp = Bayport chert; Cw = Collingwood chert
[a]Source: Deller and Ellis (1992: Tables 39–41).

Raw materials may explain some of the differences observed between Leavitt and Thedford, but behavior and/or organizational factors must apply as well. Absolute frequencies of Bayport debris differ enormously between the sites, but relative frequencies also differ substantially in virtually every debris class. Large faceted-platform flakes are more common and biface retouch ones less common at Leavitt. Combined percentages of the two faceted-platform classes are similar in the sites' Bayport debris assemblages. Combined flat-platform flake frequencies at Leavitt are far lower than the comparable figure for uniface retouch flakes alone in the Bayport debris at Thedford. The latter's tool assemblage includes more unifaces than does Leavitt, but fewer Bayport unifaces (Deller and Ellis 1992).

Channel flakes are both absolutely and relatively far less abundant at Leavitt than at Thedford. Moreover, they are confined to the dominant raw material at Leavitt; at Thedford, nearly equally proportions are found in Collingwood and other materials. The scarcity of channel flakes at Leavitt may appear puzzling, but it nicely complements their superabundance at Barnes (Voss 1977:258). Just as there is no reason to question the frequency of channel flakes at Barnes (cf. MacDonald 1983:99), there is no reason to do so at Leavitt. Viewing those two sites as parts of a larger cultural and technological system nicely underscores the fact that a single-site focus is as necessary for description as it is misleading for analysis.

A considerably larger fraction of the Leavitt assemblage is broken, possibly the result of several factors. First, plowing may have occurred more often at Leavitt than at Thedford. At the least, the Feature 4 debris assemblage implicates plowing as a major breakage factor, although possible differences between the sites in rates of plowing are unknown. Second, the relatively dense and compact soil at Leavitt may cause greater breakage of flakes as well as tools. Third, Bayport may be a more fragile chert than Collingwood, although proportionally fewer Bayport than Collingwood flakes are broken at Thedford. Fourth, occupation span or resident population at Leavitt may have been greater, and greater disturbance may have fractured some specimens (Gifford-Gonzalez et al. 1985). Flake debris, however, probably is subject to secondary disposal to remove it from habitation areas (Clark and Kurashina 1981; Gallagher 1977; Hull 1987), making this explanation unlikely. Fifth and finally, genuine differences in reduction and tool use practices may have characterized the sites, such that more reduction overall and more early or intermediate reduction occurred at Leavitt. Earlier points or stages of reduction are not as well controlled as later ones, and can yield a higher percentage of broken flakes (Magne and Pokotylo 1981:Tables 3 and 5). Although broken flakes are relatively common at Paleo-Indian sites, few (e.g., Zander [Stewart 1984:Table 1]) display such a high rate of breakage as Leavitt.

To remove the effects of different frequencies of broken flakes, Table 4.11 presents relative frequencies of major flake debris classes at Leavitt and Thedford, omitting broken flakes from the calculations. Comparing the dominant raw materials classes at the sites, the chief effect of excluding broken flakes registered in Table 4.11 as altered ratios of relative frequencies of the debris classes. Excluding broken flakes, that is, reduces the apparent difference in biface retouch and uniface retouch flake frequencies, although Thedford retains its advantage in both classes. Bayport chert relative frequencies at the sites also continue to differ substantially, but to a somewhat lesser extent; a greater relative frequency of Bayport biface retouch flakes at Thedford, when all flakes are considered, is reversed, however, when only diagnostic platform types are tabulated. Total values for each site also differ, as shown in Table 4.11. For the entire assemblages, biface retouch flakes are less than half as common at Leavitt than Thedford; in Table 4.11, they are roughly two-thirds as common. Similarly, combined flat-platform classes are nearly equal in relative frequencies in the complete assemblages, but the Leavitt values in Table 4.11 are 30% greater than comparable Thedford ones.

TABLE 4.11
Relative Frequencies of Diagnostic Flake Debris Classes at Leavitt and Thedford

	LEAVITT			THEDFORD[a]		
	Bp	Other	All	Cw	Bp	All
Faceted-platform	16.8	7.8	16.4	7.4	5.4	7.2
Flat-platform	23.6	36.4	24.2	N/A	N/A	N/A
Biface retouch	39.2	23.3	38.5	62.8	32.4	60.6
Uniface retouch	20.3	32.5	20.9	29.8	62.2	32.1

[a]Source: Deller and Ellis (1992: Tables 39–41).

Interpretations of Flake Debris

Points/Stages of Reduction Represented

Paleo-Indian sites located any considerable distance from a quarry are unlikely to include tool blanks or debris from the complete lithic reduction continuum. In this general respect, Leavitt is no exception. The scarcity of cores and the preponderance of flakes derived from advanced points in the reduction continuum establish that reduction practices at the site were skewed toward finishing and maintenance. However, Paleo-Indian assemblages can vary continuously and in complex fashion within broad limits. Analytical methods used for the flake debris analysis limit our ability to gauge the nature and scale of this variability, but it is clear nonetheless that Leavitt differs from Thedford and probably Barnes as well.

Detailed comparison with the latter site is impossible but, as noted above, mean flake weight at Leavitt is much greater than at Thedford. This observation alone suggests that the sites differ to at least some degree in reduction practices, with earlier points in reduction more extensively represented at Leavitt. The presence of cores at Leavitt supports this conclusion. Alternatively, differences in kind—reduction of nodular, not tabular, cores—may account for the differences between the sites.

Only mass analysis techniques will permit the thorough analyses and comparison of Paleo-Indian flake debris assemblages required, because they are extremely efficient and therefore feasible on large collections like Leavitt and because they analyze continuous variability in continuous fashion (Ahler 1989). Future analyses of such assemblages—and perhaps reanalysis of sites like Leavitt, Barnes and Thedford—should use such techniques in some consistent analytical design. In this way, potentially subtle and complex patterns of variability in site assemblages can be documented, studied and explicated.

Form of the Imported Assemblage

The character of Leavitt's debris assemblage permits some limited inferences about the form of the tool assemblage imported to the site. Since spent cores were found, some amount of core working and flake preform production occurred at the site. On balance, however, most material probably was imported in finished or partly reduced form.

Uniface production requires less extensive modification of preforms than does biface production, and unifaces could have been brought to Leavitt as anything from flake preforms to finished tools; without doubt some of each, as well as partially modified blanks, were imported. The large flat-platform flakes could have been struck from uniface blanks during the production process, and their incidence suggests that at least some uniface finishing from earlier-stage or -point blanks occurred. Large flat-platform flakes slightly outnumber uniface retouch flakes (Tables 4.2-4.4); if no production of unifaces from blanks took place at Leavitt, then flat-platform flakes should be found only as small retouch flakes, and not as large specimens as well. Leavitt apparently differs from Thedford (Deller and Ellis 1992) and Parkhill (Roosa and Deller 1982:11) in the form of the imported uniface assemblage, since those sites show little evidence of reduction of unfinished blanks.

Early or intermediate points in biface production also are represented in the debris assemblage, indicating that unfinished biface blanks were carried to Leavitt. Obviously, however, the scarcity of channel flakes and the abundance of biface retouch flakes suggests that a considerable fraction of the biface assemblage came to the site in finished form. Flake dorsal surfaces were not consistently examined for "remnants of the original surfaces of tool blanks" (Deller and Ellis 1992:90), so Leavitt cannot be compared to Thedford in this salient respect.

Neither is it possible to determine precisely the number of flakes struck from biface blanks in their reduction to finished tools. Nevertheless, a crude attempt to estimate this quantity can aid interpretation of the debris assemblage. By Deller and Ellis's account (1992:90) between 13 and perhaps 25 thinning flakes are removed to complete each biface. Thedford has far too few flakes of this nature to account for bifaces recovered, let alone imported, there. But Leavitt has a considerable number of such flakes, far exceeding Thedford's absolute total and relative frequency (Tables 4.2-4.4, 4.10-4.11). Only six large faceted-platform flakes are found in the non-Bayport component of the assemblage, but 261 Bayport flakes of this nature could account for the reduction from blank to nearly finished form of 10 to 20 bifaces. The comparable Thedford estimate is only one to two bifaces. Thus, more of the imported assemblage at Leavitt may have been in unfinished, partly reduced, form.

Uniface Retouch

A total of 340 uniface retouch flakes were recovered at Leavitt (Table 4.2); 45 unifaces also were found. In view of the highly organized nature of Paleo-Indian technological and the presumed high curation rate, it is unlikely that tools were produced and used to exhaustion at a single settlement. Although the relationship between the uniface assemblage and the uniface retouch flake assemblage is difficult to measure, archaeological and ethnoarchaeological data can be combined in an admittedly crude initial attempt to gauge the curation rate of unifaces at Leavitt.

Ethnoarchaeological data (Clark and Kurashina 1981; Gallagher 1977) describe the use and resharpening of end scrapers, so treatment here is confined to that class of unifaces. Twenty-four of the 45 unifaces from Leavitt (53.3%), are end scrapers (Tables 5.1-5.4). For purposes here, a similar percentage of the uniface retouch flakes—180 of the total of 340—are assumed to be from end scrapers, although the latter figure also will be used in some calculations. (This figure may overestimate the number of uniface retouch flakes struck from end scrapers, which generally have shorter bits than side scrapers and hence require fewer flake removals to resharpen [Lothrop 1986:423].) End scrapers probably were imported to Leavitt in varying degrees of use, from flake blanks to nearly exhausted specimens. It is impossible, without a thorough and extremely laborious exercise in refitting, to determine exactly how many retouch flakes were struck at the site from each end scraper. Instead, estimates of the total number of such flakes struck from each end scraper specimen can be compared to the recovered number of uniface retouch flakes to estimate in turn the fraction of all use and retouch of the end scrapers that occurred at Leavitt.

The two ethnoarchaeological studies yield dramatically different estimates of the total number of flakes removed from each specimen during its resharpening. Both report that resharpening is performed with great care to minimize attrition of the tool while simultaneously forming a new sharp edge (Clark and Kurashina 1981:308; Gallagher 1977:411). In fact, Clark (pers. comm.) suggests that actual retouch flakes are extremely small, much smaller than the debris recovered at Leavitt and interpreted as uniface retouch flakes. Obsidian is the raw material used in both ethnoarchaeological cases, which may require or permit finer retouch. The possibility that actual retouch flakes are too small to be recovered using conventional excavation techniques is acknowledged but it is assumed for purposes of this discussion that the debris identified as uniface retouch flakes was indeed produced in uniface retouch and that the recovered material includes most if not all such debris generated at Leavitt. Gallagher's (1977:Tables 1, 2) data from secondary deposits of debris and exhausted end scrapers suggest that approximately 37 retouch flakes are struck from each tool between its production and exhaustion. Clark and Kurashina (1981:309), in contrast, indicate a figure of 16.2 retouch flakes per tool (Table 4.12). In both cases, figures were calculated from published data, and were not reported as such by the authors.

TABLE 4.12
Ethnoarchaeological Data on End Scrapers and Associated Debris

Flakes	Scrapers	Ratio	Source
1131	31	36.5	Gallagher 1977: Tables 1, 2[a]
356	22	16.2	Clark & Kurashina 1981:309[b]

[a]Figures are combined from two separate secondary deposits. Retouch flakes include only material identified as "flakes," and excludes other categories of debris.
[b]Figures are from a grab sample of 393 items. Flake count includes items identified as "flakes" and "flake fragments," but not "cores" or other categories of debris. Tool count includes both intact and broken specimens.

Assuming that these figures include all retouch flakes removed from end scrapers, the 180 end scraper retouch flakes from Leavitt would account for the complete resharpening of 4.9 end scrapers using Gallagher's data or 11.1 using Clark and Kurashina's. If all 340 uniface retouch flake from the site are ascribed to end scrapers, the figures become 9.3 and 21.0, respectively. The lowest estimate of 4.9 end scrapers accounts for 20.4% of the end scraper assemblage from the site, the upper figure of 21.0 for 84.0% of the assemblage. Because side scrapers and other unifaces also were retouched at Leavitt, and because recovery of uniface retouch flake probably was not complete, the lower figures probably are more reliable. If only one-fifth, approximately, of the estimated total number of retouch flakes that the Leavitt end scraper assemblage could have generated were in fact deposited there, then, on average, end scrapers were imported to the site with approximately 80% of their maximum potential utility (Shott 1989a:24) already depleted.

Using other data, an even greater degree of prior use before importation to Leavitt can be suggested. Mean metric attributes reported by Clark and Kurashina (1981:Table 21.1) of original, unused end scrapers are surprisingly similar to those of uniface (probably end scraper) blanks found at Leavitt (Table 4.13), although the Leavitt mean was admittedly obtained by averaging two specimens, neither of whose length is close to that mean. Gallagher (1977:410) reports similar figures for original, unused specimens. Significantly, metric attributes of exhausted specimens also are similar between Leavitt and Clark and Kurashina's study, lending greater credence to the comparison. Because of this similarity, Clark and Kurashina's ethnoarchaeological data are used to estimate end scraper curation rates. As Table 4.13 shows, depletion occurs when an average of 25.4 mm of original tool length is lost through use and retouch; the relatively slight reduction in tool width can be ignored for purposes here. The loss in length multiplied by the smaller width value of 36.5 mm yields a conservative estimate of total area lost of 927.1 mm^2.

TABLE 4.13
Mean Metric Data on End Scraper Blanks and Exhausted End Scrapers at Leavitt Compared to Original and Exhausted Ethnoarchaeological End Scrapers

	LEAVITT[a]		ETHNOARCHAEOLOGICAL	
	length	width	length	width
Blanks	68.3	42.1	65.3	42.3
Exhausted	35.2	30.7	39.9	36.5

All measurements in millimeters.
[a]Only specimens 85-27-255 and 88263-12 were used to calculate the mean, since these are the only two intact Bayport blanks that probably were intended for use as end scrapers. Including other uniface blanks, however, produces a slightly different width value of 42.1 mm. No other Bayport blanks are intact, so additional values for length are not available.

Although individual flakes from Leavitt were not measured, Deller and Ellis's (1992:Table 43) mean values for platform length and width of uniface retouch flake, 2.7 and 0.7 mm respectively, can be substituted. Again, equivalence is assumed, not demonstrated, but the approximate nature of this exercise justifies the assumption. The total area of each flake platform probably is less than the product of its length and width, since platforms rarely, if ever, are rectangular. Nevertheless, the product of mean length and width, 1.89 mm^2, is used here as a generous estimate of platform area of end scraper retouch flakes. Dividing the total area lost, 927.1 mm^2, by this figure yields an estimate of 490.5 retouch flakes per exhausted end scraper. The 189 uniface retouch flakes from the Leavitt debris assemblage assigned to end scrapers account for only 38.5% of the total for a single specimen. Alternatively, the recovered end scraper retouch flakes make up 1.5% of the total of 12,262 flakes estimated from 25 exhausted end scrapers. Using even the higher uniface retouch flake count of 340, the comparable figures are 69.3% of the total for one tool or 2.8% of all uniface retouch flakes yielded by the tools. Following the same reasoning used above, these calculations suggest that end scrapers were imported to Leavitt in nearly depleted condition.

Whichever set of estimates is favored, it is clear that only a small fraction of the possible retouch flakes struck from the 25 end scrapers at Leavitt were recovered. Yet both sets of estimates ignore an additional factor that would reduce the fraction still more: the 25 recovered end scrapers almost certainly represent only a subset of all end scrapers used at the site. Any specimens imported to Leavitt but also removed from it upon abandonment because they were not yet depleted, or finished and partly used at the site, cannot be included in the tool count. It is impossible to determine how many specimens may have been part of both the site's founder and donor sets (sensu Schiffer 1975), but it is reasonable to assume that at least several were. Accordingly, the estimates calculated above are minimum ones. On balance, this exercise demonstrates that the recovered uniface retouch debris assemblage is only a fraction—perhaps a small one—of the total number of retouch flakes removed from end scrapers deposited at Leavitt. The small size of uniface retouch flake may explain part of the discrepancy, since some flakes may have escaped recovery, but considerable use of end scrapers before arrival at Leavitt also is suggested.

This conclusion is surprising, since Paleo-Indian technologies probably were characterized by high curation rates. If tools were carried from site to site and only discarded after long use-lives, then most assemblages should have more retouch flakes than can be accounted for by the exhausted tools recovered with them. Foregoing discussion suggests precisely the opposite for Leavitt and further suggests that end scrapers were discarded after only brief use. But the close agreement in metric attributes of exhausted end scrapers between Leavitt and the ethnoarchaeological case suggests considerable curation.

The apparent dilemma can be resolved by questioning the accuracy of the foregoing estimates or the validity of the assumptions used in arriving at them. In our state of limited understanding of assemblage formation processes, the estimates are reasonable (if provisional) and merit consideration until better ones are developed. The dilemma may also be explained in part by a possible bias suggested by Deller and Ellis (1992 :91). Since biface reduction and retouch produce more flake debris than do the similar processes for unifaces, any excavation strategy—such as that employed at Leavitt, Thedford, and other major Paleo-Indian sites—influenced by gross density will favor areas in which biface debris is abundant. Unless biface and uniface debris are deposited together, this bias may act to the detriment of areas dominated by uniface retouch flake. In this connection, it is noteworthy that both ethnoarchaeological studies of end scraper use document thorough collection and careful secondary disposal of debris (Clark and Kurashina 1981:308; Gallagher 1977:410-11). Finally, the dilemma might be explained by reference to other observations in the ethnoarchaeological cases: end scrapers in both cases were made, used and depleted in the space of several hours of dedicated work (Clark and Kurashina 1981:306; Gallagher 1977:411-12), although in the former case this work was distributed over a period of several days (Clark, pers. comm.). Thus, end scrapers in these cases are not curated in the sense originally meant by Binford (1973), by being carried between sites. Redefining curation to refer to degree of use regardless of the number of sites involved (Shott 1989a:24) preserves the view of high curation of Paleo-Indian tools, although it has no bearing on within-site assemblage formation processes. Tools can be used and depleted at a single location and still be highly curated. If in fact end scrapers, whether highly curated or not, were made, used and exhausted at Leavitt, then the flake debris:tool ratio suggested by Clark and Kurashina (1981) nearly accounts for all recovered uniface retouch flake at Leavitt.

Density of Flake Debris

As noted above, the flake debris assemblage from Leavitt is unusually large for a Parkhill phase site. Its extraordinary size is not the product of recovery techniques; slightly more intensive recovery methods were used at Barnes (Voss 1977:256) and Thedford (Deller and Ellis 1992:5-6), but debris densities at those sites are considerably lower than Leavitt's. Areas of excavation were similar at Leavitt and Barnes, and approximately twice as much was excavated at Thedford. Yet Leavitt's flake debris assemblage is nearly twice the size of Barnes' and over four times the size of the Thedford assemblage. Leavitt also is distinguished by a density of debris much greater than the other Parkhill phase sites.

Debris density by major excavation block and overall debris density are shown in Table 4.14. The extremely high values in the excavation blocks, especially the Small Block, are reduced somewhat when debris from outlying regions of Leavitt is included. Nevertheless, overall debris density remains quite high.

TABLE 4.14
Debris Density by Excavation Area at Leavitt

Area	Flakes	m^2	Fl/m^2
Main Block	3164	162	19.5
Small Block	1146	45	25.6
Overall	4416	247	17.9

TABLE 4.15
Flake Debris Density at Selected Parkhill Phase Sites

Site	Flakes	Excavated Area (m^2)	Density (fl/m^2)	Source
Leavitt	4416	247	17.9	this report
Barnes	2488	256	9.7	Voss (1977:257)
Thedford	1009	500	2.0	Deller & Ellis (1992)
Zander	1977	96	20.6	Stewart (1984)

Debris density is far greater at Leavitt than at Barnes and Thedford (Table 4.15). No exhaustive compilation of relevant data from Great Lakes Paleo-Indian sites was attempted, but at least one other site in the region, Zander, resembles Leavitt and in fact slightly exceeds its value. It is possible that sites near quarries, such as Fisher, have even higher densities. Interestingly, Zander is approximately the same distance from Collingwood sources as is Leavitt from its probable Bayport sources. These similar patterns of variability in debris density over distance are based on very little data, but they do suggest that high rates and/or early stages of reduction are not necessarily confined to sites that are very close to quarries.

Flake:Tool Ratios

Flake:tool ratios are a common but not necessarily reliable measure of variability in Paleo-Indian assemblages. As Deller and Ellis (1992:88) note, recovery methods influence the ratios, and sites excavated using different methods are not strictly comparable. Treatment of tool—and conceivably flake—fragments in ratio calculations also affect results; their inclusion or omission can significantly alter ratios. High but variable rates of curation in Paleo-Indian industries also produce uncontrolled variability in ratios, since it is not likely that all locations occupied by Paleo-Indians experienced identical curation rates. Occupation span also can affect the composition of tool and, by extension, flake debris assemblages at sites (Schiffer 1975: Shott 1989a). Other aspects of assemblage composition have been discussed by Deller and Ellis (1992:88-89).

These factors alone make calculations of flake:tool ratios problematic. The history of investigations at Leavitt introduces yet another complicating factor, since some tools were collected in uncontrolled fashion from areas that almost certainly lay outside the excavation grid. In contrast, all flake debris was taken from excavation units. Thus, debris and tool counts are the product of collection techniques that differ in frequency, intensity and scale.

The interpretive value of flake:tool ratios, therefore, is unclear. To provide at least a modicum of comparability with other studies, a simple set of ratios were calculated (Table 4.16) using all flake debris and all tools and tool fragments recovered at Leavitt, regardless of provenience. In effect, the figures shown in Table 4.16 ignore the possible effects of the complicating factors noted above, especially those stemming from the complex history of investigations at the site. They should be used with caution, and for general comparative purposes only.

The overall debris:tool ratio is 61.3:1. The predominance of Bayport among both debris and tools makes the ratio similar when only Bayport is considered. Thedford values are far lower (Deller and Ellis 1992:88), although contrasting ways of compiling data may partly explain the difference. Excluding Bayport, the debris:tool ratio is considerably lower, though still above the Thedford value. Confining treatment to biface retouch flakes and bifaces, the ratio closely resembles that for non-Bayport materials. To say the least, non-Bayport bifaces were imported to Leavitt as finished tools subject to resharpening only; the lowest ratio is between non-Bayport biface retouch flakes and these specimens. Bayport bifaces, in contrast, generated considerably more biface retouch debris. Among uniface retouch flakes and unifaces, the ratio is extremely low, falling in the range for the overall value at Thedford. The ratios for Bayport and non-Bayport uniface subsets differ relatively little from each other or the overall uniface ratio.

TABLE 4.16
Debris:Tool Ratios

	Debris	Tools	Ratio
All	4416	72	61.3
Bayport	4126	61	67.6
Non-Bayport	290	11	26.4
Biface	626	23	27.2
Bayport biface	608	18	33.8
Non-Bayport biface	18	5	3.6
Uniface	340	49	6.9
Bayport uniface	315	43	7.3
Non-Bayport	25	6	4.2

Obviously, ratios vary considerably among subsets of the debris and tool assemblages. If, as suggested previously, many broken flakes were in fact produced during biface retouch, then certain Table 4.16 values underestimate the true ratios between debris and tool classes. On balance, Leavitt's debris:tool ratios are quite high for a Great Lakes Paleo-Indian site, underscoring again the comparatively unusual nature of the site.

Flake Debris Weight

As noted above, aggregate debris weight by provenience unit was calculated in the analysis. Variability in weight by raw material, platform type and spatial locus would be extremely interesting to study, but only the aggregate figure is available. Accordingly, discussion in this section is brief. Gross weight and mean weight per flake in the Leavitt assemblage are shown in Table 4.17, with comparable figures from Thedford. As the table shows, mean flake weight at Leavitt is five times the Thedford figure, revealing yet another major difference between the sites. The considerably greater number of large faceted-platform and flat-platform flakes at Leavitt probably accounts for most of the difference.

The Thedford value is slightly lower than Magne and Pokotylo's 33 g experimental mean weight (1981:Table 8), which supports the view that tool reduction and retouch was the primary flake-producing activity there. The Leavitt value is nearly three times Magne and Pokotylo's figure for blank reduction flakes, but also less than one-twentieth of their figure for core reduction flakes (1981:Table 7). The Leavitt value is much closer to Magne and Pokotylo's blank reduction figure, which suggests that most flake-producing activities there also stemmed from tool production and retouch, not core reduction. In this perspective, Leavitt and Thedford differ significantly in degree, but not in kind, of flake-producing activities. Both fall in Magne and Pokotylo's (1981:Table 9) "Late Reduction" stage, although Leavitt falls near the upper end of the range. Small debris is indeed typical of Paleo-Indian assemblages, but the debris size varies.

TABLE 4.17
Debris Weight at Leavitt and Thedford

	WEIGHT (g)	
Site	Aggregate	Mean
Leavitt	4048.6	0.92
Thedford	183.2	0.18

The difference in mean flake weight is especially pronounced when the greater relative and absolute frequency of broken flakes at Leavitt is considered. Deller and Ellis (1992:87) suggest that most broken flakes at Thedford probably derived from biface reduction or retouch; since retouch flakes far outnumber reduction flakes there, most broken flakes probably could be assigned to the former class. By extension, this reasoning would apply to Leavitt as well, such that most broken flakes probably are from biface reduction or retouch. The higher relative and absolute frequency of reduction flakes at Leavitt would suggest that broken specimens should be more evenly allocated between the two faceted-platform classes. Nevertheless, biface reduction and retouch flakes generally are small and light, and most broken ones probably are as well. Despite this, mean flake weight at Leavitt is much greater than at Thedford.

Discussion

Variability in flake debris assemblages can result from several factors. Actual differences in the types and number of tools brought to or produced at sites, with presumed differences in associated tool-using activities (Shott 1989b) is one obvious factor. If this alone accounts for the difference between Leavitt and Thedford, it indicates that activities associated with unifaces—hideworking is one obvious example—were more common and/or important at Leavitt, since flat-platform flakes occur at higher relative frequency there. Conversely, biface-related activities were more prevalent at Thedford. The higher percentage of large flake classes at Leavitt suggests that tool production was more important there than at Thedford.

Differences in timing of occupation relative to the most recent resupplying of raw material is a second possible factor. The greater prevalence of tool production, as opposed to use and resharpening, at Leavitt would indicate by this reasoning that it was occupied more recently after replenishing raw material supplies than was Thedford. Ellis (1989; see also Deller and Ellis 1992) argues persuasively that the organized nature of Parkhill phase Paleo-Indian cultures resisted or overcame the entropy assumed by this explanation. Nevertheless, Goodyear (1993) marshalls considerable data suggesting that entropy and progressive conservation or recycling of raw material supplies does in fact characterize other Paleo-Indian cultures. Entropy can be resisted, but not overcome. Entropy—shortages in raw materials in this context—may produce some variability in flake debris as well as tool assemblages, but its role at Leavitt is unknown.

A third factor must also be considered. Occupation span can influence the composition of tool assemblages (Schiffer 1975; Shott 1989b) and there is no reason to exclude its effects on flake debris assemblages. Even if tool-using activities were identical in kind and frequency at Leavitt and Thedford, different rates of tool production and retouch could create some of the variability observed between the sites.

Chapter 5

Unifaces

Introduction

Although bifaces shoulder most of the typological and chronological burden in Paleo-Indian studies, the distinctive nature of Paleo-Indian unifaces is well documented. Moreover, the need for skin and hide products, a major object of work with unifaces, was probably critical in early Holocene eastern North America.

This chapter treats the uniface assemblage from Leavitt. It begins with a brief discussion of the inferred reduction process that produced most specimens recovered from the site. Under the heading of two chief processes, individual specimens are illustrated and also described at some length. This treatment should underscore not only the central tendencies that the uniface assemblage shares with Paleo-Indian industries across North America, but some of the particular aspects of the Leavitt assemblage. In this manner, due attention is paid to the modal properties of the uniface assemblage at the same time that variation within the assemblage is systematically assayed. This approach is followed in recognition of the equal importance of modal properties and variation in prehistoric cultural adaptation.

A basic distinction is made in description and analysis between distal- and proximal-margin tools, commonly and henceforth termed "end scrapers," and lateral-margin ones, commonly and henceforth "side scrapers." The distinction may seem axiomatic, and it is rarely validated, but it nevertheless requires justification. At Lindenmeier, these categories exhibit few significant differences in original technological attributes (e.g., platform attributes, overall size and form) but sharp ones in functional attributes (Wilmsen and Roberts 1978:137). Side scrapers and utilized flakes, moreover, were found to differ little in functional respects, leading Wilmsen and Roberts (1978:161) to identify them as equivalent tools differing more in degree of retouch than in specific design elements. This judgment is supported by Dibble's (1987) reanalysis of Old World Middle Paleolithic side scraper types, which are interpreted as merely arbitrary stages in a reduction continuum of large, otherwise-unmodified flakes. In Great Lakes Paleo-Indian studies, similar conclusions have been reached. Ellis and Deller (1988:128) regard side scrapers as classes of tools, not specific tool types possessing functional significance. Lothrop (1988) and Shott (1986a) echo this judgment.

End scrapers, in contrast, are generally treated as tools modified not merely by use and resharpening, but for hafting, functional and perhaps other design purposes. End scrapers, then, possess (usually) unifacial functional margins or bits perpendicular to the tool's longitudinal axis. Bits usually lie at the distal margin, but may alternatively or additionally occupy the proximal one as well (Ellis and Deller 1988:115-16). End scrapers generally are treated as a unitary functional class involved in hideworking, surely an important activity in the Parkhill phase repertoire. In Ellis and Deller's (1988) terms, they comprise a tool type or perhaps a set of such types, rather than a mere tool class. Some ethnographic data support this treatment (Clark and Kurashina 1981; Gallagher 1977; Murdoch 1893), but experimental (Brink 1978; Kamminga 1982) and archaeological (Siegel 1984; cf. Hayden 1986) studies suggest that end scrapers are somewhat more functionally diverse or versatile than standard archaeological treatment would suggest. Microscopic use-wear analysis might settle the issue with respect to the Leavitt assemblage, but it was not attempted in this study. Results of such work may be problematic in any event (Ellis and Deller 1988:122-23; Hayden 1986).

Ethnographic end scrapers are almost invariably hafted (Clark and Kurashina 1981; Gallagher 1977; Hayden 1979; Murdoch 1893; Nissen and Dittemore 1974). Although archaeologists have long assumed the same of their prehistoric specimens, systematic inspection for hafting evidence in the absence of organic preservation is a more recent development (Cauvin 1987; Mansur-Franchomme 1987; Rule and Evans 1985). Such evidence is adduced from close inspection of Leavitt specimens, as noted in both the descriptive and analytical sections to follow.

Retouched flakes are rare in the assemblage and the somewhat more numerous side scrapers are not systematically analyzed in this study. Instead, analysis will focus primarily on end scrapers. Reduction practices employed to produce uniface, especially end scraper, blanks will be sketched briefly. Size and form of end scrapers will be described and comparisons made with other Parkhill phase assemblages. Haft attributes will be summarized and haft size and form inferred. Degrees of use and curation rate will be estimated by measuring exposed length of specimens as recovered and comparing this to ethnographic data on end scrapers in various stages of use and depletion (Grimes and Grimes 1985; Shott 1989a). Finally, brief functional analysis by means of macroscopic use-wear identification is attempted (see also Ellis and Deller 1988 on possible morphological evidence of tool function).

The Leavitt uniface assemblage includes 24 end scrapers, 15 side scrapers, several miscellaneous specimens, and a number of highly fragmentary items that probably are pieces of end or side scrapers. Attributes of unifacial tools are presented in Tables 5.1-5.4. (Some fragmentary specimens are listed in the tables but are not described in detail below.) Uniface flake blanks are summarized in Table 5.5. Uniface attributes are defined as follows.

Uniface Attributes

Selection of attributes by which to code and analyze tools was based on several considerations. Because many Paleo-Indian as well as other specialists employ the attributes first defined by Wilmsen (1970), a degree of comparability between assemblages virtually requires following the same course. Additional attributes, however, were defined to accomodate the unique properties of Great Lakes Paleo-Indian assemblages. Finally, others were used because of their relevance to the research program under which Leavitt was studied (Shott 1986a).

All tools are produced by the reduction of nodular or tabular masses of chert. Usually, tools are produced from flake blanks, which are struck from the larger masses of cores. Many are then modified for hafting, or otherwise modified in some way for use. In this study, an effort is made to distinguish sets of tool attributes. The first set corresponds to the flake blank from which the tool is formed. This includes blank and platform attributes. A second set of haft attributes and a third set of functional attributes are recorded as well. All attributes were used in the original study of the Leavitt assemblage (Shott 1986a), but some are not used in this report. Nevertheless, all are defined in the interests of complete presentation of data. Attributes of the flake blank are defined first.

Discrete Attributes

Material: the chert or other raw material from which the tool was fashioned. Bayport, Ten Mile Creek, Upper Mercer, and quartzite, the most common raw materials, are described in Chapter 2.

Part: the section of the tool. Classes include intact, proximal, medial and distal. For unifaces, two different observations were made, one for the original flake blank and a second for the tool itself. That is, intact tools can be—often are—fashioned from deliberately snapped or broken flake blanks.

Polidding and heat: the presence or absence of potlidding (Purdy 1975) or heat stress fracture, and color alteration produced by heating. Potlidding is unmistakeable and is considered accidental damage wrought by overexposure to heat, often after a tool has been used. Color alteration, usually evident as a reddish hue imparted to the specimen by oxidation, is sometimes difficult to detect. A conservative policy was adopted here, and only clear cases of heat alteration were coded as positive for this attribute. Such heating usually is considered deliberate, designed to improve knapping and use properties of the specimen (Crabtree and Butler 1964).

Nodule attributes: the Leavitt assemblage is composed primarily of Bayport chert, which occurs generally in nodular form. Bayport nodules frequently possess a series of concentric rings. The number of such rings visible on a tool was recorded although, frankly, this information was not used often in description and analysis. It is possible to determine if the flake blank intersected the nodule center when the cross-section of the complete central ring is visible. In such instances, the attribute "nodule center" was recorded as present.

Cortex: the presence/absence of tabular or nodular cortex, a remnant of the original core surface.

Termination: flakes terminate normally by feathering, or alternatively by hinging or stepping (Wilmsen 1970:12). Following Ellis (1984:544), those classes of flake termination were recorded. Obviously, flake termination could be coded only for intact flake blanks and

TABLE 5.1
Uniface Flake-Blank Attributes

				OVERALL			PLATFORM													
Spec.	Matl	a	b	Length (mm)	Width (mm)	Thickness (mm)	Wid. (mm)	Thickness (mm)	Ang.	Bulb Thickness (mm)	c	d	X-sec t	X-sec l	e	Face Angle l	Face Angle r	Potlid d	Potlid v	Heat
88261	BP	4	.	.	54.1	12.0	.	.	.	.	.	.	1	0	.	.	.	-	-	-
88273	BP	4	.	.	59.0	9.3	.	.	.	.	.	.	3	0	.	.	.	-	-	+
85-27-268-2	BP	4	.	.	18.3	3.8	.	.	.	.	.	.	2	5	.	.	.	-	-	-
90210	BP	1	3	50.9	38.7	9.6	5.8	2.0	75	5.8	-	2	7	3	1	50	60	-	-	-
88261-16	BP	1	3	30.0	33.0	6.3	.	.	.	5.1	-	4	1	0	2	60	70	-	-	-
88269-14	BP	4	2	.	30.0	10.3	.	.	.	5.3	-	-	3	9	.	50	65	-	-	-
85-27-190/275	BP	4	.	.	28.2	7.9	.	.	.	.	.	.	2	0	.	50	50	-	+	-
88235	BP	1	1	50.1	34.5	9.3	5.8	2.0	70	8.2	-	2	2	7	.	40	40	-	-	-
88268	BP	2	.	.	36.3	13.4	5.4	1.8	90	11.5	-	3	5	.	3	65	50	-	-	-
90211	BP	3	.	.	40.1	11.0	.	.	.	.	.	.	2	0	.	65	80	-	-	-
90213	BP	2	.	76.5	29.2	9.6	.	.	.	9.9	-	.	5	6	.	40	75	-	-	-
85-27-68	BP	4	.	.	25.2	6.6	.	.	.	.	.	.	4	0	.	.	.	-	-	-
85-27-324	BP	4	.	.	49.9	8.7	.	.	.	.	.	.	7	4	1	.	.	+	-	+
85-27-126	BP	1	.	57.8	31.6	11.0	10.0	4.1	20	5.4	+	2	2	0	.	45	60	-	-	-
88263-16[a]	BP	1	5	69.8	50.7	12.3	.	.	.	8.1	-	.	2	8	1	70	65	-	+	+
88263-16[a]	BP	2	.	.	45.7	7.8	.	.	.	8.1	-	.	2	0	3	70	65	-	-	-
85-27-37	BP	4	.	.	27.1	8.2	.	.	.	.	.	.	3	0	.	.	.	-	-	-
88260-3	BP	3	.	.	24.9	8.9	.	.	.	6.1	+	.	4	8	.	.	.	-	-	-
85-27-8	BP	2	.	.	28.2	5.4	.	.	.	4.7	-	.	6	0	3	.	.	-	-	-
88260-8	BP	3	.	.	30.7	5.7	.	.	.	.	.	.	2	8	.	.	.	-	-	-
88261-22	BP	1	2	61.7	41.0	8.1	.	.	.	7.9	-	4	4	9	2	90	65	-	-	-
90208	BP	1	3	42.6	30.4	11.7	4.8	3.7	85	7.6	-	2	6	0	.	40	50	-	-	-
88263-A	BP	2	2	.	51.4	8.7	17.6	.	.	8.4	-	4	1	9	4	40	55	-	-	-
85-27-13	BP	4	3	.	22.7	10.0	.	.	.	.	.	.	.	.	.	.	.	-	-	-
88260-4	BP	2	2	.	23.7	6.4	.	.	.	5.2	-	-	2	0	.	30	55	-	-	-
85-27-1-17	TM	4	2	.	31.2	10.1	.	.	.	.	.	.	4	9	.	80	.	+	-	+
88260-10	BP	1	2	42.5	30.3	7.2	.	.	90	8.1	+	.	5	7	.	-	.	-	-	-
90209	BP	2	2	41.0	31.4	11.0	.	.	.	6.2	+	.	2	0	.	45	55	-	-	-
85-27-1-5	BP	3	4	.	26.5	5.7	.	.	.	.	.	.	7	5	.	.	.	-	-	-
85-27-317	BP	4	1	.	30.3	6.3	.	.	.	.	.	.	6	4	.	60	70	-	-	-
90212	BP	2	1	.	33.4	12.8	.	.	.	11.8	-	4	2	0	4	85	80	-	-	-
88261-19	BP	4	1	.	26.4	9.7	.	.	.	.	.	.	2	0	2	.	.	-	-	-
85-27-16	BP	1	2	35.6	23.1	10.0	.	.	.	.	.	.	2	0	.	55	60	-	-	-
85-27-85	BP	2	1	.	32.7	8.0	.	.	.	.	.	.	2	0	.	.	.	-	-	-
85-27-15	BP	4	2	.	45.2	11.0	.	.	.	.	.	.	7	0	.	.	.	+	-	-
85-27-120	BP	3	1	.	20.6	4.2	.	.	.	.	.	.	.	0	.	.	.	-	-	-
88224	BP	1	2	39.5	27.9	9.6	4.8	.	70	7.1	+	2	3	0	.	.	.	-	-	-
85-27-71	BP	3	2	.	16.4	6.4	.	.	.	.	.	.	3	9	.	.	.	-	-	-
88261-11	QZ	4	1	.	65.2	9.8	.	.	.	.	.	.	2	0	.	.	.	-	-	+
88254	QZ	1	5	74.6	44.9	15.3	.	.	.	7.7	+	.	2	0	4	40	65	-	-	-
88260	UM	3	2	.	28.7	7.0	.	.	.	7.7	-	.	7	0	.	.	.	+	+	+
88290	BP	1	3	38.7	42.5	7.0	14.6	0.2	.	12.3	-	4	4	0	1	70	50	-	-	-
85-27-289/204	TM	1	1	39.5	28.7	13.8	.	.	.	.	.	.	7	0	2	.	.	-	-	-
88261-15	BP	2	3	.	49.3	8.2	7.8	2.6	70	7.1	-	2	6	9	4	50	50	-	-	-
85-27-87	BP	1	2	35.1	22.5	8.0	3.7	1.4	60	4.6	-	2	4	9	.	85	85	-	-	-
85-27-143/69	BP	2	2	.	31.8	9.5	12.1	6.1	65	8.1	-	2	.	.	.	.	.	+	+	-
85-27-176	BP	4	2	.	.	5.2	.	.	.	.	.	.	.	.	.	.	.	-	-	-
88261-14	BP	2	3	.	40.3	9.8	5.4	1.7	60	4.8	-	2	.	.	.	.	.	-	-	-
88360-9	BP	2	.	.	29.1	9.3	.	.	.	.	.	.	.	.	.	.	.	+	-	+

Material: BP = Bayport, UM = Upper Mercer, TM = Tenmile Creek, QZ = quartzite; **a:** condition (1 = whole, 2 = proximal, 3 = medial, 4 = distal); **b:** number of dorsal facets; **c:** bulb thinning (-absent, +present); **d:** platform type (1 = faceted, 2 = flat, 3 = ridge, 4 = hinged); **X-sec:** cross-section; **t** = transverse (1 = bi-convex, 2 = plano-convex, 3 = trapezoidal, 4 = triangular, 5 = offset triangular, 6 = concave, 7 = irregular); **l** = longitudinal (ordinal values from flat [0] to highly curved [9]); **e:** flake termination (1 = normal or feather, 2 = hinge, 3 = step); **face angle:** l = left, r = right; **potlid:** d = dorsal, v = ventral (-absent, +present); **heat:** - absent, + present

[a]Used, broken, rehafted and reused—coded once for each use.

TABLE 5.2
Uniface Haft Attributes

Spec.	Condition	LENGTH (mm) l	LENGTH (mm) r	Abrasion l	Abrasion r	Edge angle l	Edge angle r	Face angle l	Face angle r	a	Thinning length (mm)	Notch l	Notch r	THICKNESS prox. (mm)	THICKNESS dist. (mm)
88261	4	.	.	-	-	30	90	160	150	.	.	+	+	12.0	10.1
88273	1	49.3	25.7	-	-	70	75	30	60	5	31.8	+	+	2.0	9.7
85-27-268	1	11.4	12.0	-	-	40	30	90	75	0	0.0	-	-	3.2	.
90210	1	39.8	22.3	-	-	90	50	50	60	1	14.4	+	+	3.5	7.1
88261-16	1	.	.	-	-	.	.	.	.	0		-	-	.	.
88269-14	1	9.6	27.7	+	+	60	90	115	105	1	11.9	+	-	3.0	6.7
85-27-190/275	1	.	.	.	.	.	.	.	.	.	.	.	.	.	.
88235	1	24.6	19.0	-	-	35	70	180	110	0	0.0	+	+	2.3	9.7
88268	1	34.0	30.7	-	-	30	45	180	135	3	18.6	+	+	3.3	12.8
90211	2	23.8	24.6	-	-	.	.	90	80	.	0.0	+	+	8.0	9.1
90211	1	11.5	7.0	-	-	70	30	.	.	0	0.0	+	+	8.0	9.7
90213	1	.	.	-	+	.	.	.	.	0	0.0	+	-	.	.
85-27-68	4	.	.	.	.	.	.	.	.	.	.	.	.	.	.
85-27-324	1	0.0	0.0	-	-	.	.	.	.	.	.	-	-	.	.
85-27-126	1	28.1	19.5	-	-	50	55	130	125	4	23.2	-	-	2.3	8.5
88263-16[a]	1	12.2	12.9	-	-	45	50	.	.	5	15.8	+	+	5.6	8.1
88263-16[a]	1	5.6	6.9	-	-	90	85	60	70	4	13.1	-	-	2.3	4.4
85-27-37	1	14.4	12.8	-	-	55	60	60	90	2	0.0	+	+	5.0	7.5
88260-3	1	.	.	.	.	.	.	.	.	.	.	.	.	.	.
85-27-8	1	.	.	.	.	.	.	.	.	.	.	.	.	.	.
88260-8	4	.	.	.	.	.	.	.	.	.	.	.	.	.	.
88261-22	1	.	.	.	.	.	.	.	.	.	.	.	.	.	.
90208	1	21.4	21.1	-	-	70	65	120	140	0	0.0	-	-	3.7	9.8
88263-A	1	17.8	24.2	-	+	40	45	-	-	6	35.0	+	-	5.0	7.8
85-27-13	4	.	.	.	.	.	.	.	.	.	.	.	.	.	.
88260-4	1	9.2	11.7	+	+	60	60	100	135	.	.	+	+	1.8	5.7
85-27-1-17	1	29.7	33.5	-	-	30	25	80	70	0	.	+	-	7.2	9.8
88260-10	1	.	32.4	.	.	60	85	80	45	2	12.3	-	-	4.9	8.9
90209	1	15.0	14.6	+	+	60	55	80	85	1	27.9	-	-	2.8	7.5
85-27-1-5	1	0.0	0.0	-	-	40	75	80	50	0	0.0	-	-	5.4	0.0
85-27-1-5	1	0.0	0.0	-	-	75	99	80	85	0	0.0	-	-	1.1	0.0
85-27-317	1	3.9	7.3	-	-	90	65	60	70	0	0.0	+	+	4.3	6.4
90212	1	0.0	0.0	-	-	55	90	75	90	2	19.0	-	-	1.8	11.7
88261-19	2	.	27.6	.	-	75	75	75	60	4	19.2	.	+	2.1	9.2
85-27-16	1	21.7	18.3	-	-	45	65	55	60	2	21.5	+	+	2.9	8.4
85-27-85	1	20.0	17.2	-	+	90	75	50	50	5	16.6	-	+	2.7	8.2
85-27-15	1	14.9	10.3	+	-	99	75	60	70	0	0.0	-	-	8.4	8.8
85-27-120	3	.	.	.	.	.	.	.	.	.	.	.	.	.	.
88224	1	21.0	17.4	+	+	65	85	40	75	2	17.4	-	+	2.5	9.2
85-27-71	4	.	.	.	.	.	.	.	.	.	.	.	.	.	.
88261-11	4	.	.	.	.	.	.	.	.	.	.	.	.	.	.
88254	1	0.0	0.0	-	-	.	.	.	.	.	.	-	-	.	.
88260	3	.	.	.	.	.	.	.	.	.	.	.	.	.	.
88290	1	15.7	19.8	-	-	50	40	.	.	0	0.0	+	-	4.6	9.0
85-27-289/204	1	0.0	0.0	-	-	.	.	.	.	.	.	-	-	.	.
88261-15	1	0.0	0.0	-	-	.	.	.	.	.	.	-	-	.	.
85-27-87	1	0.0	32.0	-	+	30	60	.	.	3	24.6	-	-	2.5	7.8
85-27-143/69	1	.	0.0	.	-	.	65	.	50	1	6.6	.	+	2.4	9.0
85-27-176	4	.	.	.	.	.	.	.	.	.	.	.	.	.	.
88261-14	2	.	.	.	.	.	.	.	.	.	.	.	.	.	.
88260-9	4	.	.	.	.	.	.	.	.	.	.	.	.	.	.

Condition: 1 = whole, 2 = proximal, 3 = medial, 4 = distal; **l** = left, **r** = right; - absent, + present; **a:** number of dorsal facets
[a]Used, broken, rehafted and reused. Therefore coded once for each use.

TABLE 5.3
Uniface Bit Design Attributes

Spec.	Midline Length (mm)	a	Butt Width (mm)	bit #	Butt: Bit Wid. (mm)	Bit Wid. Angle	Bit Wid. (mm)	Bit Wid.: Bit (mm)	Max. Thick-ness (mm)	b (mm)	ANGLES ret.	ANGLES use	ANGLES face	Corner l	Corner r
88263-16[a]	69.8	0	13.8	1	.	0	14.1	2.5	7.5	6.0	60	90	120	.	.
88263-16[a]	.	.	.	2	.	180	15.9	0.0	6.1	5.7	70	90	110	.	150
88263-16[a]	39.0	0	13.8	1	.	180	15.9	0.0	6.1	5.7	70	90	110	.	150
88263-16[a]	47.6	90	19.5	1	43.3	95	14.1	2.5	7.5	6.0	60	90	120	.	140
85-27-37	23.3	0	24.5	1	13.5	95	24.9	9.9	5.8	2.5	60	110	120	160	.
88260-3	29.0	30	13.3	1	21.7	85	16.6	0.0	8.9	4.9	60	85	120	90	110
.	.	.	.	2	.	160	7.4	0.0	5.6	2.6	75	90	130	110	170
85-27-8	29.4	0	27.4	1	24.0	80	16.4	5.9	4.9	2.4	50	80	140	.	150
88260-8	19.1	15	.	1	.	.	12.8	2.6	3.5	4.2	60	65	120	.	140
.	.	.	.	2	.	.	16.1	1.6	4.3	3.1	60	80	120	140	.
88261-22	34.3	90	47.2	1	34.3	210	51.4	5.2	5.9	4.4	65	80	130	105	170
90208	42.6	0	4.8	1	35.5	30	14.8	2.1	11.3	11.3	50	60	130	180	140
.	.	.	.	2	35.3	85	22.9	4.4	7.0	6.4	60	80	120	140	110
.	.	.	.	3	32.8	140	17.6	1.9	9.4	6.5	65	100	125	110	150
88263-A	47.0	0	17.0	1	41.6	100	32.0	0.0	8.5	6.8	50	90	130	.	130
85-27-13	.	.	.	1	.	.	.	.	10.0	4.9	70	90	110	.	.
88260-4	24.9	30	9.8	1	18.5	90	17.9	5.2	5.3	3.5	65	90	125	90	140
.	.	.	.	2	19.4	120	11.4	2.7	5.1	4.9	50	90	130	.	.
85-27-1-17	43.0	5	17.1	1	35.7	85	30.7	8.3	8.1	4.6	90	95	110	90	80
88260-10	42.5	0	2.8	1	36.9	95	30.0	3.4	8.0	5.0	65	85	125	90	90
90209	43.0	10	9.4	1	24.7	25	16.0	0.0	2.3	1.0	55	90	125	180	40
.	.	.	.	2	40.8	80	29.0	4.3	11.0	4.3	75	90	105	40	70
.	.	.	.	3	34.9	160	11.4	0.0	3.3	1.5	55	80	125	70	180
85-27-1-5	22.7	0	16.7	1	19.7	85	23.1	2.2	5.6	2.3	75	85	105	80	150
88261	39.7	25	45.2	1	40.1	60	53.1	3.7	10.9	4.0	60	90	140	110	75
.	.	.	.	2	44.9	.	28.8	2.8	6.9	5.9	60	85	160	.	.
88273	71.0	155	18.9	1	59.1	75	49.7	6.7	9.4	8.0	60	80	135	85	60
.	.	.	.	2	.	.	36.7	5.8	9.1	5.3	65	90	60	60	.
85-27-268	16.0	15	14.2	1	11.0	85	19.0	4.5	3.7	2.4	70	90	110	110	70
90210	39.1	45	6.3	1	53.4	25	19.4	4.4	9.1	4.0	65	85	130	110	110
.	.	.	.	2	34.7	130	23.9	6.3	9.2	10.0	50	90	145	150	145
88261-16	30.0	0	13.2	1	14.5	.	26.9	0.0	1.3	0.0	60	60	120	110	65
.	.	.	.	2	28.9	115	14.0	3.9	2.5	3.3	75	85	105	.	.
88269-14	37.8	0	7.5	1	.	0	9.8	0.0	7.8	3.2	70	90	125	0	95
.	.	.	.	2	41.3	95	28.8	2.7	10.3	2.7	70	90	110	90	95
.	.	.	.	3	.	180	15.0	0.0	10.7	2.3	70	90	110	95	0
85-27-190/275	26.0	45	0.0	1	20.7	100	38.4	2.4	7.9	8.0	50	100	130	45	45
88235	50.1	0	6.9	1	39.2	55	35.5	0.9	9.8	4.2	70	90	110	170	110
.	.	.	.	2	50.1	100	19.2	2.0	8.8	4.9	60	75	120	110	110
88268	34.3	0	8.1	0	.	.	.	.	.	.	.	.	.	.	.
90211	42.7	0	24.4	1	.	165	26.6	2.8	4.8	1.4	80	90	100	.	165
	42.7	0	24.4	2	.	165	47.3	5.7	4.8	1.4	45	45	.	.	165
90212	76.2	180	13.3	1	.	180	69.7	.	7.1	.	40	60	160	180	180
85-27-68	26.0	20	.	1	.	110	25.1	3.2	6.6	3.2	50	75	130	75	110
85-27-324	42.3	85	28.2	1	45.7	120	43.0	8.7	6.1	7.5	60	75	160	130	150
85-27-126	57.8	0	21.1	1	.	.	.	.	.	.	60	105	120	180	120
.	.	.	.	2	53.6	110	19.3	2.1	7.7	3.9	60	90	120	120	120
.	.	.	.	3	.	.	.	.	.	.	50	90	130	120	180
85-27-317	31.3	0	14.8	1	20.9	25	17.2	0.0	4.4	3.9	45	90	135	170	120
.	.	.	.	2	29.5	85	28.3	5.5	5.1	3.8	70	85	110	120	80
.	.	.	.	3	14.5	150	17.5	0.0	6.0	3.5	60	90	120	80	160
90212	33.9	0	22.7	1	22.8	30	30.6	0.0	10.7	8.8	55	90	125	140	90
88261-19	34.3	60	7.4	1	.	.	.	.	.	.	.	.	.	.	.
85-27-16	35.5	20	5.1	1	35.5	55	18.7	3.3	7.1	5.9	60	80	120	125	110

TABLE 5.3 (cont.)

Spec.	Midline Length (mm)	a	Butt Width (mm)	bit #	Butt: Bit Wid. (mm)	Bit Wid. Angle	Bit Wid. (mm)	Bit Wid.: Bit (mm)	Max. Thick-ness (mm)	b (mm)	ANGLES ret.	ANGLES use	ANGLES face	Corner l	Corner r
	.	.	.	2	28.6	105	19.8	2.9	7.2	5.9	60	80	120	110	100
85-27-85	33.2	30	1.6	1	18.1	105	32.5	9.9	8.0	3.9	70	85	110	95	160
85-27-15	30.1	45	39.7	1	25.4	60	47.6	4.1	11.0	3.4	50	90	130	150	105
85-27-120	17.8	0	.	1	.	.	17.8	4.0	4.2	3.3	60	75	120	.	.
88224	39.5	0	11.5	1	33.9	5	19.3	0.0	9.0	6.2	65	110	115	180	95
	.	0	.	2	35.5	90	14.3	1.6	9.4	6.0	70	90	110	95	140
85-27-71	39.9	.	17.0	1	.	.	39.4	0.0	5.6	2.7	70	75	110	.	.
	.	.	.	2	.	.	19.1	0.0	4.5	3.4	60	.	120	.	.
88261-11	30.2	0	65.2	1	0.0	.	65.2	9.9	8.4	6.2	60	90	120	.	.
88260	33.6	0	13.4	.	.	.	.	.	.	.	.	.	.	.	.
88290	36.8	160	14.1	1	36.8	100	10.1	0.0	.	.	.	80	100	180	180
85-27-289/204	39.5	0	38.8	1	24.0	90	30.2	0.0	5.9	5.4	75	75	105	80	110
88261-15	36.1	80	.	1	.	.	52.7	0.0	4.1	4.1	50	65	130	180	65
85-27-87	35.1	0	10.0	1	31.7	85	22.5	3.4	6.9	6.3	60	70	120	85	85
85-27-143/69	31.9	50	7.8	1	28.5	80	30.7	3.3	9.5	6.1	65	75	115	.	.
85-27-176	.	.	.	1	.	.	.	.	5.2	2.1	80	100	.	.	.
88261-14	.	.	5.4	1	.	.	.	.	.	.	.	.	.	.	.
88260-9	.	.	.	1	.	.	.	.	.	.	.	.	.	.	.

a: angle of longitudinal axis, midline axis; **b:** distance from point of maximum bit thickness to edge of bit (bit thickness:bit)
[a]Used, broken, rehafted and reused—coded once for each use.

distal fragments lacking extensive distal-margin retouch.

Cross-section: viewed from the proximal end of the specimen with the dorsal surface up. Following Ellis (1984:542), nine states were observed for this attribute: plano-convex, bi-convex, triangular, offset-triangular, wedge, trapezoid, convex-trapezoid, concave and irregular. Longitudinal section was coded on an ordinal scale from zero (flat) to nine (highly curved), corresponding to a series of circle segments of decreasing diameter.

Metric and Angular Attributes

All metric values are measured in millimeters (mm) unless otherwise noted.

Length: the maximum length of each specimen. For unifaces, length was measured on the longitudinal axis of the original flake blank (Wilmsen 1970:14).

Width: the maximum width perpendicular to the longitudinal axis.

Thickness: maximum thickness perpendicular to both length and width. On unifaces retaining the original flake bulb of percussion (Wilmsen 1970:19), maximum thickness was recorded below the bulb, not on it.

Weight: specimen weight was recorded in grams.

Width and thickness positions: the distance from the flake-blank platform or the tool base to the points of maximum width and thickness.

Face angle: the angle formed by the juncture of the platform with each lateral margin of the flake-blank (Ellis 1984:548; Wright 1981a). The measurement was taken when viewing the specimen from the dorsal face. Separate measures were taken for each lateral margin.

Facets: the number of facets on the dorsal surface from prior flake removals. Facets struck from the specimen after its removal (e.g., bit retouch facets) are not included in this figure.

Platform Attributes

All flake blanks are struck from cores. The point or area on the core to which force was applied by the knapper to remove the flake is termed the platform (Wilmsen 1970:15). A series of both discrete and metric attributes of flake platforms was recorded for each specimen (Fig. 5.1).

Width and thickness: maximum width and thickness of the platform. Width is indicated by the distance along the platform between flake margins; thickness is the distance between dorsal and ventral faces of the flake.

Angle: the angle formed by the intersection of the platform surface and the ventral face. This is referred to as the interior platform angle by some investigators

TABLE 5.4
Uniface Bit Functional Attributes

Specimen	BIT CURVATURE		EDGE DAMAGE			Haft length	Weight
	long.	tran.	form	type	distr.		
88261	0	1	1	2	3	.	38.9
	0	0	1	2	3	.	.
88273	0	0	2	1	2	28.8	49.2
	0	0	1	2	2	.	.
85-27-268	1	1	2	2	2	.	1.3
90210	0	1	2	2	2	20.8	19.8
	1	1	2	2	1	.	.
88261-16	0	0	1	.	.	.	6.1
	0	0	3	2	2	.	.
88269-14	0	1	1	2	3	.	13.9
	1	0	2	1	2	19.2	.
	0	0	1	2	3	.	.
85-27-190/-275	0	0	1	2	2	.	6.1
88235	1	1	1	1	3	18.9	21.2
	2	1	2	2	2	.	.
88268	.	.	.	1	2	19.8	15.6
90211	0	0	1	2	2	24.4	22.5
	0	0	2	2	2	6.9	.
90213	0	1	1	1	2	.	22.4
85-27-68	1	1	2	2	3	.	4.3
85-27-324	0	0	2	2	2	.	16.6
85-27-126	0	0	1	2	3	.	21.8
	1	0	1	3	2	25.7	.
	0	0	1	1	2	.	.
88263-16[a]	0	0	2	2	2	.	35.9
	0	0	1	2	2	15.8	.
	0	0	1	2	2	15.8	15.6
	0	0	2	2	2	.	20.5
85-27-37	1	1	2	2	2	12.3	6.0
88260-3	1	0	0	2	3	.	7.0
	0	0	1	2	3	.	.
85-27-8	1	2	2	2	2	.	5.4
88260-8	0	0	2	1	3	.	3.5
	1	0	1	2	2	.	.
88261-22	1	2	2	2	2	.	22.7
90208	0	0	2	2	3	.	14.2
	0	0	2	2	3	.	.
	1	1	1	2	3	.	.
88263-A	1	0	1	2	3	22.5	21.3
85-27-13	0	0	2	2	3	.	3.6
88260-4	0	0	2	2	3	16.8	3.6
	0	1	2	2	3	.	.
85-27-1-17	1	1	2	2	2	33.3	11.9
88260-10	1	0	2	2	3	24.7	12.5
90209	0	0	1	1	3	.	13.3
	1	1	2	2	3	20.8	.
	0	0	1	2	3	.	.
85-27-1-5	0	1	2	2	3	.	4.9
	0	0	2	2	3	.	.
85-27-317	0	0	1	2	2	.	6.5
	2	1	2	1	3	.	.
	0	0	4	2	3	.	.
90212	0	0	1	3	3	.	17.1
88261-19	.	.	.	.	.	19.6	8.8
85-27-16	1	1	2	1	3	17.3	8.4
	1	0	1	1	2	.	.

TABLE 5.4 (cont.)

Specimen	BIT CURVATURE long.	BIT CURVATURE tran.	EDGE DAMAGE form	EDGE DAMAGE type	EDGE DAMAGE distr.	Haft length	Weight
85-27-85	2	2	2	1	2	.	8.8
85-27-15	2	2	1	2	3	.	21.4
85-27-120	0	0	1	1	3	.	1.8
88224	0	0	1	2	3	.	14.2
	2	1	1	3	2	.	.
85-27-71	0	0	1	2	2	.	2.8
	0	0	0	2	2	.	.
88261-11	0	0	2	3	2	.	26.0
88260	.	.	.	.	.	.	8.1
88290	1	1	1	1	3	.	13.1
85-27-289/204	0	0	.	1	2	.	17.4
88261-15	2	2	1	1	3	.	21.7
85-27-87	2	2	2	1	3	29.2	5.8
85-27-143/69	0	0	2	2	3	13.5	6.3
85-27-176	.	3	.	2	3	.	9.6
88261-14	2	2	2	1	2	.	11.6
88260-9	2	2	2	3	3	.	3.4

Specimens with two or more bits feature a corresponding number of lines in the table. Measurements are given in millimeters and grams.
Bit curvature: long. = longitudinal; tran. = transverse (0 = straight, 1 = slight, 2 = pronounced)
Edge form: 0 = concave, 1 = straight, 2 = convex, 3 = irregular
Edge damage type: 1 = scalar, 2 = step
Edge damage distribution: 1 = isolated, 2 = patchy, 3 = continuous
[a]Used, broken, rehafted and reused—coded once for each use.

TABLE 5.5
Summary Data on Uniface Flakes Blanks

Spec.	Matl.	a	b	Len.	Width	Thickness	PLATFORM Width	PLATFORM Thickness	PLATFORM Angle	Bulb Thickness	c	d	e	f	X-sec	Face Angle l	Face Angle r	# Facets	Weight
85-27-255	BP	1	+	54.8	39.9	7.7	7.6	3.5	65	5.9	-	1	+	3	pc	45	50	10	17.9
88261	BP	2	-	57.2	49.3	8.2	7.8	2.6	70	7.1	-	2	-	4	cv	50	50	3	21.8
88261	BP	2	-	33.8	38.7	8.7	5.0	1.4	75	5.3	-	2	-	4	ir	40	45	3	11.4
88268	BP	2	+	44.8	36.2	13.7	5.4	1.8	90	11.3	-	3	+	4	ot	65	50	1	15.6
88263-12	BP	1	+	81.9	46.6	11.9	7.7	2.2	60	8.6	-	2	+	1	ot	45	45	1	45.8
88254	QZ	1	+	74.6	44.9	15.3	.	.	.	7.7	+	.	.	.	pc	.	.	5	60.3
85-27-169	BP	2	-	34.7	21.1	7.4	.	.	.	5.8	-	1	-	.	pc	.	.	7	7.7

All measurements in millimeters, grams; **a** = condition, **b** = cortex, **c** = bulb thinning, **d** = platform preparation, **e** = platform cortex, **f** = flake termination; **material:** BP = Bayport; QZ = quartzite; **condition:** 1 = whole, 2 = proximal, 3 = medial, 4 = distal; + present, - absent; **platform preparation:** 1 = faceted, 2 = flat, 3 = ridge; **termination:** 1 = feather, 2 = hinge, 3 = step, 4 = snap; **cross-section:** pc = plano-convex, cv = concave, ot = offset triangular, ir = irregular

(Dibble and Whittaker 1981). Wilmsen (1970:14) calls it "angle *beta.*"

Bulb thickness: the maximum thickness of the flake bulb of percussion.

Bulb thinning: the presence/absence of flake scars on the bulb of percussion resulting from deliberate attempts to thin the bulb. Number of distinct scars was not counted.

Cortex: the presence/absence of cobble or tabular cortex on the platform. The percentage of the platform occupied by cortex was not noted.

Preparation: platforms exhibit one of several forms of preparation, reflecting the history of the core before the flake's removal (Ellis 1984:539; Wilmsen 1970: Fig. 3). Faceting indicates the presence of flake scars from the prior use of the core. Flat platforms exhibit no faceting

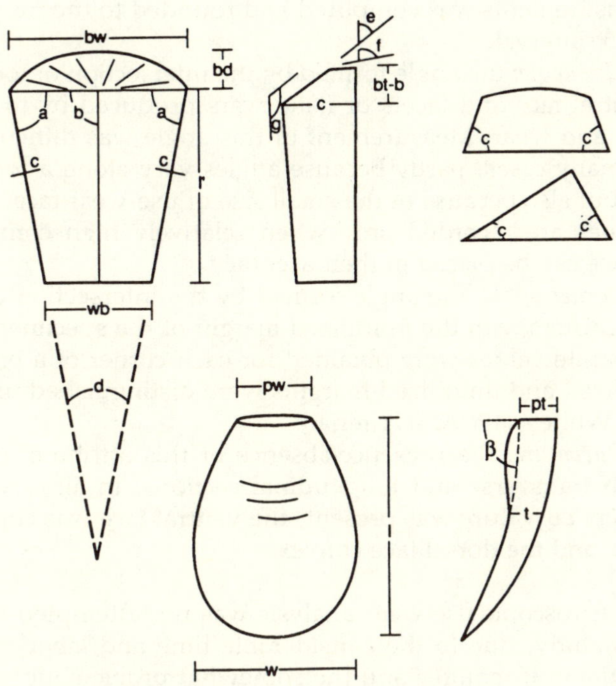

Uniface Variables
bw= bit width
bd= bit depth
I'= haft length
a= corner angle
b= bit width angle
c= margin edge angle
wb= width of butt
d= face angle
e= retouch angle

f= use angle
t= bit thickness
bt-b= bit thickness to bit
g= dorsal surface angle
pw= platform width
l= axis length
w= width
pt= platform thickness
= platform angle
t= maximum thickness

Figure 5.1. Uniface variables.

or surface features of any kind, and indicate that the core platform, or at least that part from which the specimen was struck, had not been previously flaked. Hinging indicates that the flake platform was removed from the specimen by spalling or hinging, probably during the removal of the flake. Usually, the flake bulb of percussion was retained in such instance, and its thickness could be measured. Similarly, the presence/absence of flake scars on the bulb also could be determined. Ordinarily, however, other platform attributes could not be observed on hinged-platform specimens.

Abrasion: the presence/absence of abrasion or grinding on the platform. Platforms were often ground before knapping in order to increase friction between core and hammer, and to promote greater control over flake production (Ellis 1984:539; Wilmsen 1970:16).

Haft Attributes

Haft attributes were observed on many unifacial specimens. Since hafting and the curation strategies it often implies have important morphological effects on stone tools (Keeley 1982:800-801), careful consideration and detailed evaluation of these attributes are warranted. The following were employed in this study.

Length: length of the tool haft from the butt or proximal end to the distal termination of the haft element. For many specimens, the latter point was indicated by the presence of shallow but distinct marginal notches, by the extent of proximal thinning facets, or by the extent of lateral margin abrasion from the butt. In a number of cases, haft length could not be determined satisfactorily, and therefore was not coded.

Lateral abrasion: the extent of lateral margin abrasion from the proximal end of the tool. Such abrasion is observed frequently on Paleo-Indian tools, especially fluted bifaces (Wilmsen 1970). Close inspection of Leavitt specimens often revealed the presence of this attribute on unifaces. Abrasion was measured separately for each tool margin.

Edge angle: the lateral margin edge angles on the haft element of the specimen (Wilmsen 1970:10). Again, separate measurements were taken for each margin. Since edge angles tend to vary across a single tool margin, up to three separate measurements were taken from each margin, and the mean value was recorded. As with utilized and retouched margins, measurement was carried out using polar coordinate paper to the nearest 5° interval (Parry 1987; Wilmsen 1970:17). Haft margin edge angle is not to be confused with tool margin edge angle, since the latter is affected by the manner and degree of use which a tool experiences. Haft margin angles were measured only within the haft element: that is, that segment of the specimen so identified by the presence and extent of other haft attributes.

Face angle: the lateral margin face angles on the haft element of the specimen (Wright 1981a). All particulars of this measurement are the same as for flake blank margin edge angles.

Dorsal thinning: the presence/absence of dorsal thinning from the tool proximal end. Two measurements were taken: the number of distinct facets, if any, and the mean length of those facets.

Notches: the presence/absence of notches at the presumed distal end of the haft element. Again, a separate observation was made for each tool margin.

Thickness: thickness at both proximal and distal ends of the haft element. The distal end was defined by the position of marginal notches, the extent of dorsal thinning, or the extent of lateral margin abrasion.

Butt width: width of the specimen at its proximal end. Where a tool retained its flake-blank platform, this attribute coincides with platform width. For flake medial and distal fragments, it corresponds to width of the flake blank at the point of fracture.

Functional Attributes

The use and retouch of tools produces another set of attributes. The following set were used in this study.

Midline length: the longitudinal axis of a tool can differ from the longitudinal axis of the flake blank from which it was produced. The midline length—longitudinal axis of the tool, not necessarily the flake blank—is defined as the line that bisects the butt and the bit or utilized margin. Where multiple bits were present, the distal-margin one was used to determine midline length.

Axis angle: the angle formed by the intersection of a specimen's flake-blank and tool longitudinal axes, measured to the nearest 5° interval.

On unifaces, one or more distinct marginal sections—bits—may be used and/or retouched. Tool bits are identified by the presence of a continuous distribution of resharpening facets and, usually, at least some visible attrition from use. The following attributes were employed to characterize tool bits.

Number: simply the number of distinct bits. Distinct bits were designated if an angle greater than 10° was formed by their intersection.

Width: the maximum width of each bit: that is, the length of the specimen margin that it occupies. This quantity is measured as the straight-line distance—the bit width line—between opposite ends of the bit.

Butt-bit width: the distance from the tool butt or proximal end to the midpoint of the bit.

Bit width angle: the angle formed by the intersection of each bit width with the specimen's flake-blank longitudinal axis.

Convexity: the distance between the bit width line and the furthest projecting point along the bit.

Thickness: maximum thickness of the tool bit.

Bit thickness-bit: the distance between the point of maximum bit thickness and the furthest projecting point on the bit. The latter is the same point used to determine bit convexity.

Retouch angle: the angle formed by the intersection of the tool ventral face with the retouch or resharpening facets present on the bit. Since the angle frequently varies along the length of a bit, the mean value of three measurements was computed and rounded to the nearest 5° interval.

Use angle: the angle formed by the intersection of tool ventral face and facets or flake scars produced by tool use and wear. Measurement of this angle was difficult in many cases, partly because angles vary along a tool bit but also because of the small size of use-wear facets. Values are recorded only when relatively high confidence can be placed in their accuracy.

Corner angle: the angle formed by the intersection of bit corners with the unutilized margin of the specimen. Separate values were obtained for each corner of a bit. Utilized and unutilized margins were distinguished using White's (1969:24) criteria.

Curvature: the presence/absence of this attribute for both transverse and longitudinal sections. In all cases where curvature was present, the ventral face was concave and the dorsal face convex.

Microscopic use-wear analysis was not attempted in this study, due to the considerable time and labor investment it requires and the somewhat problematic results it often produces (Cross 1983; Ellis and Deller 1988:122-123). As an alternative, Parry's (1987: Fig. 5.2) macroscopic tool margin morphology and wear or damage attributes were employed.

Edge shape: a series of ordinal states was used, from concave to pointed; an additional category of irregular shape was included. Edge shape has a bearing on the shape and size of incision or other attrition which a tool produces when applied to other material (Parry 1987).

Scar type: scalar, step and crescent or lunate (Keeley 1980:24-25). The scar types are identified with distinct sets of task applications (Keeley 1980:15-84). These scars are not to be confused with those produced by deliberate resharpening of tools.

Scar distribution: the distribution of scars or facets produced by tool use. Categories include continuous, discontinuous or patchy and, rarely, isolated (Keeley 1980; Parry 1987). Parry identifies these with different task applications and modes of tool use.

Bifacial Reduction

The proposed reduction sequence for biface-core blanks is shown in Figure 5.3. There, and in Figures 5.8 and 6.2, all tools are from the Leavitt assemblage itself unless otherwise noted. To note otherwise, the biface core depicted in the upper left corner is a hypothetical reconstruction of a fragment recovered at the site. As such cores were reduced, they would yield progressively smaller and perhaps more excurvate flake blanks.

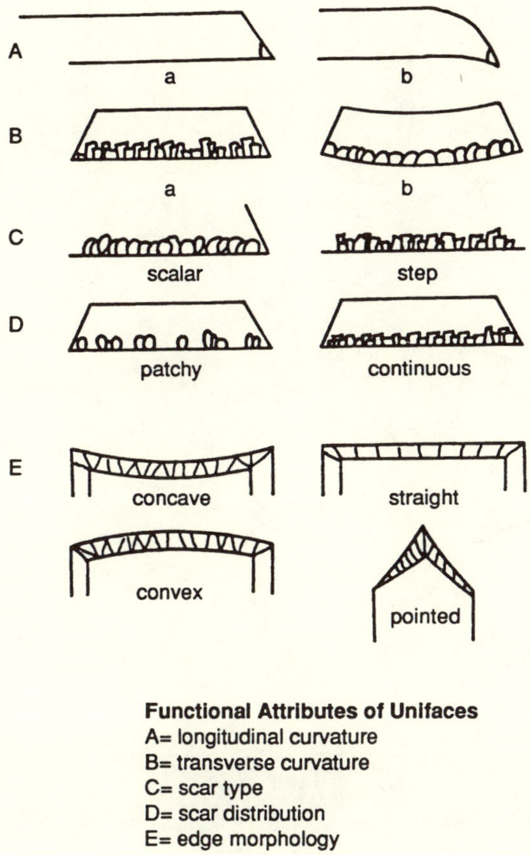

Figure 5.2. Functional attributes of unifaces.

The specimens in the second column of Figure 5.3, for instance, might have been struck from such a core at earlier to later stages as arranged from top to bottom. Blanks were struck across the face, top or bottom, of large biface cores from well-prepared platforms. Blanks themselves probably possessed well-defined platforms, although most platform segments have been removed from finished specimens. Blanks also tend to have expanding margins, pronounced longitudinal curvature, and extensive dorsal faceting from prior flake removals from the core, which typically originate from all directions. Because such blanks can be struck from biface cores of varying size and form and at various stages of reduction, the size and form of blanks can vary considerably, imparting similar variation to tools fashioned from them. Blanks also can be snapped and finished into two tools, or the proximal segment with its bulb of percussion can be discarded.

How Bayport chert nodules are reduced to bifacial cores is not addressed in this scheme, but they could be produced intentionally from split nodules. As reduction proceeds, blanks of decreasing size may be removed from their margins, yielding shorter and less curved products (e.g., 88261-16, Fig. 5.12a). The end product of this reduction sequence could be a core blank exhibiting extensive dorsal faceting and a bi-convex cross-section but little longitudinal curvature (e.g., 88261-15; Fig. 5.6a). Specimens are described according to the scheme presented in Figure 5.3. The left-hand column of specimens includes all for which original blank attributes were observable. This includes both finished tools like 88263-16 (Fig. 5.4a) and unmodified blanks like 85-27-255 (Fig. 5.4e). Specimens in this column are ordered in size from top to bottom. More extensively retouched specimens, for which hafting modifications often obscure original blank attributes, are shown in the right column, again ordered from top to bottom by size. Thus, unifaces are arranged not necessarily by degree of use but by extent of modification from the original flake-blank form.

88263-16 (Fig. 5.4a). This specimen was fashioned from a blank struck across the top of a bifacial core. Dorsal faceting is extensive and from all directions, and longitudinal curvature is pronounced. The platform has been removed and the resulting scar slightly reworked from the dorsal surface. The right margin is unifacially retouched along its entire length, but the left margin bears only slight retouch. The flake blank is fractured transversely near its midpoint, perhaps deliberately for the production of two tools. The proximal segment bears slight evidence of use after fracture while the distal portion is unifacially retouched at the corner formed by the fracture. In addition, its left margin is heavily retouched near the distal end, while the proximal end is not retouched. The two margin segments are separated by a cavity left by a vein inclusion, not a deliberate notch. On balance, the specimen probably was used first as an intact flake; after fracture, the distal portion was again used extensively. Specimen 88263-16 appears twice in Tables 5.1 and 5.2, first for the blank and haft attributes of the original flake and then for the attributes of the distal fragment as reoriented for use. It appears four times in Tables 5.3 and 5.4, once each for the original tool, the two utilized segments of the distal fragment and the one utilized segment of the proximal fragment.

88263-A (Fig. 5.4b). The platform of this blank has been removed by a hinge fracture, and part of the left margin has been snapped off by a bend fracture. The resulting specimen is asymmetrical in form, and its distal margin is heavily retouched.

88263-20 (Fig. 5.4c). Technically a flake blank (and so

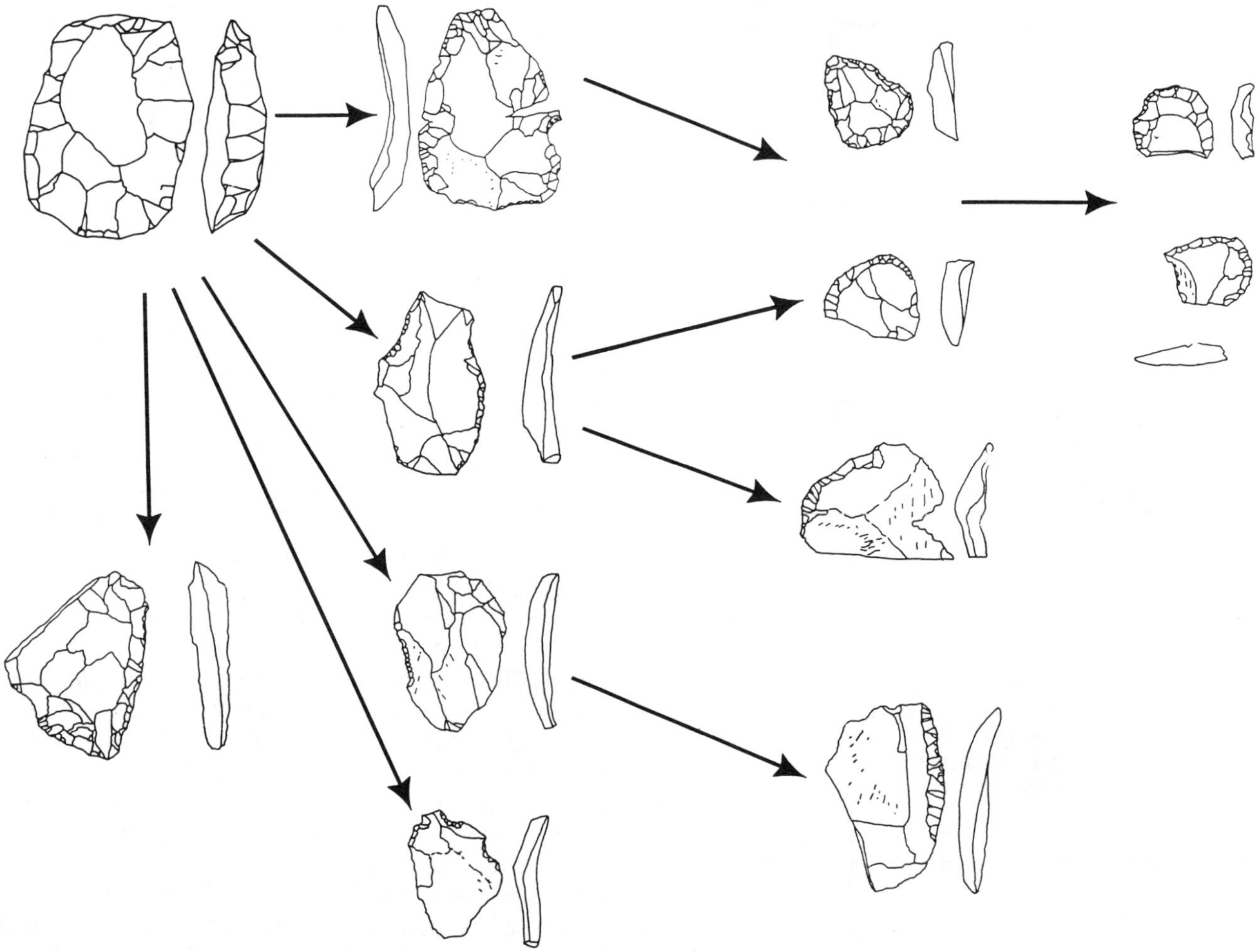

Figure 5.3. Reduction sequence for biface core blanks. The core depicted in the upper left corner is a hypothetical reconstruction of a fragment recovered at Leavitt.

not included in Tables 5.1-5.4), this specimen lacks its distal segment and the remaining portion bears only moderate evidence of use on part of the left margin and nearly all of the right one. The transverse cross-section forms an offset triangle, indicating that the blank was struck across the face of a core prepared by prior chipping of a longitudinal ridge.

88261-22 (Fig. 5.4d). Lacking both platform and one margin, this fragmentary specimen from a lustrous, waxy Bayport nodule bears extensive steep-angled retouch on its right margin. A flute-like flake was struck from the distal end, presumably to thin the right-margin bit. Longitudinal section is markedly excurvate.

85-27-255 (Fig. 5.4e, Table 5.5). This item, of Bayport chert, is a thin blank struck from a prepared platform on a biface core. Slightly excurvate in longitudinal section, it terminates in a bend fracture. The dorsal surface bears a series of at least seven expanding facets, each emanating from a different point on the margin of the core. Thus, prior flaking of the core used its entire margin. It is possible that at least some prior flaking was performed to prepare this flake for removal; the intersection of the prior facets forms a well defined ridge normal to the flake's longitudinal axis. Specimen 85-27-255 was struck from an abraded and faceted platform. The ventral surface bears a relatively thin and diffuse bulb of percussion. The specimen probably was a blank for a thin end scraper. It bears no definite traces of use, although the left margin has faceting produced by the plow.

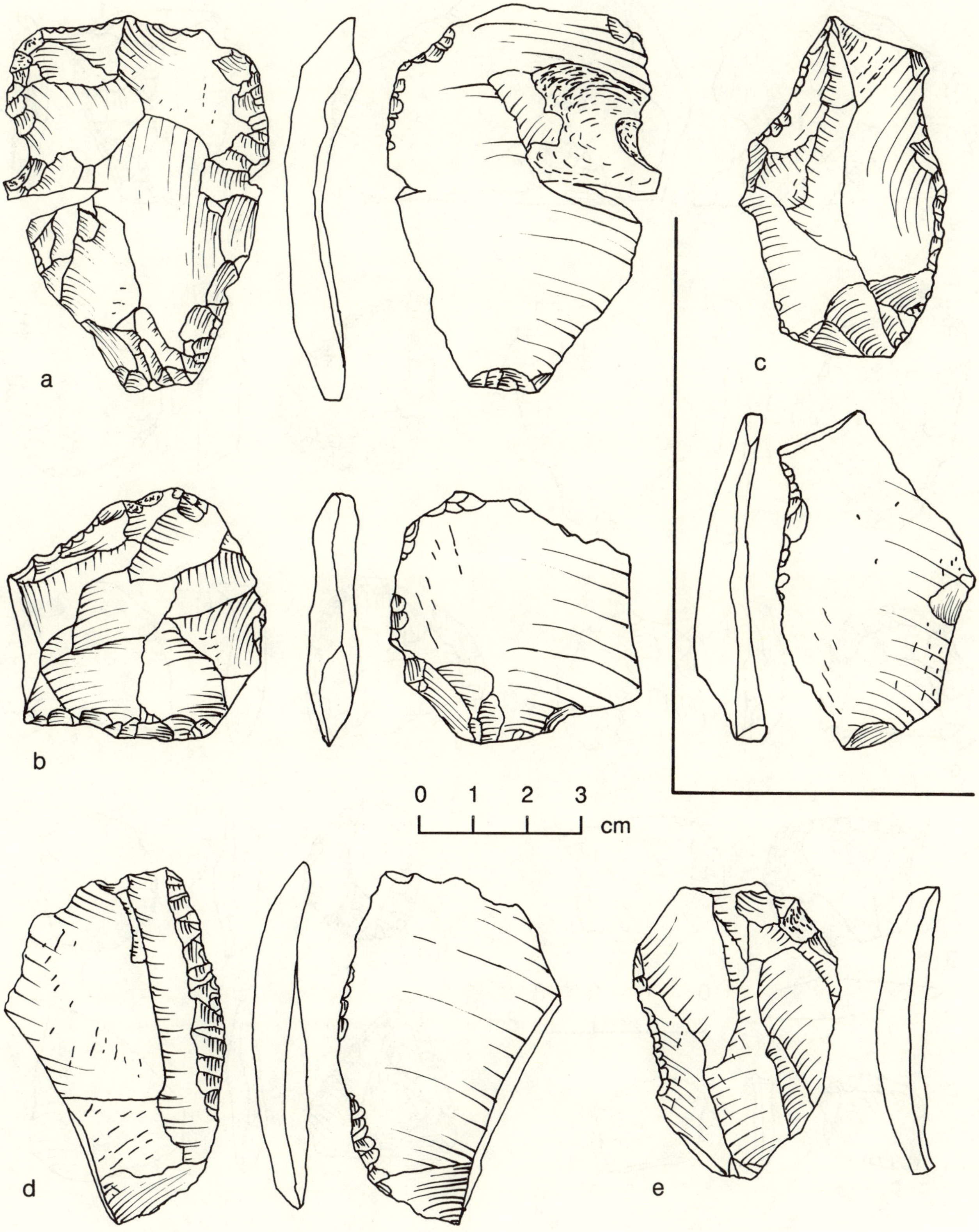

Figure 5.4. Unifaces from biface core blanks. *a*, 88263-16; *b*, 88263-A; *c*, 88263-20; *d*, 88261-22; *e*, 85-27-255.

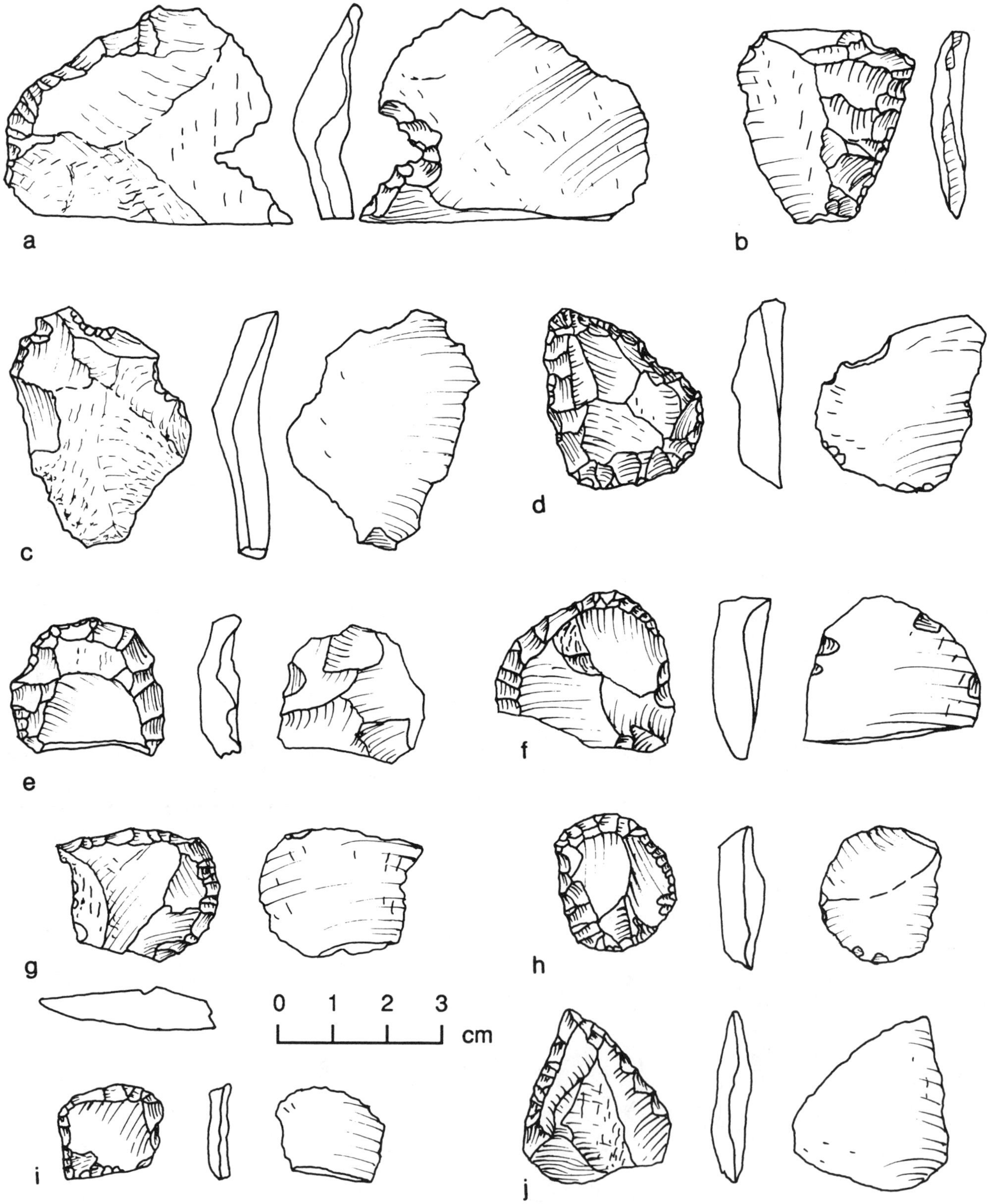

Figure 5.5. Unifaces from biface core blanks. *a*, 85-27-324; *b*, 85-27-169; *c*, 85-27-1-4; *d*, 85-27-16; *e*, 85-27-37; *f*, 85-27-85; *g*, 85-27-1-5; *h*, 88260-4; *i*, 85-27-268; *j*, 88261-18.

85-27-324 (Fig. 5.5a). This distal portion of a large flake blank bears a transverse bend fracture. Its reddish hue suggests that the blank was heat-treated after removal, though the core itself may have been so treated before the blank was removed. A deep, ragged and fairly broad notch was formed from the dorsal surface just below the fracture plane along the right margin. The notch may be functional, though it may also represent some unidentified form of haft preparation. The opposing left margin bears heavy retouch and use-wear, and is markedly curved in cross-section.

85-27-169 (Fig. 5.5b, Table 5.5). The platform of this fragment was removed by hinging, and the dorsal face bears one large facet parallel to the longitudinal axis and a series of smaller ones perpendicular to it that originate at the right margin. That margin also bears a thin remnant of the flat platform from which the latter facets originate. Thus, the specimen may have been struck along the edge of a flat-platform core to rejuvenate the core, rather than a biface core. Nevertheless, it is longitudinally excurvate and has expanding margins, both hallmarks of biface-core flake blanks. Slight retouch and use-wear is found on the bent fracture plane.

85-27-1-4 (Fig. 5.5c, Table 5.5). A smaller and somewhat asymmetrical version of 85-27-255, this blank is markedly curved in longitudinal section and bears slight use-wear on the distal margin.

Malkin Uniface No. 1 (not illustrated). A flake struck from a well prepared platform, this specimen is probably a small uniface blank. Similar in platform preparation, size and form to UMMA specimen 85-27-255, it bears at least six dorsal facets in a convergent pattern. Longitudinal cross-section is moderately excurvate. The flake platform is faceted, lenticular in form, and heavily abraded. At least two small margin segments may bear use-wear, but no deliberate retouch is found. These three attributes strongly suggest that the specimen was struck from a small biface core.

85-27-16 (Fig. 5.5d). The platform has been removed from this tool, which bears marginal retouch and dorsal thinning in its proximal area to facilitate hafting. Approximate distal limits of hafting are marked by a left-margin inflection and a matching but slight right-margin notch. The tool's corners and distal margins are retouched for use.

85-27-37 (Fig. 5.5e). This tool is fashioned from the distal segment of a flake blank broken transversely by bending. The blank's original cross-section was offset triangular. Margins are essentially parallel and are retouched both dorsally and ventrally to facilitate hafting, producing a finished cross-section trapezoidal in form. The distal bit is curved and heavily retouched. It was rejuvenated by ventral flaking.

85-27-85 (Fig. 5.5f). This specimen is the distal segment of a flake blank broken obliquely by bending. The retouched bit curves across the left and distal margins. The specimen has been thinned from the pointed butt to facilitate hafting. Converging haft margins are formed by the fracture plane and the original right margin. The original blank curved down distally, and the orientation of the tool gives it marked transverse curvature. Cauvin et al. (1987: Fig. 2) illustrate several Near Eastern Mesolithic end scrapers that resemble this specimen in the oblique fractures that produce converging haft margins. They regard these as deliberate modifications for hafting in hollowed bone or antler handles (1987:257-68).

85-27-1-5 (Fig. 5.5g). Struck from a lustrous and waxy Bayport nodule similar to specimen 88261-22, this specimen was fashioned from the bend-fractured distal portion of the original flake blank. Retouching and use lie on the original right margin, and the tool's butt occupies the left one. The prominent spur found at the original left distal corner is an original attribute, not one formed by retouch, but it may nevertheless have been functional. The original distal and tool left margin is retouched, perhaps to facilitate hafting but also perhaps as a distinct functional bit used before or after the specimen was hafted.

88260-4 (Fig. 5.5h). A small, double-bitted tool, this specimen's flake blank bears a longitudinal ridge formed by converging facets that originated on opposite margins, both roughly perpendicular to the flake's longitudinal axis. Both proximal and distal margins were retouched and used. The latter probably was used first; it is retouched to a steep angle approaching the notches that mark the end of the haft, and bears extensive use-wear. As originally designed and used, the tool probably was depleted and then removed and inverted for further use, with the proximal margin serving as the bit. A shallow, expanding ventral facet may have been formed to thin this segment of the tool, either for original hafting or to rework the proximal edge for use. The proximal bit is retouched to a relatively low angle and is very heavily abraded. The parallel lateral margins are retouched and heavily abraded for hafting; they also are symmetrically notched, probably at the haft:blade juncture.

85-27-268 (Fig. 5.5i). The thin blank of this specimen is fashioned from a flake struck from the face of a biface core. Longitudinal section is moderately excurvate. Despite its appearance, the flake blank is not a blade. Instead, the dorsal face is marked by facets originating from different directions and perpendicular to the flake's longitudinal axis. The tool is a distal fragment, either snapped by bending deliberately for hafting and use or broken in the haft during use. The bit is curved in both sections and is steeply retouched and heavily used.

88261-18 (Fig. 5.5j). The distal portion of a thin flake blank, this specimen is triangular in plan and unifacially retouched on two converging margings to form a point. It bears a superficial resemblance to the "Mungai knife" recovered at Meadowcroft Rockshelter (Adovasio et al. 1978: Fig. 9A), but the extremely limited modification of both specimens makes conclusions about age, function or cultural identity problematic. Specimen 88261-18's association with numerous demonstrably Paleo-Indian tools argues convincingly for its cultural affinity, but it probably is best considered an expediently retouched flake and so is not listed in Tables 5.1-5.4.

88261-15 (Fig. 5.6a). This specimen is a biface worked unifacially on two margins. The blank may have been a very large flake, but probably was a core, perhaps one produced at the completion of the process of biface-core reduction. The specimen is roughly bi-convex in cross-section and is transversely fractured by bending. The left margin bears a wide, shallow notch just below the fracture plane, and the corresponding right margin location may have been notched. On the specimen as recovered, that area has been reworked by retouch of the oblique distal margin. Edges of the fracture plane are lightly abraded. Thus, specimen 88261 may have been deliberately bent and notched for hafting and use as a large beveled tool, technically a biface but functionally a uniface. Numerous retouch attempts on the distal margin terminated in step fractures; together with the overall form, this suggests that the specimen was used to the point of depletion. The left margin below the notch is beveled to the same face as the distal one, but is somewhat irregular in form.

In addition to large, curved flakes, biface cores may also have yielded large, relatively straight or flat flakes. Two large unifaces that are essentially flat in longitudinal section, bi-convex in cross-section and extensively faceted on the dorsal surface from all directions may represent such flake blanks.

88273 (Fig. 5.6b). This ovoid specimen is extensively thinned ventrally at its proximal end and so lacks its platform. It also bears some dorsal thinning flakes that extend over half the tool's length. The blank's right margin is straight, its left one convex. The latter is notched near its midpoint and a shallow, minute notch lies opposite it on the right margin. Together with the dorsal and ventral proximal thinning, these attributes probably indicate modification for hafting. Below the notch, both margins are steeply beveled to the ventral surface, forming either a single bit that converges to the distal point or two separate bits that converge there. Different types of use-wear on the margins and slight ventral retouch at the tip that separates them suggest the latter. (The original flake blank runs across the center of the Bayport nodule, suggesting that it may have been struck across the flat face of a split cobble. If so, it is not a blank struck from an exceptionally large biface core, but from a nodular or tabular core.) In plan form, specimen 88273 closely resembles a backed biface from the Dixon site (Ellis and Deller 1988: Fig. 4a), although, as noted, it is unifacial on its functional margin.

90211 (Fig. 5.6c). This medial fragment was bend-fractured at both ends and bears a crazed, perhaps heat-induced, fracture on one lateral margin. The original cross-section probably was plano-convex, and the longitudinal section was certainly flat. The remaining margin is extensively retouched along its entire length and exhibits slight ventral faceting as well. It may have been hafted or mounted along the damaged lateral margin in some slotted apparatus, exposing the retouched margin for use.

Malkin Uniface No. 2 (Fig. 5.7). This tool resembles the preceding specimen. It has a lunate outline form, a thin, contracting presumed haft segment, and a curved, steeply beveled bit exhibiting heavy unifacial resharpening and wear. Defined by its beveled form, the bit is confined to a relatively small length of the curved margin. Presumed haft margins are abraded.

Nodular or Tabular Core Reduction

The proposed reduction sequence for many Leavitt unifaces starts with a split nodular core or, alternatively, some form of tabular core (Fig. 5.8). It is also possible that continuous reduction transforms a nodular core to a tabular one. Unless tabular Bayport chert (Ozker 1982:86) was used by Leavitt artisans, however, tabular cores had to be manufactured from spherical nodules; most Bayport chert does not occur in such form. No complete nodular or tabular core was found at Leavitt, so no prototype appears in Figure 5.8. Instead, arrows lead from the left margin to specific tools representing blanks that may have been removed from such cores in earlier (top) to later (bottom) reduction stages.

Flake blanks struck from nodular cores may vary considerably in length, width, and thickness (e.g., 88263-

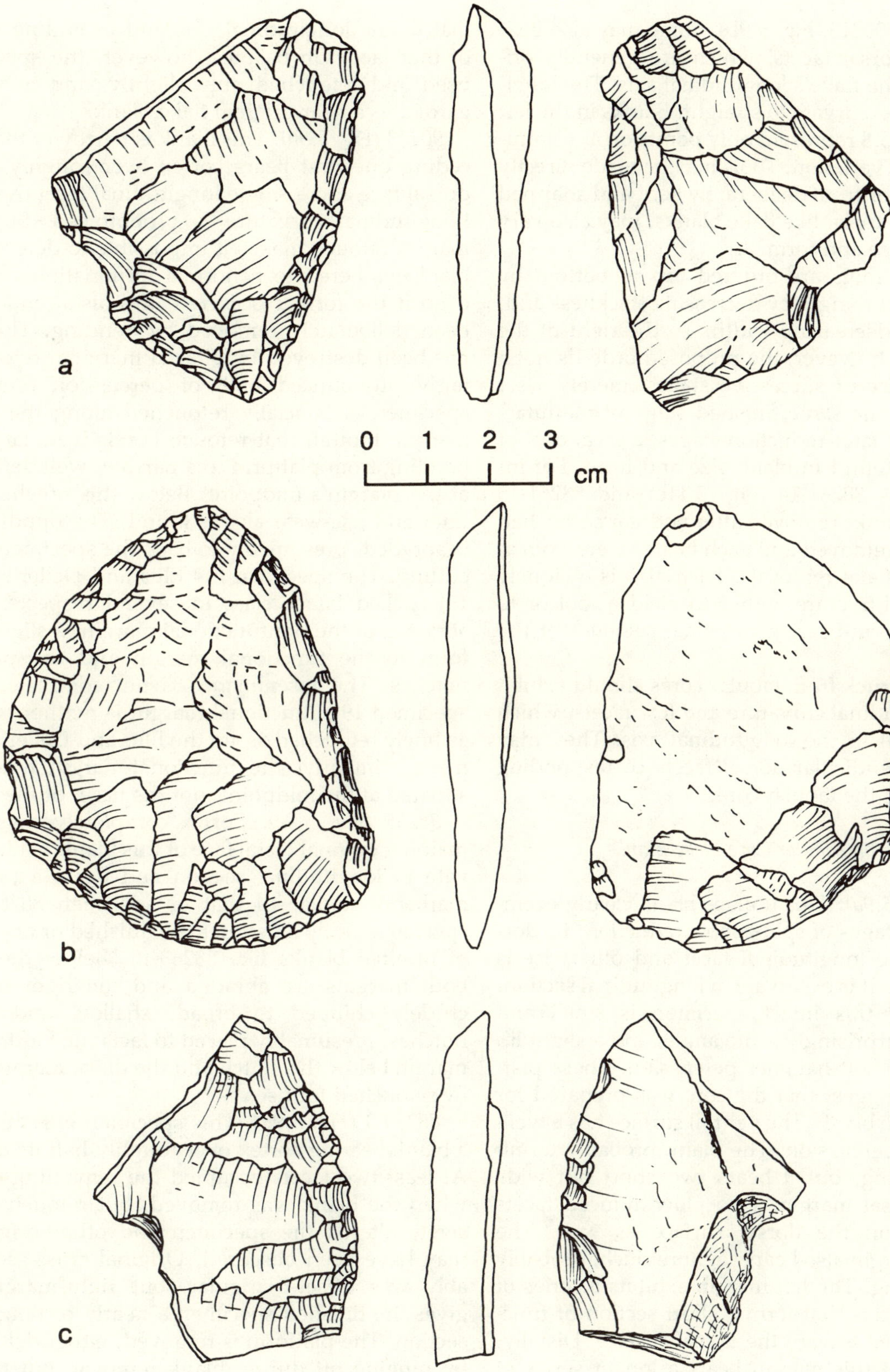

Figure 5.6. Unifaces from biface core blanks. *a*, 88261-15; *b*, 88273; *c*, 90211.

12, Fig. 5.9a, and 90213, Fig. 5.9b). Some may also bear two or several dorsal facets, which are generally oriented normal to the flake's longitudinal axis. The longitudinal section is excurvate to straight. Blanks in the left column of Figure 5.8 represent only points on a continuous range of such variation. Tools may be made directly from such blanks or from deliberately bent and snapped blanks. Therefore tools, like flake blanks, may also vary considerably in size and form.

In Figure 5.8, tools are ordered top to bottom by blank type and left to right by decreasing thickness and, to some degree, decreasing width. To the right of the lefthand column, however, the proposed order is not a reduction sequence of successive stages, merely a set of variants all at the same finished stage of manufacture. Especially at later reduction stages, a great deal of variation can be found in blank size and form. For instance, specimens 88261-14 (Fig. 5.11e) and 88261-15 (Fig. 5.11d) are blanks removed after nodular cortex had been completely removed and each bears facets from at least three prior flake removals. Each also is obliquely snapped by bend-fracture, either to yield a tool or to remove the platform-bearing proximal segment of the blank.

Flake blanks struck from tabular cores should exhibit little or no longitudinal curvature and few facets, which should be normal to the longitudinal axis. They may also exhibit perpendicular dorsal facets corresponding to distinct faces of the tabular core.

Nodular or Tabular Core Flake Blanks

88263-12 (Fig. 5.9a). This uniface blank clearly exemplifies the early stages of split-cobble reduction. Its dorsal face bears one longitudinal facet and otherwise is covered by cortex. It is excurvate in longitudinal section. The platform of this intact specimen is small and abraded, has a surprisingly acute angle, and a slight lip that may indicate soft-hammer percussion. These platform attributes suggest that the core was prepared for the removal of the blank. The ventral surface has a well-defined bulb of percussion. The blank probably terminated in feathering, but it bears two short but wide facets on its dorsal margin. Two plow-induced facets appear distally on the dorsal surface as well. The abraded right margin also bears slight retouch, probably to facilitate hafting. The left margin exhibits a series of extremely fine facets that form a short section of functional edge beveled toward the dorsal surface. Distally, a short section of this margin bears a longer series of small, less regular and bifacial retouch facets. The dorsal cortex surface bears a series of distinct striations normal to the longitudinal axis and extending the length of that face. On balance, however, the specimen was used and retouched only slightly, and it may be regarded as a near-original flake blank.

90213 (Fig. 5.9b). This blank is narrower than the preceding one, but bears cortex over roughly half of its dorsal face and a single longitudinal facet over the rest. Longitudinal curvature is pronounced. Slight distal-margin retouch makes it impossible to determine if the blank feathered to a normal termination or snapped; even if the former occurred, the distal end may have been deliberately removed by bending. The platform has been destroyed by bifacial marginal retouch, but a fairly pronounced bulb of percussion remains. The specimen is bifacially retouched along the entire left margin, though that retouch is relatively large and expanding from platform to a narrow, well defined notch at the margin's midpoint. Below this notch, retouch is finer and use-wear also is found. The opposite margin is abraded, presumably to back the specimen for use in cutting. The specimen fits Ellis and Deller's (1988:114-15) backed biface class in several respects, including abrasion of the nonfunctional margin, a slightly convex form to the functional margin and the presence of notches. The resemblance is not complete, however; specimen 19's functional margin is neither beveled nor as finely retouched as are the Ellis and Deller type specimens. Similarly, the functional-margin notch is here situated at the midpoint, not the base, of the specimen.

88235 (Fig. 5.9c). Cortex completely covers the remaining original distal face of this blank, which is excurvate in longitudinal section and bears a platform remarkably similar to that of specimen 88263-12. This specimen nicely illustrates the finished or depleted form of original blanks like 88263-12. Below the platform, both margins are abraded and the right one also is crudely chipped to broad, shallow and ill-defined notches, presumably placed to facilitate hafting. The left margin below this notch and the distal margin are heavily retouched for use.

88260-3 (Fig. 5.9d). This specimen is fashioned from a blank bearing cortex over roughly half its dorsal face. At least two facets occupied the remaining dorsal face when the blank was removed, but retouch has extensively altered the specimen and other original facets may have been obscured. Original cross-section probably was offset-triangular, but right-margin retouch gives the finished specimen a nearly rectangular cross-section. The platform is removed, either deliberately or by hinging off during blank removal, but the bulb of percussion remains. Roughly parallel lateral margins are retouched and abraded to within 5-7 mm of the dis-

Figure 5.7. Malkin Uniface 2.

tal bit, which is steep-angled and bears extensive retouch and use-wear.

88224 (Fig. 5.9e). This blocky specimen bears cortex only on its abraded, flat platform, which is partly thinned by a ventral facet. Two original dorsal facets originate from opposite margins. Longitudinal curvature is slight. The parallel margins are retouched and heavily abraded and the thick distal bit is slightly excurvate and heavily retouched and used. Its left corner bears what may be a wide, shallow notch that narrows and isolates it from the tool margin.

88260-10 (Fig. 5.10a). The dorsal face of this specimen bears two facets as well as nodular cortex. Longitudinal curvature is slight. Although the bulb of percussion remains, the platform has been removed by a combination of ventral thinning and a burin-like spall struck from the platform itself. This burinated margin and the original left margin converge to a pointed butt as in the bifacially derived specimen 85-27-85 (Fig. 5.5f). As in that case, these modifications probably are for hafting (Cauvin et al. 1987:257-68), a judgment strengthened by abrasion of the margins to within 6-8 mm of the distal bit and a single dorsal-face thinning flake struck probably from the burin-like facet. The bit bears extensive retouch and use-wear as well as a slight spur at its right corner. Whether or not such end scraper spurring is a Paleo-Indian diagnostic property, it may be functional or merely the incidental by-product of resharpening. This topic will be addressed below at greater length. Deller and Ellis (Deller and Ellis 1992: Fig. 48) illustrate similar specimens from the Thedford site.

85-27-87 (Fig. 5.10b). This specimen bears dorsal cortex nearly perpendicular to its single dorsal facet. Longitudinal curvature is pronounced and the flake platform is steep-angled and abraded. Margins expand slightly and at least the cortex-covered right one is abraded. The prominent dorsal ridge formed at the cortex:facet intersection is thinned by two flakes struck from the proximal end, probably for hafting. The heavily retouched and used bit is curved in both transverse and longitudinal sections, and its left corner is snapped off by bending, perhaps in a failed attempt at rejuvenation (e.g., Wilmsen and Roberts 1978:98, Fig. 92).

85-27-143 and 85-27-69 (Fig. 5.10c). This specimen bears cortex only on its large, flat and abraded platform. Original dorsal faceting is obscured by subsequent retouch. The finished tool bears a single distal bit oblique to its longitudinal axis. The platform thus occupies part of the tool's right margin, which is notched just below it. The bit is heavily retouched and the tool reduced to a point approximately 7 mm below the notch. Thus, it probably was depleted, though subsequent heat-induced fracture produced a fragment that was retouched and used unifacially along a fracture edge. That fracture also destroyed the specimen's left margin.

85-27-317 (Fig. 5.10d). This specimen bears a narrow strip of cortex and a single wide facet on its original dorsal face. Longitudinal cortex is pronounced, the platform is snapped off by bending, and both lateral margins were retouched and slightly abraded. The finished tool is trapezoidal in cross-section. Right-margin retouch produced a broad, shallow notch halfway between butt and the heavily used distal bit, but the left margin is not notched.

Blanks for the following specimens may have been produced in the manner inferred for the preceding, but it is likelier that they were removed from some kind of tabular Bayport core. Most are thick, curved slightly or not at all in longitudinal section, and bear cortex-free dorsal facets perpendicular to their longitudinal axes and lying at right or obtuse angles to each other. Some bear remains of what may be edges of the original tabular core.

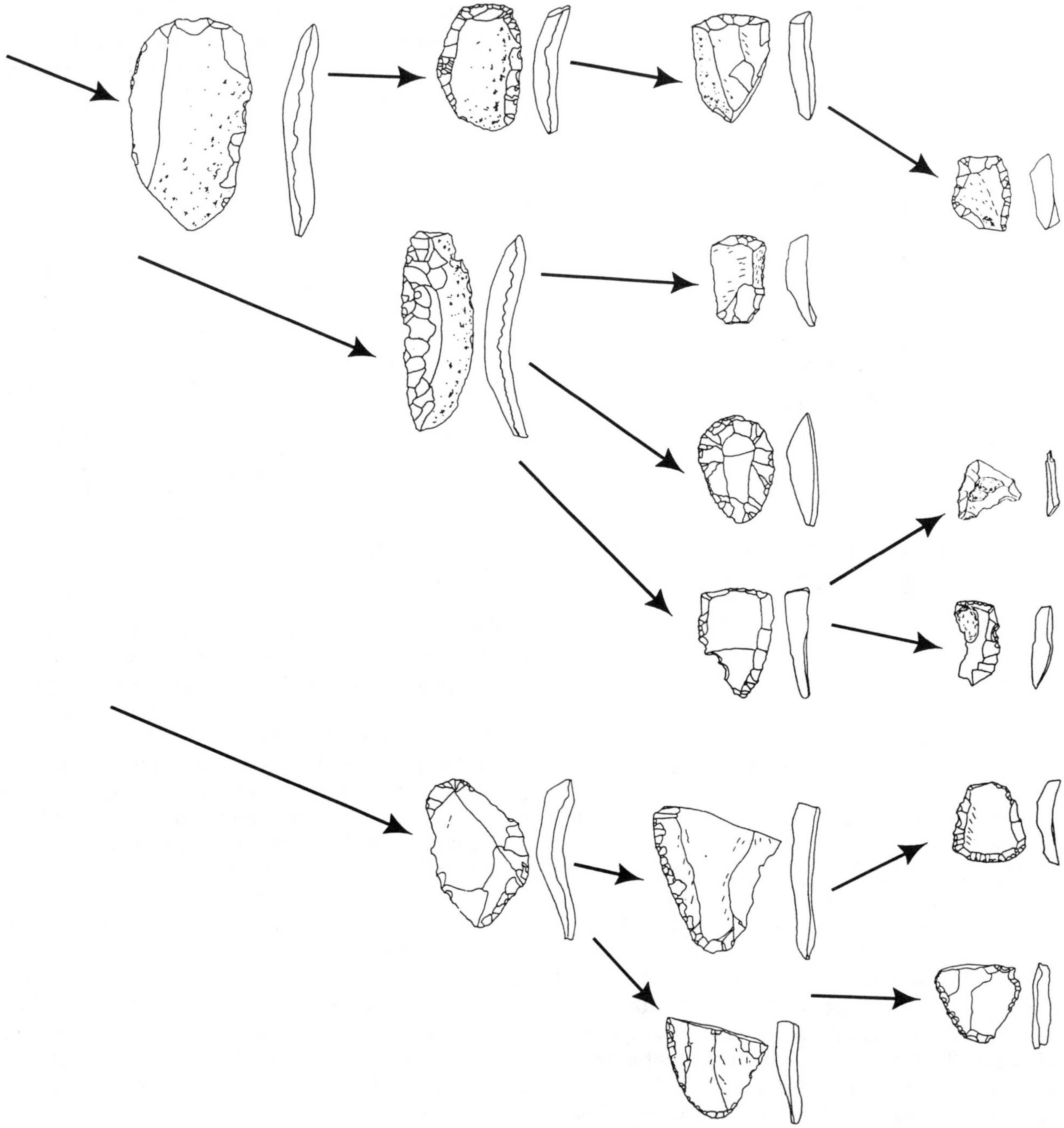

Figure 5.8. Reduction sequence for tabular core blanks. No complete nodular or tabular core was found at Leavitt, so no prototype appears in the figure. Instead, arrows lead from the left margin to specific tools representing blanks that may have been removed from such cores in earlier (*top*) to later (*bottom*) reduction states.

90212 (Fig. 5.10e). The proximal segment of a thick, blocky flake, this specimen exhibits little longitudinal curvature. The platform is crushed and the dorsal face bears one longitudinal facet partly overridden by an irregular facet produced by a massive and poorly controlled blow struck from the fracture plane of the bend-fractured flake. That plane bears slight retouch and use-wear, and the left margin is heavily retouched, presumably for use as a side scraper. The right margin formed by the irregular facet also bears slight use-wear. The

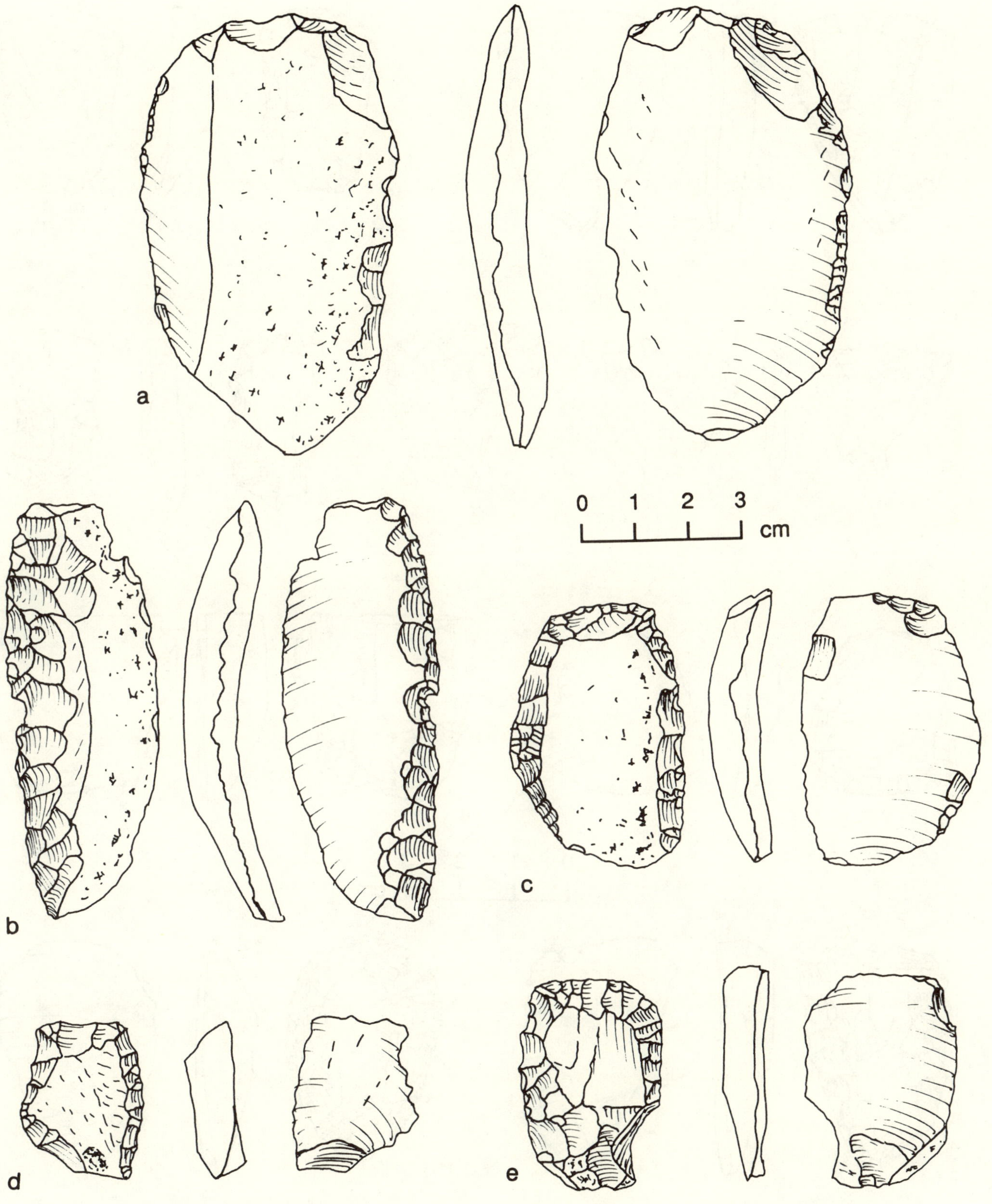

Figure 5.9. Unifaces from tabular core blanks. *a*, 88263-12; *b*, 90213; *c*, 88235; *d*, 88260-3; *e*, 88224.

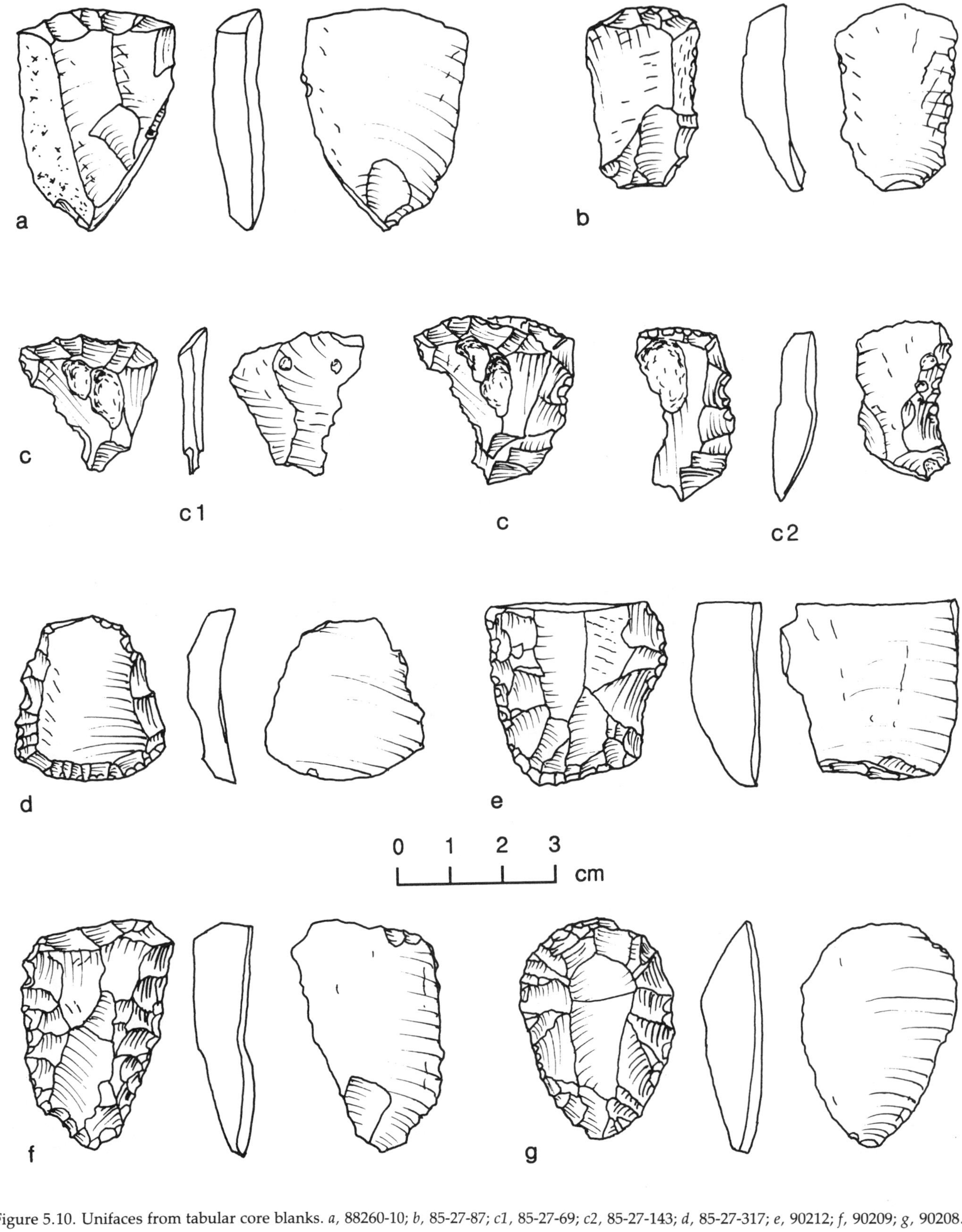

Figure 5.10. Unifaces from tabular core blanks. *a*, 88260-10; *b*, 85-27-87; *c1*, 85-27-69; *c2*, 85-27-143; *d*, 85-27-317; *e*, 90212; *f*, 90209; *g*, 90208.

specimen may have been deliberately bent and snapped and then used as a side scraper; if so, the irregular facet may have been produced to facilitate hafting on the opposite margin. The tool later may have been used expediently on the other margins, though retouch and use-wear there could also have been for hafting purposes.

90209 (Fig. 5.10f). This blocky flake blank is slightly excurvate in longitudinal section, and bears two original dorsal facets forming a shallow triangular cross-section. The platform was removed in the process of ventral thinning of the bulb. Proximal thinning also occurred on the dorsal face, and the expanding margins are retouched and abraded to within several mm of the distal bit. The latter is slightly oblique to the tool's longitudinal axis, and is thick, steep-angled and extremely heavily retouched and used. These properties all suggest heavy use and depletion. The bit's right corner also bears a short, possibly functional, spur.

90208 (Fig. 5.10g). This tear-shaped specimen bears two dorsal facets forming an obtuse angle and an offset-triangular original cross-section. Marginal retouch gives the finished tool a trapezoidal cross-section. The specimen is slight excurvate in longitudinal section. The platform is flat, abraded, steep-angled and covered with cortex; a fairly prominent bulb of percussion lies below it on the ventral face. Abrasion of the margins is slight, but abrasion of dorsal facet ridges is heavy. The convex bit is heavily retouched and used; opposite the platform it is fairly acute, but it steepens abruptly toward the right corner.

85-27-126 (Fig. 5.11a). This ovoid specimen is a combined end and side scraper that resembles uniface blanks illustrated by Gallagher (1977: Fig. 2) and by Clark and Kurashina (1981: Fig. 21.3). The former source (1977:408) briefly describes a kind of tabular core reduction at least broadly consistent with the reduction sequence inferred here. Clark and Kurashina (1981:307) report a less systematic practice. The specimen's bulb was removed by flaking, and the distal bit bears a single ventral retouch facet at one corner.

88269-14 (Fig. 5.11b). Original blank form of this specimen is obscured by extensive marginal retouch, but the dorsal face retains a single longitudinal facet, and a right-angled ridge probably was formed by its intersection with another facet near the blank's left margin. The specimen exhibits slight longitudinal curvature and the platform is removed by chipping from both faces; a remnant of the flake bulb is visible on the ventral face. Original margins are parallel, but removal has produced a tool with irregular and asymmetrical margins that converge to a pointed butt. Margins are retouched and heavily abraded to within 10 mm of the steeply retouched bit, which bears only moderate use-wear.

90210 (Fig. 5.11c). This distinctive implement is the rare Leavitt uniface that resembles a well-documented Great Lakes Paleo-Indian type, Ellis and Deller's (1988:116-17, Figs. 5d, 11) asymmetrical end scraper. The flake blank was struck from a small core, probably of tabular form. The dorsal face bears only four prior facets fairly evenly spaced along the circumference, suggesting a biface core. But the two longest facets are nearly perpendicular, and are divided by a ridge running the length of the flake, properties typical of block-core blanks. Transverse section is wedge-shaped. Longitudinal section is markedly convex, and the specimen bears unifacial retouch on both margins along the haft segment. A single thick, convex bit is found at the blank's distal edge. The specimen conforms to Ellis and Deller's (1988) type in both sections, possibly in blank type, and in asymmetrical bit placement. Unlike this specimen, however, type specimens bear thin, nearly flat bits placed well to the left of the longitudinal axis.

88261-15 (Fig. 5.11d). This is the proximal fragment of a large, expanding, thin flake. The platform is abraded but flat and has a comparatively high interior angle. The dorsal surface bears three facets, all normal to the longitudinal axis and forming two well defined ridges running the length of the specimen. A pronounced bulb of percussion is found on the ventral surface. The specimen has a bend fracture which may have been deliberate. The dorsal left margin is extensively, finely and unifacially retouched for use as a side scraper, and marginal retouch invades the fracture plane. The functional edge is excurvate; most edge wear is unifacial, discontinuous and stepped. This specimen illustrates the difficulty in distinguishing between blanks and tools. Although well made, the retouched margin probably could have been produced in a few moments' use. Specimen 88261 may be a uniface blank, or a discarded and expedient worked proximal fragment of a larger flake blank. I favor the former interpretation. If correct, it suggests that deliberate fracture was an element of tool design and production.

88261-14 (Fig. 5.11e). Similar in form to the preceding, this specimen also is a proximal fragment of an expanding flake. It bears three dorsal facets in a similar pattern, and has a similar platform and bulb of percussion. Finally, it too is retouched on its left margin and retouch invades the fracture plane. Although retouch in this case is less controlled, use-wear is fine, regular, unifacial and continuous.

88268 (Fig. 511f). Similar in plan form to the above two specimens, this is a proximal fragment of a large

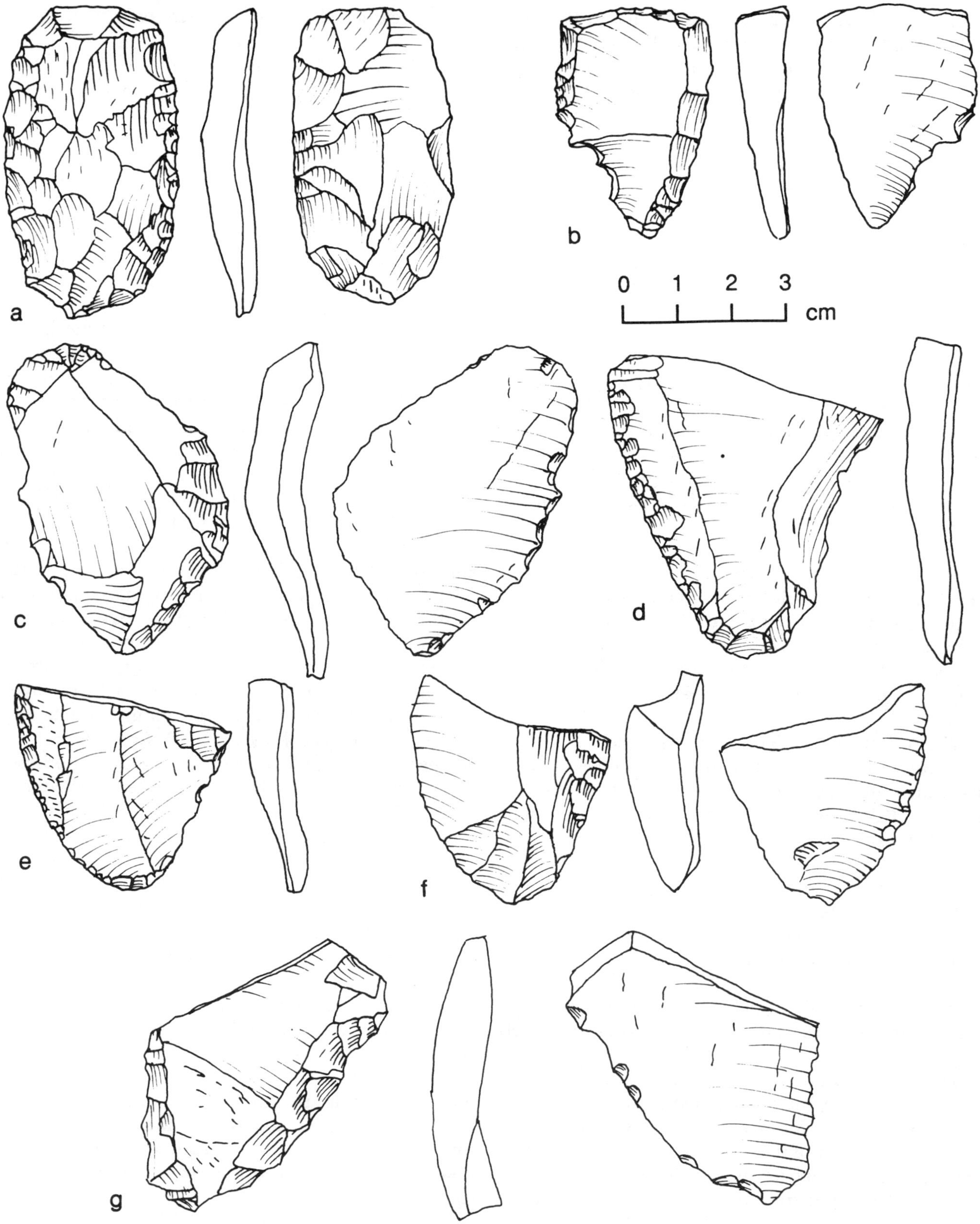

Figure 5.11. Unifaces from tabular core blanks. *a*, 85-27-126; *b*, 88269-14; *c*, 90210; *d*, 88261-15; *e*, 88261-14; *f*, 88268; *g*, 85-27-15.

expanding flake. It bears two large dorsal facets normal to the longitudinal axis, however, and is thicker than the preceding two specimens. Cross-section is distinctly triangular. Fine proximal retouch on the dorsal face suggests platform preparation, but the platform itself has been removed by subsequent flaking. The bulb is thick, with a shallow scar. The dorsal right margin bears massive unifacial retouch, but the left margin has only fine, irregular bifacial use-wear. The right margin may represent backing for use as a knife. The distal fracture plan bears slight use-wear traces.

85-27-15 (Fig. 5.11g). This unusual specimen is a distal fragment that terminated at the corner of a tabular core. Thus, it bears two distinct margins, both perpendicular to the longitudinal axis. The flake blank is markedly excurvate in longitudinal section and is retouched and used along its lateral margins as a side scraper.

Malkin Uniface No. 3 (not illustrated). This specimen bears all the attributes of a classic Paleo-Indian end scraper. It is fashioned from a long, narrow, and thick flake blank, and the cross-section is offset-triangular. Flake blank and tool longitudinal axis coincide. Evidence of hafting is found in a single broad and shallow notch on the left margin, margin abrasion from the butt to this notch, and the removal of the bulb of percussion from the ventral surface. The right margin bears no evidence of modification to facilitate hafting. Approximate haft length, judging from the attributes observed on the left margin, is 27.4 mm. A single bit occupies the distal edge of the tool. Maximum flake thickness is just below the bit, which is well defined and heavily used. Bit retouch is steep, at approximately 90°, and use angle probably exceeds 90° (exact angle measurements were not taken). Use-wear is nearly continuous, and consists principally of step facets. Most use-wear is dorsal, but the ventral surface of the bit exhibits slight wear. Unlike other tools in the Malkin collection, Specimen 4's provenience is fairly precise. It was found along the property's western boundary, west of the house now standing on Harry Leavitt's property. Although not from the site area proper as defined here, the specimen could have been from a separate Paleo-Indian locus west of the excavated area. Since that area now is Mr. Leavitt's yard, it could not be investigated.

Miscellaneous Artifacts

88261-16 (Fig. 5.12a). Probably struck from a tabular core, this specimen was truncated upon removal by a hinge fracture. It has several longitudinal dorsal facets below a snapped platform. The left margin bears unifacial retouch and use-wear and the distal right corner has been retouched to form a spur.

85-27-71 (Fig. 5.12b). A long, narrow utilized edge distinguishes this specimen from all others at Leavitt. Retouch is entirely unifacial, and it forms what resembles a drill bit. The specimen closely matches Ellis and Deller's (1988:119, Fig. 5g, h) description of hafted perforators. As a distal fragment, original haft form cannot be determined. Wilmsen and Roberts (1978: Fig. 79) also illustrate a similar specimen from Lindenmeier.

85-27-84 and 85-27-129, conjoined (Fig. 5.12c). This specimen is the distal section of a long flake struck along a ridge formed by converging facets on a bifacial core. The platform is hinged off and the remaining section fractured as well into the two recovered pieces. After fracture, the longer medial fragment, 85-27-84, was retouched and used on its right margin. Similar Lindenmeier specimens were reduced in width by approximately 1.3 mm per retouch episode (Wilmsen and Roberts 1978:99, Fig. 93d). Because the original lateral margins of the flake were convex and converged toward the distal end, medial fragment 85-27-84 is wider than distal fragment 85-27-129 even after undergoing retouch. Therefore, width reduction by retouch cannot be measured. The specimen measures 47.1 mm by 20.5 mm by 6.4 mm. A similar conjoined but complete specimen, 85-27-62 and 85-27-79, was formed on a similar flake and it too bears slight use-wear.

88260-9 (Fig. 5.12d). This specimen illustrates the process of uniface bit rejuvenation. It is a bit removed from its original tool by a blow struck from one corner, probably in bipolar fashion while the tool was seated on an anvil. Wilmsen and Roberts' (1978) Figure 92d illustrates a similar Lindenmeier specimen.

Unifaces of Other Material

Several unifaces were not made of Bayport chert. Too few were recovered to permit generalizations concerning reduction sequences or patterns of use, so individual specimens are briefly described.

85-27-1-17 (Fig. 5.12e). This heat-treated distal specimen of Collingwood(?) chert bears two parallel facets normal to its longitudinal axis. The cross-section is offset-triangular and the longitudinal section is moderately excurvate. The proximal segment may have been taken off by bend fracture to facilitate hafting. The distal margin is steeply retouched. Because fairly coarse-grained cortex occupies that margin, use-wear cannot be observed. The left margin bears a broad, shallow notch just above the bit, probably for hafting.

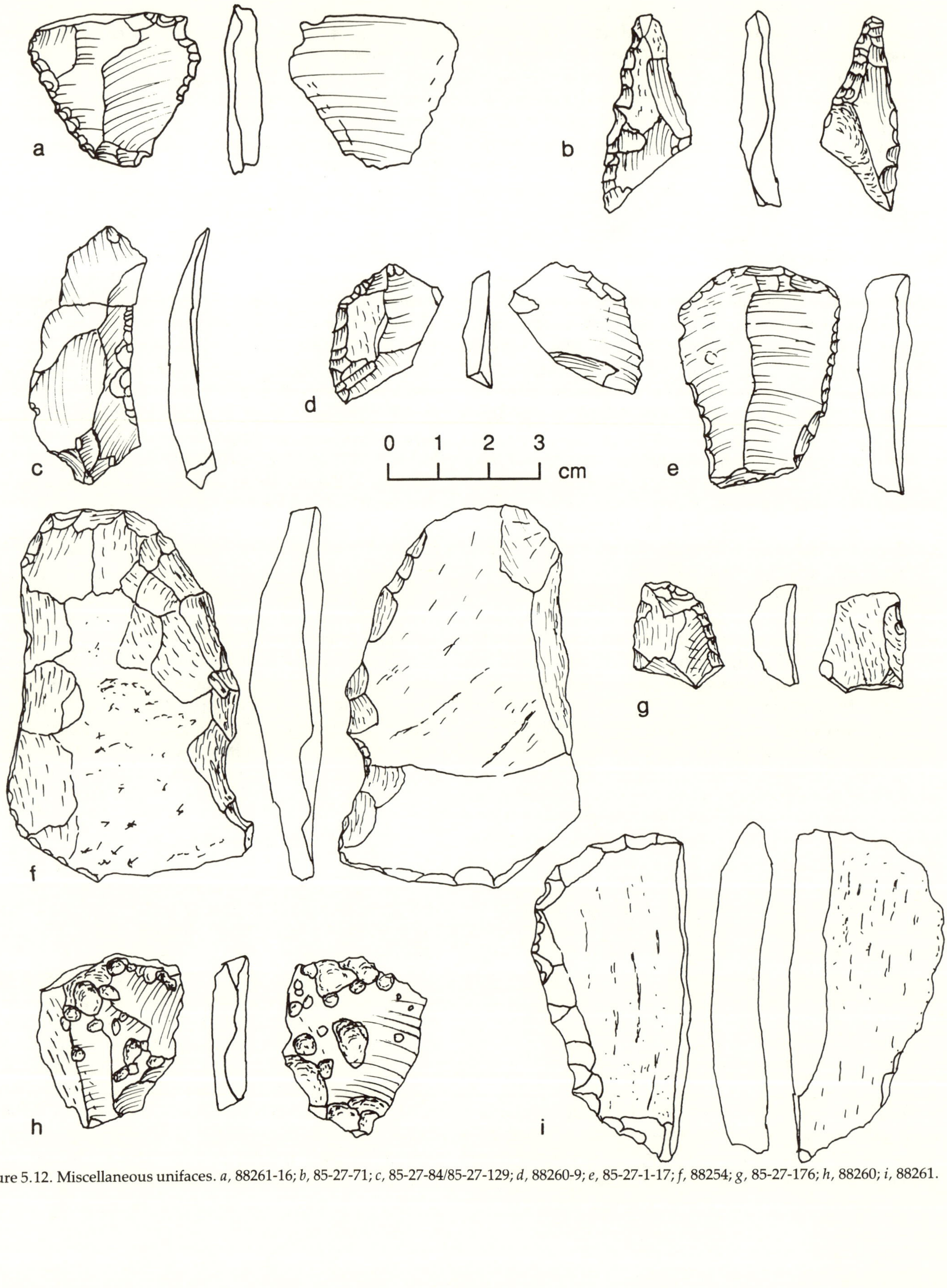

Figure 5.12. Miscellaneous unifaces. *a*, 88261-16; *b*, 85-27-71; *c*, 85-27-84/85-27-129; *d*, 88260-9; *e*, 85-27-1-17; *f*, 88254; *g*, 85-27-176; *h*, 88260; *i*, 88261.

88254 (Fig. 5.12f). The only quartzite blank in the Leavitt assemblage, this specimen is a large flake bearing cobble cortex along a central ridge and over most of the distal section of its dorsal surface. The flake platform is missing and probably was removed deliberately by chipping. Two pronounced ripples are found on the ventral face and the flake terminates in what appears to be a step fracture. The ventral surface has two small facets. Slight dorsal faceting at the distal margin may be deliberate or post-occupational. The flake appears to be a core platform rejuvenation flake, with the smaller ventral facet being the edge of the core platform. Flakes struck from that platform have left facets on one margin. Facets originating on the opposite margin, however, were probably produced after the flake was removed from the core. They are massive and expanding, imparting a sinuous form to that margin which nevertheless bears no obvious evidence of use. Apart from removal of the flake's platform, it bears no sign of preparation for hafting. The Leavitt assemblage contains no quartzite uniface for which this specimen could have served as a blank. It is possible but by no means demonstrated that it could have been a biface blank.

85-27-176 (Fig. 5.12g). This quartz or quartzite specimen was fashioned from a small, blocky flake blank. It is a side scraper with a narrow distal margin that may have been retouched for use. If so—and faceting is difficult to detect on refractory material like quartzite—the specimen may have served also as a narrow bit end scraper (Ellis and Deller 1988:117-18).

88260 (Fig. 5.12h). This Upper Mercer specimen is badly heat-damaged by potlidding and retains none of its original margins. Its size, thickness and pattern of dorsal faceting (three nearly parallel longitudinal facets) all suggest, however, that is was a uniface. Assuming as much, it is the only Upper Mercer uniface found at Leavitt, though specimens of at least broadly similar form, as far as can be determined from this fragmentary specimen, are common at the earlier Gainey site (Simons et al. 1984: Figs. 4, 9).

88261-11 (Fig. 5.12i). Possibly heat-treated, this quartzite specimen is fashioned from a laterally split blank. The left margin is retouched and bears extensive use-wear. Coarse-grained materials like quartzite are well suited to demanding use on hard materials (Crabtree and Davis 1968; Hayden 1979:42-46).

Conjoinable Fragments

A number of specimens found at Leavitt could be cross-mended or conjoined to other specimens. Most cross-mends are formed between fragments of flakes. Several, however, were tools before fracture, or one or both fragments were used after fracture occurred. Conjoined specimen 85-27-143 and 85-27-69 already has been described (Fig. 5.10c). Unless noted otherwise, the following cross-mends are between fragments thought to have been broken during use when the site was occupied.

85-27-289 and 85-27-204. Of Ten Mile Creek chert, this specimen is a large irregular flake or piece of lithic shatter itself fractured into two pieces. One lateral margin is perpendicular to both faces of the piece, is thick, and forms a natural backing for the opposite margin. The latter is a functional edge bearing two large invasive scars that are essentially broad, shallow notches. Each has a series of irregular use-wear facets superimposed upon it. The fracture bisects the specimen transversely, and also bisects the larger of the two notches. There is no evidence of continued use and wear along the original functional edge or the fracture plane on either fragment.

85-27-190 and 85-27-275. The original tool is itself a radial fracture (Frison and Bradley 1980:97-98) of a large bifacial core flake blank. Triangular in outline form, it has a unifacial functional edge on the margin which is not a fracture plane. The ventral surface bears several potlid fractures indicating exposure to heat. The functional edge bears extensive resharpening and use facets, and appears to have been used heavily. The specimen was broken near one corner, and the thin, wedge-shaped fragment (85-27-275) was removed. Neither fragment appears to have been utilized after fracture.

85-27-84 and 85-27-260 are unutilized fragments of a large flake removed along the dorsal spine or ridge of a bifacial core. Given the size, form and excurvate cross-section of the conjoined flake, it could have served nicely as a flake blank for an end scraper. However, the flake broke where an incipient hinge fracture probably weakened it, although it continued until terminated by a second hinge. A small flake removed earlier from the core partly overlapped the larger conjoined flake, forming the only set of three conjoined flakes found at Leavitt. That is, the third flake is not a third fragment of a single original flake, but a distinct flake produced in an earlier removal from the core. It overlaps the larger flake and also is unutilized. Notably, the platforms of the two flakes are separated by a small triangular gap, a marginal remnant that probably served to define and isolate a platform for subsequent flake removal from the opposite face. This flaking pattern is inferred for later-stage bifaces at Leavitt (e.g. specimen 88259), but this reconstructed specimen provides the only direct evidence for the practice. Although the specimen is the only set of three articulating flakes identified at the site, others may and probably do exist in the lithic debris assemblage. Systematic inspection of the assemblage for other cross-mends and articulating surfaces, however, was beyond the time and budget limits of this study.

Assemblage Characteristics

In this section, general metric and other characteristics of Leavitt unifaces are explored. Emphasis is placed on end scrapers as defined previously, because side scrapers are regarded as a disparate class of tools rather than a coherent type (sensu Ellis and Deller 1988:128) or set of types. The Leavitt assemblage includes not only the specimens described and illustrated above, but a number of additional broken specimens (Tables 5.1-5.4). These too are included in analysis, so tool counts often exceed the number of specimens described individually. Because they were not measured, Malkin collection specimens are omitted from all subsequent discussion.

End scrapers are a common element of Paleo-Indian assemblages. Although they also appear in later industries, they seem more abundant in the earliest North American cultures. This abundance has not been lost on archaeologists, who have made end scrapers an important part of most analyses of Paleo-Indian assemblages. Certain forms of end scrapers have even come to be regarded as diagnostic of Paleo-Indian occupation, though this issue remains open to question. Whatever the case, analysis of Paleo-Indian end scrapers in some detail is a worthwhile exercise, and an attempt is made here using the Leavitt assemblage.

Any such analysis must view end scrapers as functional tools, but also as tools generally modified for hafting. Most archaeologists implicitly classify end scrapers as hideworking tools, a judgment that might be accurate at a gross level (cf. Siegel 1985), although hideworking itself encompasses a fairly wide range of activities. A brief assay of end scraper function is made here, although its provisional nature is emphasized. But end scrapers usually are hafted, and morphological and contextual evidence for hafting is more readily gleaned from the Leavitt assemblage. Whatever its specific function(s):

> the Paleoindian endscraper is principally designed to concentrate heavy force against a narrow and resistant working surface. The steeply canted, high angle, markedly convex distal edge emphasizes durability over sharpness, while the positioning of the working edge along the main axis of the tool sacrifices a broad working element to take advantage of the amplified edge loading made possible by a longitudinal transmission of force. Employment of a haft is a similar technological convention, magnifying the tool's potential for distal load application by extending the length of direct line force transmission from the arm and hand through the handle and long axis of the tool; in consequence, both heavier and more precise energy conversions are made possible. [Rule and Evans 1985:214-15]

In the following analysis, end scrapers will be viewed both as functional tools and as hafted tools.

Mean metric attributes and bit retouch angle of end scrapers and side scrapers are presented in Table 5.6. Although side scrapers are not further examined here, it is interesting to note that they do not appear more variable as a class than do end scrapers. Specifically, side scraper and end scraper variation as measured by the coefficient of variation, a measure of dispersion that corrects for differences in mean values, are equal for most attributes. Only tool midline length and butt width are substantially more variable among side scrapers than end scrapers. Because side scrapers are viewed as a class for which a wide variety of flake blanks could be selected—a judgment supported by other analysts (Ellis and Deller 1988; Wilmsen and Roberts 1978:161)—they are expected to show great variation. This expectation, however, is supported only weakly in the Leavitt assemblage.

Frequency distributions of major metric and angular attributes appear in Figures 5.13-5.14. Midline length of intact end scrapers is widely dispersed, though only a single mode (and one outlier) is evident. If anything, the distribution is left-skewed, but the opposite would be expected in a homogeneous set of extensively used and curated tools. That is, very few specimens should lie below some minimum length value, most should cluster around it, and some—those not used to depletion but instead lost or abandoned—should be dispersed above the minimum value (e.g., Grimes and Grimes 1985: Fig. 7). The distribution of Leavitt values suggests instead that what are classed as end scrapers there may represent several functional types. Maximum width is approximately normal in distribution, though slightly right-skewed; it also features a second mode composed of three outliers (specimens 85-27-324, 88263-A and 88263). Maximum thickness also is approximately normal but slightly left-skewed, and butt width normal but with an outlying mode. Haft length also is slightly right-skewed, and haft circumference is approximately normal. Metric value distributions at Leavitt are surprisingly variable considering the small size of the assemblage. Few can be considered normal, and several are bimodal. This general pattern stands in marked contrast to results obtained at major Paleo-Indian sites like Lindenmeier (Wilmsen and Roberts 1978: Figs. 81-90), where approximately normal distributions were observed for most attributes. Either sample vagaries distort a set of underlying normal distributions or Leavitt end scrapers do not conform to a single morphological type.

Bit width angle, a measure of the departure from perpendicular orientation to specimen long axis, is unimodal but right-skewed. Most end scraper distal bits fall within 10° of perpendicular, though it bears noting that secondary bits may lie at acute or obtuse angles to specimen longitudinal axis. Bit retouch angle is distributed approximately normally around a mean value of 64.8 (Fig. 5.14b). Not surprisingly, use-wear angle of end scraper bits exhibits a higher mean of 85.7° and a somewhat left-skewed distribution that nevertheless varies narrowly around that mean.

Mean metric attributes of end scrapers by flake-blank type are presented in Table 5.7. Flake axis length is not necessarily tool midline length, and the significance of the difference between flake-blank classes is problematic. Thickness and midline length values are very similar but, not surprisingly, specimens fashioned from biface-core blanks are somewhat wider than those deriving from tabular cores. Most other attributes also are similar, although biface core blank end scrapers are somewhat more extensively reduced, and the standard deviation of their reduction ratio is much lower. Distributions of values are approximately normal for most attributes, but maximum width of biface core blank specimens is markedly bimodal, as is maximum width of all end scrapers combined. On balance, Leavitt end scrapers made from biface core and tabular core flake blanks do not differ substantially in most metric attributes.

In one possibly important respect, however, a clear difference appears. Virtually no biface core blanks retain their original flake platform, while a number of the tabular core specimens do. Perhaps hafting of the former was hindered by the platform, which was therefore removed.

TABLE 5.6
Mean Metric Attributes of End Scrapers and Side Scrapers

	End Scrapers			Side Scrapers		
Attribute	N	$\bar{x}$	s.d.	N	$\bar{x}$	s.d.
Axis length	9	39.2	7.1	4	52.3	9.8
Midline length	20	35.2	8.8	9	39.9	9.4
Max. width	24	30.7	8.8	13	37.7	10.8
Thickness	24	8.4	2.1	13	10.2	2.1
Butt width	22	12.8	7.4	12	23.2	19.0
Bit width	22	22.4	7.9	10	39.4	14.7
Retouch angle	23	62.2	10.0	11	61.8	11.2
Haft length	9	21.2	7.0	6	17.6	5.9
Haft circum.	12	6.2	1.1	—	—	—

In millimeters.

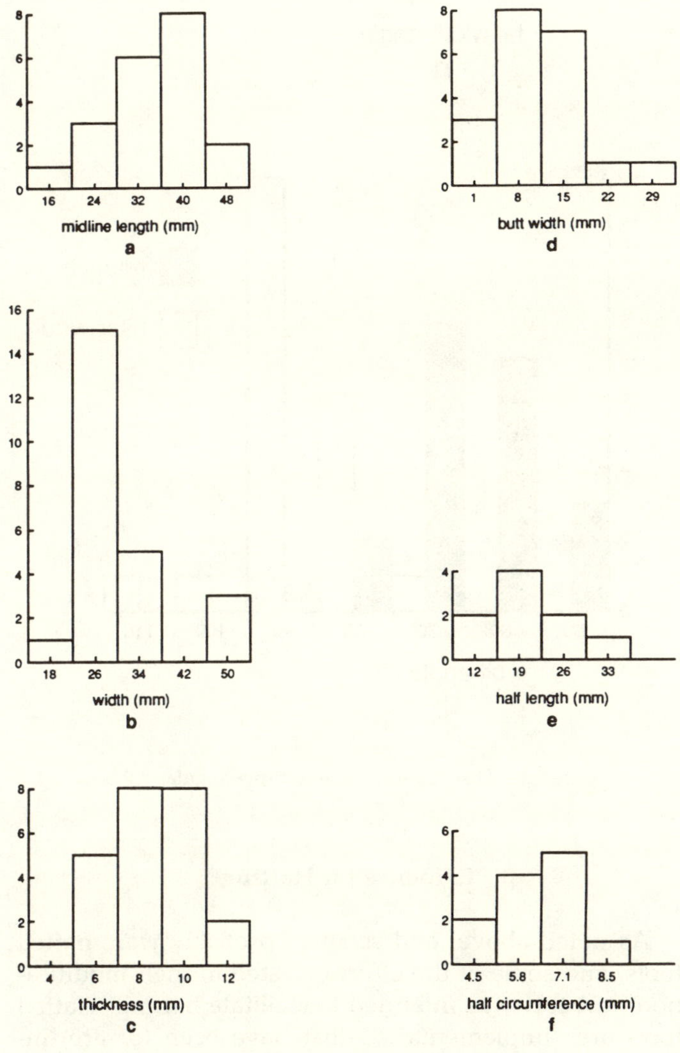

Figure 5.13. Distribution of end scraper metric values.

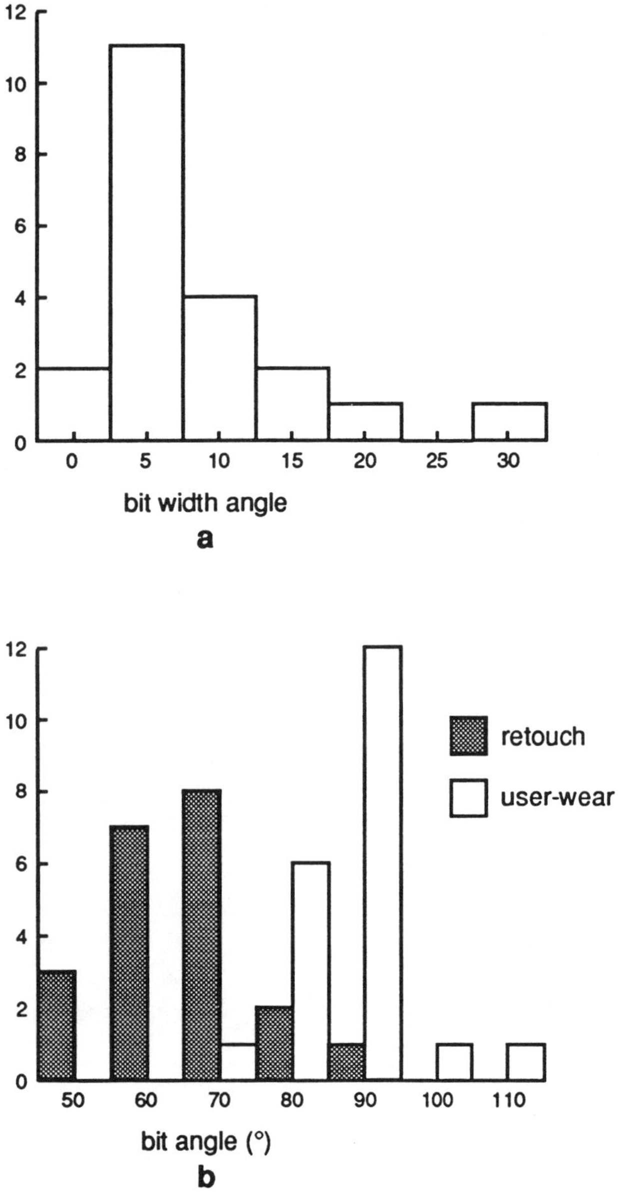

Figure 5.14. Distribution of end scraper angular values.

TABLE 5.7
Mean Metric Attributes of End Scrapers Made from Biface Core and Tabular Core Flake Blanks

Attributes	Biface Core Blanks			Tabular Core Blanks		
	N	x̄	s.d.	*N*	x̄	s.d.
Axis length	2	52.7	24.2	8	41.7	9.8
Midline length	7	38.6	16.2	14	37.1	10.4
Width	8	35.3	12.0	14	29.7	7.2
Thickness	8	8.4	2.0	14	8.8	2.4
Butt width	7	13.2	7.7	13	12.6	6.8
Bit width	9	22.9	6.5	13	25.6	13.0
Retouch angle (°)	9	61.7	8.7	14	59.3	8.9
Haft length	4	17.0	4.2	5	19.3	8.5
Haft circum.	3	5.7	0.3	9	6.1	1.0

In millimeters.

Evidence for Hafting

As noted above, end scrapers probably were hafted tools, and some of the effort invested in their modification probably was intended to facilitate hafting. Hafted tools are "implements . . . that have been (or are) inserted into or attached by some means to another element, usually a handle or shaft" (Keeley 1982:799). Haft modification, as Rule and Evans (1985) note, serves the dual functions of tightly securing scraper to haft, thereby greatly increasing mechanical efficiency in tool use, and producing a close fit to narrow specifications for pre-existing handles. Haft varieties include sockets, bindings and adhesives, or some combination of the three (Keeley 1982:799). Hafting evidence can be adduced from several morphological attributes of archaeological specimens, as well as from ethnographic observation. The following discussion employs both sources of information.

Hayden (1979:Table I) suggests that "prehafting modification" is nearly ubiquitous in the Alaskan ethnographic collection he studied, though details of the evidence are not offered. Other Alaskan specimens studied by Nissen and Dittemore (1974:69) bear lateral retouch that narrowed flake blanks sufficiently to fit them to pre-existing hafts. Gallagher observed such lateral trimming of end scraper haft segments, which in his Ethiopian study area was designed to "reduce the piece sufficiently so that it will fit, proximal end in, into the hole in the wooden handle" (1977:410). Gallagher also observed thinning of the blank's bulb of percussion for similar reasons.

Morphological and microscopic end scraper attributes have been linked by Old World scholars to the hafting of end scrapers. Presumably hafted in socketed handles, French Middle Paleolithic end scrapers exhibit "organized striature," polish and/or crushing of dorsal ridges over two-thirds of the length of dorsal faces (Beyries 1988:219-20). These patterns of wear suggest hafting in wood or bone with leather strips. Alaskan ethnographic specimens provide an apt analogy for such practices (Hayden 1979; Nissen and Dittemore 1974:69), which fit tools snugly into their handles. Deliberate snapping or burination of haft segments to produce converging margins are gross morphological attributes that also may have facilitated hafting (Beyries 1988; Cauvin et al. 1987: Fig. 2).

Rule and Evans' (1985) treatment of end scraper hafting at the Shawnee Minisink site is the first major study of hafting practices in a Paleo-Indian context. Like analysts of ethnographic specimens, Rule and Evans regard retouch of lateral margins, sometimes "conveying the impression of multiple working edges" (1985:213), as a common form of modification for hafting (see also Grimes and Grimes 1985:40; Frison and Todd 1987:245; and Keeley 1982:801). In addition, the Shawnee Minisink collection contains many end scrapers with notches and/or crushing on one or both margins, and thinning of the dorsal face at the butt, usually proximal, end (Rule and Evans 1985:216). Similar notching is found on Horner site specimens, but is regarded as functional, not haft-related (Frison and Todd 1987:246). Only detailed microscopic wear studies can distinguish the alternative possibilities. For present purposes, the modifications of Leavitt unifaces described earlier in this chapter, which resemble those observed at Shawnee Minisink, are treated as evidence for hafting.

There is one additional line of evidence for hafting: bend or snap fractures of unifaces immediately proximal of the bit, which are unlikely to occur in hand-held specimens because sufficient loading for fracture could not easily be imposed just by hand. As Grimes and Grimes note in discussing hafted flakeshavers, "During use the combination of compressive force through the major axis of the tool and bending force perpendicular to it periodically result in a transverse snap. In a rigid haft, this failure generally occurs at the point where the tool emerges from the socket" (1985:41; see also Frison and Todd 1987:246).

Rule and Evans (1985:215-18) report the frequency of various hafting modification in the Shawnee Minisink assemblage. Although they clearly indicate that lateral-margin retouch is a common form of such modification (1985:216), they do not report its frequency. They do, however, record the frequency of notching and face thinning, data which appear in Table 5.8. Comparable Leavitt data also appear there. As in other respects, the Leavitt assemblage thus displays strong similarities to another Paleo-Indian assemblage. Note in particular the nearly equal frequencies of face thinning, although the frequencies of thinning alone and of thinning combined with notching do not agree. Nevertheless, general similarity is revealed, suggesting that haft modification practices were common to Paleo-Indians across eastern North America.

Rule and Evans (1985:218) also report that face-thinning extends on average a distance of 16.2 mm from the butt of Shawnee Minisink end scrapers. The comparable Leavitt value is 18.3 mm, again a similar result. Such thinning probably marks the minimum length or extent of the scraper that was enclosed in the haft. Again, similar hafting practices are suggested for the two sites.

TABLE 5.8
End Scraper Hafting Modifications at Shawnee Minisink and Leavitt

	Shawnee Minisink (Total = 89)		Leavitt (Total = 24)	
Attribute	*N*	%	*N*	%
NOTCHED	52	58.4	11	45.8
single-notch	20	22.5	6	25.0
double-notch	32	35.6	5	20.8
THINNED	46	51.7	12	50.0
thinning only	27	30.3	4	16.7
with notching	19	21.3	8	33.3

Source for Shawnee Minisink data: Rule and Evans (1985).

Spurs

As noted above, spurs on one or both corners of end scraper bits are a common feature of Paleo-Indian assemblages. The association is apparently strong enough that spurs have acquired a diagnostic status in Paleo-Indian uniface industries (Rogers 1986; cf. Morris and Blakeslee 1987). Leavitt is no exception to this general pattern; as described previously, several specimens (90209, 88260-10, 85-27-1-5) bear such a spur. The non-exclusive association of end scraper spurs with Paleo-Indian assemblages is well established, but the function or other meaning of spurs remains in question. Clearly, they are regarded as functional elements of tools by some (e.g. Wilmsen 1968:157), perhaps most, Paleo-Indian specialists. Although this matter cannot be resolved definitively, least of all in the analysis of a single assemblage, it is worth noting that the status and role of Paleo-Indian end scraper spurs must be established rather than assumed.

Rule and Evans (1985:214) discuss end scraper spurs from Shawnee Minisink. They note that at least some spurs are fortuitous, being formed directly below notches by tool fracture at the haft:blade juncture, where notches are common. Although Rule and Evans (1985:214) conclude that even if such spurs are then used, their illustration of "primary spurred" specimens (1985: Fig. 9.2b) is not convincing. It clearly shows a spur formed between and dividing two notches on the same margin of an end scraper haft element, which does not protrude beyond the rest of the margin. It is difficult to envision how this spur may have been used, since it was effectively recessed on the tool margin. Nissen and Dittemore (1974:69,71) note fortuitous notching on two of nine ethnographic specimens that they examined, clearly regarding it as an incidental consequence of resharpening of the tool. Concerning one of these specimens, they conclude that:

> It is doubtful that this spur was intentionally left on the scraper for use as a graver. With the scraper hafted as it is, it would be nearly impossible to use the spur as a graver. [1974:71]

That is, the spur did not protrude past the edge of the haft, and the hafted specimen could not have been manipulated in any way allowing the user to isolate and thereby use the spur as a graver.

Clark and Kurashina (1981:309) report "sharp projecting corners" on the bits of resharpened and depleted Ethiopian end scrapers. Although these may not be spurs in the sense denoted by Paleo-Indian specimens (J.D. Clark, pers. comm.), the observation nevertheless documents another instance in which scraper bits are transformed incidentally by resharpening. Gallagher also illustrates depleted specimens that bear incidental, nonfunctional spurs (1977: Fig. 13a,e).

Although spurs may be designed functional elements of Leavitt end scrapers, it is worth noting that the most prominent spur is found on specimen 88260-10 which also, as the following section discusses, is among the most heavily resharpened and reduced in the assemblage. This suggests that the specimen's spur may be the incidental by-product of resharpening, not a deliberate design element.

Curation Analysis

It is doubtful that many end scrapers at Leavitt or any other site were abandoned or lost in pristine condition. Instead, it is far more likely that most were used to the point of depletion and then abandoned. Some evidence from the assemblage supports this expectation.

Specimen 88263-12 (Fig. 5.9a) clearly is a uniface flake blank in the early stages of use. It bears a striking resemblance, as noted above, to used specimen 88235 (Fig. 5.9c) which is considered a depleted tool. The specimens share extensive dorsal cortex, expanding proximal margins, well prepared, faceted platforms with low platform angles, longitudinal curvature and asymmetrical triangular cross-section. In addition, specimen 88235 bears a series of at least three massive, broad and short facets on its lightly abraded right margin, probably struck to prepare the blank for hafting. As noted, similar facets are situated on the right margin of specimen 88263-12, although somewhat more distally. They too are lightly abraded.

Metric attributes of the specimens are compared in Table 5.9, where considerable similarity is found in platform attributes, width and thickness. The latter, however, are somewhat reduced in the used specimen compared to the blank. But the greatest difference is found in length, not surprising in view of the manner in which specimens like 88263-12 and 88235 were used. That is, they were retouched for use at their distal margins and subsequently resharpened on those margins. Thus, length should be the most reduced dimension in used specimens, and this brief comparison bears out that prediction.

A more systematic exploration of the degree of end scraper retouch can be accomplished using ethnographic data supplied by Clark and Kurashina (1981: Table 21.1). Mean metric attributes of depleted specimens in their sample appear in Table 5.10 along with similar data supplied by Nissen and Dittemore (1974). Gallagher (1977:410) reports remarkably similar values—original length at 60-70 mm, width at 40-50 mm—and depleted length can be estimated from his Figure 13 at approximately 35 mm. Mean metric attributes of Leavitt end scrapers also are presented in Table 5.10, where values remarkably similar to Clark and Kurashina's Ethiopian data are found. Clark and Kurashina (1981) provide only summary data, not measurements by specimen, so *t*-tests for equality of means cannot be performed. Instead, the close agreement is taken as prima facie evidence for essential equivalence in metric attributes between Leavitt specimens and Clark and Kurashina's data. Tool thickness is an exception to this conclusion, although Nissen and Dittemore's (1974) value is similar to the Leavitt one.

Mean metric attributes of unused specimens also are similar. Table 5.11 compares Clark and Kurashina's mean values for unused specimens to the mean values for Bayport uniface blanks from Leavitt. Again, only thickness values differ significantly, though it must be emphasized that the Leavitt data are from unmodified flake blanks and the Ethiopian data are from unused specimens already modified somewhat for hafting. As the table shows, width and thickness decline little with use; not surprisingly, length is the most reduced attribute of these distal-margin tools. (The "increase" in bit retouch angle registered in Table 5.12 simply reflects the fact that the same specimens were not measured before use and after depletion. Instead, unused specimens and a distinct set of depleted ones, which evidently differed in retouch angle, were measured.)

In Table 5.12, ratios of used to unused specimens in

TABLE 5.9
Comparison of Blank 88263-12 and Depleted End Scraper 88235

				PLATFORM				Face Angle	
Specimen	Len.	Width	Thickness	Wid.	Thick.	Angle	Bulb Thick.	l	r
88263-12	81.9	46.6	11.9	7.7	2.2	60	8.6	45	45
88235	50.1	34.5	9.3	5.8	2.0	70	8.2	40	40
% red.	61.2	74.0	78.1	—	—	—	—	—	—

% red. = the percentage by which 88235 dimensions are reduced compared to 88263-12 dimensions.
In millimeters and degrees.

TABLE 5.10
Metric Attributes of Used Leavitt and Ethnographic End Scrapers

			LEAVITT	
	C & K	N & D	*N*	x̄
Length	39.9	—	20	35.2[a]
Width	36.5	38.5	24	30.7
Thickness	14.8	8.6	24	8.4
Retouch angle (°)	56.6	57.7	23	62.2

All measurements in millimeters.
C & K = Clark and Kurashina 1981; N & D = Nissen and Dittemore 1974
[a]Tool midline length.

the two data sets are compared. Although there is general agreement in ratios, it is nevertheless clear that the ethnographic values consistently exceed those from Leavitt. Higher values indicate less reduction, so Leavitt's lower values indicate greater reduction relative to original size. Some of the disparity might be attributed to differences between samples in original, unused specimens noted in the preceding paragraph. On balance, however, Leavitt end scrapers were reduced at least as much as the ethnographic specimens and perhaps somewhat more. It is conjectural to identify the functions of the Ethiopian specimens—initial working of hides—with Leavitt end scrapers, but this comparison strongly suggests that Leavitt end scrapers were hafted in a manner similar to the Ethiopian tools.

Gallagher (1977:411) reports that end scrapers in his Ethiopian study area were used, resharpened and thereby reduced at a rate that removed over 10 mm of tool length per hour. Although this may seem considerable, it is clear elsewhere in his account that tools were used intensively and that they were resharpened carefully in order to minimize loss through resharpening (1977:411-12; see also Clark and Kurashina 1981:308). It is questionable to assume the same rate of reduction at Leavitt in view of the time, space and cultural contexts separating it from the Ethiopian examples. Purely as an illustrative exercise, however, assume that Gallagher's reduction rate is exactly 10 mm per hour and that the same rate obtained at Leavitt. From Table 5.11, original length of Leavitt end scrapers was 68.3 mm; from Table 5.10, depleted length was 35.2 mm. This yields a mean figure of 33.1 mm removed per end scraper and 3.31 hours of use per specimen. Considering just the 24 specimens for which most attributes can be recorded, a total of 79.44 hours (3.31 × 24) of use is indicated. Again, it must be emphasized that this figure is offered purely for heuristic purposes. As our understanding of the tool-use practices and assemblage formation processes characterizing Paleo-Indian assemblages im-

TABLE 5.11
Metric Attributes of Unused End Scrapers

Attribute	C & K	Leavitt
Length	65.3	68.3[a]
Width	42.3	42.1
Thickness	16.8	10.0
Retouch angle (°)	44.2	—

In millimeters.
C & K = Clark and Kurashina 1981
[a]Tool midline length.

TABLE 5.12
Rates of Reduction in Ethnographic and Leavitt End Scrapers

	ETHNOGRAPHIC			LEAVITT		
Attribute	unused	used	ratio	unused	used	ratio
Length	65.3	39.9	.611	68.3	35.2	.515
Width	42.3	36.5	.863	42.1	30.7	.729
Thickness	16.8	14.8	.881	10.0	8.4	.840
Ret. angle (°)	44.2	56.6	1.280	—	62.2	—

In millimeters.
Ethnographic data from Clark and Kurashina (1981).

proves, it may be possible to use reasoning of this sort independently to estimate occupation span. Of course, end scrapers would not be in use for every moment of a site's occupation, but occupation span could be estimated from these figures and similar estimates of the rate of use of tools.

End Scraper Depletion at Leavitt

In their analysis of flakeshavers from Bull Brook I, Grimes and Grimes (1985) demonstrate the effects of depletion and other discard processes on the metric attributes of archaeological specimens. Like end scrapers, flakeshavers are hafted, distal-margin tools, although they differ from end scrapers in form and possibly function. In fact, morphologically and metrically, flakeshavers form a more cohesive functional type than do end scrapers. The distribution of flakeshaver length at Bull Brook I (Grimes and Grimes 1985: Fig. 7) is right-skewed. Although many specimens fall below an inferred minimum functional length, most lie near the minimum value and a sizeable minority are scattered over a fairly wide range of still-functional values. Grimes and Grimes (1985:42-43) interpret this distribution as the combined product of several discard processes including, but not limited to, depletion. Some specimens—those widely dispersed above the value for minimum functional length—were discarded by loss or abandonment before they reached the state of depletion marked by the minimum functional length. In this set of tools, length is a fairly accurate measure of degree of use and therefore curation (Shott 1989a), and curation of flakeshavers was extensive but not complete at Bull Brook I.

Because end scrapers at Leavitt are highly variable in metric attributes compared to Bull Brook I flakeshavers, they do not form a single morphological type. Flakeshavers can safely be assumed to have nearly identical haft lengths and minimum functional lengths (Grimes and Grimes 1985:40-41), but the same assumptions cannot be made for Leavitt end scrapers. Therefore, midline length is not a meaningful measure of degree of use. However, this quantity can be approximated as the ratio of midline length to haft length (hereafter, "ratio"). Since midline length of distal-margin tools like end scrapers decreases with use, but haft length remains unchanged, smaller values of the ratio indicate greater use of the specimen. Therefore, the ratio varies inversely with curation or degree of use; as use, resharpening and, consequently, reduction in length occur, rate of curation rises.

Figure 5.15 shows a complex distribution of ratio values among Leavitt end scrapers. These data are far too limited to attach great confidence to them. However, modes are present at values of 1.2 and 1.8, and both are right-skewed. On a much smaller scale, the Leavitt distribution seems to fit the pattern found at Bull Brook I and the one expected in view of our understanding of curation rates in Parkhill phase assemblages (Shott 1986a, 1989d, 1990). Figure 5.15 also suggests, however, the presence of two end scraper classes with respect to the ratio, which may represent distinct design types. The higher mode is composed entirely of specimens derived from biface-core blanks, and the mean ratio for such blanks is 2.1 (s.d. = 0.2) as compared to a value for tabular core blanks of 2.6 (s.d. = 2.1). Although mean values do not differ greatly, the depletion or extent of use postulated for tabular core blank specimens was considerably more variable than that for biface core blank end scrapers.

Wilmsen (1968:127) proposed that bit retouch angle of end scrapers should increase with their degree of use. That is, retouch angle should increase with the number of resharpening episodes, an undeniable property of biface resharpening. However, ethnographic data do not strongly support this proposition when applied to unifacial end scrapers (Nissen and Dittemore 1974:71). Only weak support is found in the Leavitt assemblage, where the ratio varies inversely with bit retouch angle ($tau = -.34$, $p > .10$). Again, as the ratio declines in value, curation or degree of use increases, and retouch angle covaries weakly with this increase. Apparently, Leavitt artisans sought to maintain a constant retouch angle, but that angle tended nevertheless to increase or steepen slightly with resharpening.

A stronger and inverse relationship is found between the ratio and bit width angle. Ignoring the direction in which a bit width angle diverges from the perpendicular, and considering instead only the absolute value of the divergence, this attribute is correlated with the ratio ($r = .66$, $p = .04$). End scraper bits tend to become more perpendicular with use and resharpening, and those with skewed or canted bits tend to be less extensively reduced.

Form and Function of End Scrapers

As noted previously, end scrapers generally are regarded as hideworking tools, a view with not inconsiderable ethnographic support (Clark and Kurashina 1981; Gallagher 1977). However, it may mask a substantial amount of variation in the function of this tool type (Marshall 1985; Siegel 1985). Rather than assume that

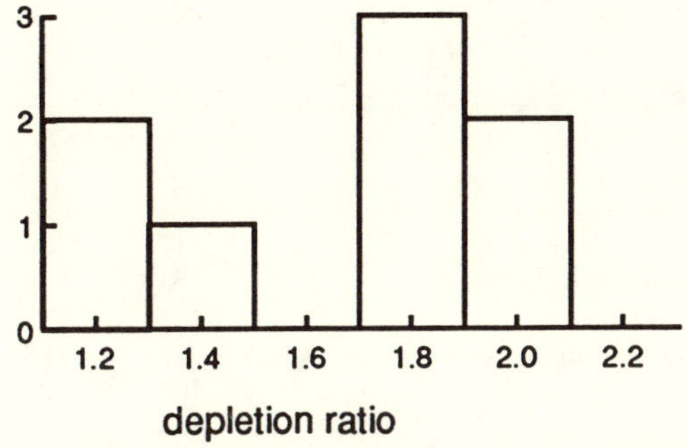

Figure 5.15. Distribution of end scraper depletion-ratio values.

all end scrapers shared a single function, or even that they were equally versatile in function (Shott 1986b), it is worth exploring at least briefly the possibility that more than one morphological and functional class of end scrapers exist in the assemblage.

Tool typologies can be defined on many grounds. In recent studies of Ontario Paleo-Indian assemblages (Ellis 1984; Ellis and Deller 1988, 1992:55-67), a number of presumably functionally distinct tool types were defined. Unfortunately, that typology cannot be applied successfully to Leavitt because, as preceding specimen descriptions suggested, most defined types are present at Leavitt in small numbers if at all. In fact, no subjectively obvious typologies emerge from inspection of the assemblage.

As an alternative, a mathematically rigorous but somewhat mechanical polythetic clustering algorithm was employed to identify end scraper types. Such an approach is consistent with the decidedly polythetic nature of Paleo-Indian tool classes (Ellis and Deller 1988), it avoids the problem of nonreplicable results which subjective typologies often produce, and it permits rigorous evaluation of results. Its disadvantages, however, also must be acknowledged. Polythethic algorithms attach equal weight to all attributes even if some are more meaningful discriminators than are others. They also are agglomerative and hierarchical in their operation. That is, successive steps in the clustering routine are predetermined to some extent by earlier results, and when a case has been assigned to a particular group or type, it cannot be reassigned later in the analysis.

Advantages and disadvantages in mind, analysis was performed using a standard variance-minimization polythetic algorithm with the Euclidean distance measure (Sokal and Sneath 1973:241). Because of the small sizes of the assemblages and the fact that fragmentary specimens lacked data for some attributes, it was necessary to confine analysis to a small set of attributes. Details are provided in Shott (1986a:238-41). Briefly, two major end scraper classes were identified, and two others with one or two members also were defined.

Functional Use-Wear Analysis

The problem of function is addressed here through macroscopic use-wear variables as described above. Functional classes were identified through the use of a monothetic subdivisive classification algorithm (Whallon 1971). Earlier, Parry (1987) used this approach to identify distinct functional classes of tool margins. Both theoretical and practical considerations guided the use of this technique, and the operation of this algorithm is discussed at length elsewhere (Parry 1987:70-71; Whallon 1971). It was chosen for this study because of its demonstrated utility, the interpretive clarity of the results it produces, and its ability to rank attributes by the contribution they make to the definition and discrimination of types.

Monothetic subdivisive classification operates on binary data representing simple presence or absence of specific attribute states. Data transformation for analysis here is described at length in Shott (1986a:243-44). Since the algorithm also initially operates by subdividing the data into groups defined by the presence or absence of a single attribute, it permits the analyst to specify which attribute to use for initial classification. Several different approaches were attempted; results generally were similar, but the best results were obtained by specifying initial division by edge damage type.

Types were identified with the following properties, and tentative functional interpretations are provided by Parry (1987:71, Table 28).

Type 1: step damage, bit curvature, and patchy to continuous damage on convex margins. The working of hard materials is suggested.

Type 2: similar to Type 1, differing only in the absence of bit curvature and the prevalence of straight over convex margins.

Type 3: scalar damage, a slight tendency for transverse bit curvature, and continuous use-wear damage. Both convex and straight margins are common. This type appears to represent a class of task applications involving scraping and cutting of materials of medium hardness.

Type 4: similar to Type 3, but lacking curved bits. Also exhibits low retouch angles and straight, with some convex, margins. The working, especially cutting, of soft material is indicated.

Assuming that the functional attributions described above are correct, it appears that Leavitt end scrapers may be a single functional type at the grossest level of cutting and scraping applications, but a set of rather distinct functional subtypes is indicated. As Siegel (1984) has noted, end scrapers may be functionally versatile tools.

However, the strength of association between discrete functional attributes of tools is not especially great. Compared to the Gainey site, functional attributes at Leavitt are weakly associated (Shott 1986a:247-48). This finding supports theoretical expectations concerning the organization and structure of the Leavitt assemblage, which is characterized by considerable functional versatility. That is, results are consistent with a situation in which tools were applied to a range of tasks, not exclusively to the same task.

The correspondence of morphological and functional tool types must be considered briefly. The four functional types are tabulated against morphological classes discussed above in Table 5.13. Analysis presented elsewhere (Shott 1986a:249) demonstrated that functional types essentially cross-cut or vary independently of morphological ones. At least in the Leavitt end scraper assemblage, form and function of tools are weakly related.

TABLE 5.13
Percentage Composition of Morphological Classes by Functional Attributes

	FUNCTIONAL CLASS			
Attribute	I	II	III	IV
Longit. curvature, pres.	70	17	100	0
Longit. curvature, abs.	30	83	0	100
Transv. curvature, pres.	100	0	78	11
Transv. curvature, abs.	0	100	22	89
Damage type, step	100	100	0	0
Damage type, scalar	0	0	100	100
Distribution, isolated	6	0	0	0
Distribution, patchy	47	50	33	62
Distribution, continuous	47	50	67	38
Retouch angle, low	47	60	50	89
Retouch angle, high	53	40	50	11
Morphology, concave	0	7	0	0
Morphology, straight	30	53	45	62
Morphology, convex	70	33	55	38
Morphology, pointed	0	3	0	0
Morphology, irregular	0	3	0	0

As a practical matter, the functional classes identified by patterned covariation of attributes are equated with specific task applictions. This equation cannot be evaluated independently, so it stands as a proposition, not a settled matter. It is possible, in fact, that the classes identified include a range of task applications or, alternatively, that some are specific to a task application and others cover a range of applications.

Use-Wear and Degree of Use

If end scrapers were used for a variety of task applications regardless of their degree of use, then no strong correlation should be observed between the curation ratio and use-wear attributes. That is, specimens would not be used preferentially in certain applications when new and in others when used extensively. Instead, the tasks to which individual specimens were applied would vary randomly. This is apparently the case in the Leavitt assemblage.

Type of use-wear (scalar or step facets) and distribution of use-wear (isolated facets, patchy distribution or continuous distribution) do not significantly covary with the degree of reduction measured by the ratio of midline length to haft length (see below for greater discussion of this ratio), or with bit retouch angle or use-wear angle. Thus, types of use-wear vary independently of degree of use (F = .33, significance = .59, df = 7), of functional retouch angles of bits (F = .31, significance = .58, df = 18), and of use-wear angles (F = 0.00, significance = 1.00, df = 18). In addition, more use-wear facets are not necessarily found on more heavily used (F = .38, significance = .56, df = 8) or steeper-angled (for retouch angle, F = .11, significance = .75, df = 19; for use-wear angle, F = 1.09, significance = .31, df = 19) specimens. This is not very surprising, since end scraper bits probably were resharpened often, a practice which removes accumulated evidence of use. Thus, the kind and amount of use-wear accumulated on specimens at the point of discard reflects not their entire history of use, but the vagaries of how long and in what fashion they were used between last resharpening episode and discard.

Versatility in the Leavitt Assemblage

It was noted in passing that a number of Leavitt end scrapers and side scrapers possess two or more bits. In an earlier study (Shott 1989d), the number of bits per Leavitt specimen was compared to similar data from the Gainey site, and systematic differences between the assemblages were explained as the product of organizational factors related to settlement mobility. In effect, the stronger constraints of more frequent movement (i.e., higher mobility frequency; see Shott 1986b:21) at Leavitt favored not only greater overall use and curation of tools than at Gainey, but probably use in a wider range of task applications as well. That analysis agrees with results obtained above, and documents the rates of tool use and degree of versatility that characterized the uniface assemblage at Leavitt.

Conclusion

Leavitt unifaces have been described both for simple documentary reasons and to indicate both the properties they share with other Paleo-Indian uniface assemblages as well as the unique ones they possess. Analysis has ranged widely but unevenly to consider hafting evidence and the effects of hafting on tool form and use, rates of use and depletion, functional versatility, and the correspondence of morphological and functional classes. No claim is made for comprehensiveness; other kinds and degrees of analysis—microscopic use-wear analysis for one—may also be undertaken profitably with this assemblage.

Leavitt end scrapers exhibit remarkable similarities to ethnographic and other archaeological ones. If nothing else is clear from this analysis, end scrapers should no longer be viewed as a unitary functional category but as a general morphological class characterized by substantial form and functional variation.

Chapter 6

Bifaces

Introduction

Bifaces, especially fluted ones, hold a strong appeal to Paleo-Indian specialists. Their craftsmanship and value in establishing time-space systematics justifies this appeal, although it sometimes results in the neglect of other components of Paleo-Indian assemblages. At the same time, the celebrated qualities of Paleo-Indian biface industries—distinctive raw material preferences, technical virtuosity in production—create an exaggerated notion of their unity. Time-space variants are indeed recognized, though their status as indicators of underlying cultural variation is sometimes obscured.

It is hoped that in this treatment of bifaces, the properties they share with other continental Paleo-Indian assemblages will emerge. Simultaneously, however, detailed descriptions of individual specimens are offered to emphasize not merely the modal properties but some of the systematic variation characterizing Paleo-Indian assemblages and the behavior that produced them. Comparisons with other assemblages, both from the Great Lakes and elsewhere, also are offered to underscore this variation and possibly to identify its causes. In this manner, the small Leavitt assemblage will be documented in some detail, and its conformity to Paleo-Indian norms can be assayed. In addition, however, a basis for the systematic documentation of variation will be established.

The Leavitt Paleo-Indian assemblage includes 22 bifaces that are intact or sufficiently large for most attributes to be observed. Metric and other data are presented in Tables 6.1-6.4. Limited data on some fragmentary specimens are listed in Tables 6.1-6.4, but those specimens are not described in detail. Several later-period diagnostics also were found at Leavitt; they are briefly described as well.

The Biface Assemblage

Biface Attributes

Most attributes of the flake blank, including platform, number of dorsal facets and overall blank dimensions, are obliterated in the process of biface production. Consequently, it is impossible to observe and measure them. Some attributes—materials, flake blank part, nodule attributes, maximum width and thickness, width and thickness positions, weight, base width, potlidding and heat, haft attributes and tool use attributes—are common to bifaces and unifaces and were defined in Chapter 5. The following are additional attributes of bifaces (Fig. 6.1).

Fracture: the type of fracture of broken specimens. Categories include bend fracture, hinge fracture, and other.

Length: maximum length of the specimen from base to tip, or base to most distal point of broken specimens. Only the values for intact specimens are used to calculate the mean of this attribute.

Basal concavity: the distance between a line formed by joining opposite basal corners and the base at its midsection. This attribute measures the amount of material removed from the base during thinning and fluting.

Face angle: following Wright (1981a), the angle formed by the intersection of each tool margin with the base. Margins that expand from the base have face angles exceeding 90°; contracting margins have face angles less than 90°. Each tool margin or corner is measured.

Eight Leavitt bifaces are fluted, thus bearing the distinctive property of Paleo-Indian assemblages. The following attributes were measured on each face of fluted specimens.

TABLE 6.1
Biface Flake Blank Attributes

Spec.	Matl.	Cond.	Wt.	Length	Width	Thickness	Base Width	Base Concavity	Face Angle l	Face Angle r	Potlid o	Potlid r	Heat
FLUTED BIFACES													
90070	BP	1	13.2	72.7	26.4	6.2	25.0	5.2	91	90	-	-	-
90072	BP	2	14.4	55.4	31.3	7.8	25.1	.	.	.	-	-	-
88264-5	BP	2	6.4	.	.	6.2	21.8	5.3	90	.	+	-	-
88264-7	BP	2	4.6	38.1	19.3	6.2	17.4	2.3	.	.	+	+	+
90071	BP	2	2.5	30.6	15.6	4.6	13.1	3.6	100	100	+	-	-
85-27-100	BP	2	11.0	.	33.7	5.7	27.0	7.8	100	95	-	-	-
88255	QZ	1	16.5	59.7	26.0	9.7	22.1	0.8	90	90	-	-	-
85-27-334-1	BP	3	9.2	.	30.7	7.5	.	.	.	.	-	-	+
NON-FLUTED BIFACES													
90073	UM	4	13.8	.	32.0	7.6	.	.	.	.	-	-	-
90074	BP	2	38.1	.	48.9	10.7	.	.	.	.	-	-	+
85-27-292	BP	4	16.8	52.6	36.3	10.2	.	.	.	.	-	-	-
85-27-48	BP	1	15.3	50.2	30.4	8.6	14.1	0.0	.	.	-	-	-
88290	BP	2	15.7	.	41.2	10.6	23.4	0.0	.	.	-	-	-
85-27-8	BP	2	4.8	.	24.9	5.8	13.2	.	.	.	-	-	-
85-27-8	BP	1	11.3	44.9	26.1	11.5	21.7	0.0	90	90	-	-	-
88280	BP	2	5.0	.	25.4	6.5	.	.	.	.	-	-	-
85-27-334-4	TM	1	9.1	34.2	23.3	9.5	25.9	0.0	55	115	-	-	-
85-27-334-21	TM	1	3.7	33.1	19.7	6.3	12.8	0.0	.	80	-	-	-
88259	BP	1	28.2	70.7	37.4	9.5	19.9	0.0	60	55	-	-	-
85-27-1-35	TM	5	6.4	.	.	.	.	.	.	.	-	-	-
88286	BP	2	2.4	.	20.3	4.8	.	.	.	.	-	-	-
85-27-309	QZ	2	2.3	.	19.1	3.7	.	.	.	.	-	-	-

All measurements in millimeters and grams. **Material:** BP = Bayport, UM = Upper Mercer, TM = Tenmile Creek, QZ = quartzite, UN = unknown; **Condition:** 1 = whole, 2 = proximal, 3 = medial; 4 = distal; 5 = longitudinal fracture; **Face angle:** l = left, r = right; **Potlid:** o = obverse, r = reverse; -absent, + present; **Heat:** -absent, + present

Number: the number of flutes visible. Each flute channel was treated separately in the measurement of all of the following attributes, except for channel width in which the total width formed by all channels in combination was measured.

Length: maximum length of the flute from base to termination. Note that this is a minimum value for original flute and channel flake length, since the basal concavity is formed in part by fluting itself, and channel flakes often originate below the remaining base.

Width: maximum width perpendicular to the longitudinal axis of the flute.

Termination: the manner in which each flute terminated. Categories include snap, hinge, feather and other.

Channel width: maximum width of the channel formed by one or more flutes perpendicular to the specimen longitudinal axis.

As with unifaces, some biface attributes used in earlier analysis (Shott 1986a) but not here are nevertheless defined and data on them is reported for purposes of complete data presentation.

Tool Descriptions

As is the case with unifaces, all bifaces are made from Bayport chert unless otherwise noted. Also like unifaces, the following descriptions are organized around a schematic diagram of biface production (Fig. 6.2). The lefthand column there denotes thinning-stage flake blanks of various sizes. Finished specimens follow to the right, arranged from top to bottom in descending order by size, and left to right by degree of modification.

90074 (Fig. 6.3a). The distal fragment of an extremely large biface, this specimen bears an oblique bend fracture. Parts of the chert matrix exhibit discoloration from oxidation, indicating that the biface was heated, probably by design. Probably fashioned from a large flake blank, original length is impossible to estimate, but the form is ovoid. Primary facets are large and expanding, and both margins bear resharpening facets as well. Both margins are slightly beveled and irregular in outline, with resharpening confined to the same face. In both cases, resharpening intersected the fracture surface and partly reworked it, clearly indicating at least some use

TABLE 6.3
Biface Fluting Attributes

	OBVERSE				REVERSE				CHANNEL WIDTH	
Specimen	Flute #	len.	wid.	term.	Flute #	len.	wid.	term.	obv.	rev.
90070	1	39.4	9.6	2	1	39.6	7.5	2	14.0	13.8
	2	29.0	10.0	1	2	32.1	6.8	3	.	.
	3	25.2	4.9	2	.	.	.	.	.	.
90072	1	43.0	18.5	2	1	23.3	11.6	3	18.5	11.6
88264-5	1	29.4	15.2	.	1	23.5	14.4	.	15.2	14.4
88264-7	1	13.4	6.0	1	1	12.7	8.2	2	9.0	8.2
90071	1	14.6	10.2	.	1	26.4	9.9	.	10.2	9.9
85-27-100	1	37.2	16.1	.	1	37.2	10.7	.	19.2	17.4
	2	26.3	5.9	.	.	.	.	.	.	.
88255	1	25.0	12.9	1	.	.	.	.	12.9	.
85-27-334-1	.	.	.	.	1	.	15.3	1	.	15.3

Measurements in millimeters; termination: 1 = step, 2 = hinge, 3 = feather or normal; obv. = obverse, rev. = reverse

TABLE 6.2
Biface Haft Attributes

	Length		Edge Angle		
Spec.	l	r	l	r	Distal Thickness
FLUTED BIFACES					
90070	29.0	28.1	40	40	6.1
90072	0.0	0.0	.	.	.
88264-5	0.0	.	50	.	.
88264-7	14.0	12.7	40	40	5.1
90071	19.4	11.2	65	60	4.0
85-27-100	0.0	0.0	—[a]	—	.
85255	0.0	0.0	60	65	7.1
85-27-334-1	.	.	.	.	.
NON-FLUTED BIFACES					
90073	.	.	.	.	.
90074	0.0	0.0	.	.	.
85-27-292	.	.	.	.	.
85-27-48	.	.	45	40	.
88290	0.0	0.0	50	35	.
85-27-8	0.0	0.0	.	.	.
85-27-8	0.0	0.0	40	70	.
88280	0.0	0.0	.	.	.
85-27-334-4	0.0	27.6	75	70	9.5
85-27-334-21	7.1	17.2	50	50	6.3
88259	30.2	36.9	40	50	8.5
85-27-1-35	.	.	.	.	.
88286	.	.	.	.	.
85-27-309	.	.	.	.	.

Measurements in millimeters, l = left, r = right
[a]Denotes an unfinished specimen, rather than missing data.

after fracture. The base is not resharpened, ground or otherwise finished. The specimen resembles several bifaces from the Barnes site and perhaps the nearby Vibber Cache (Wright and Roosa 1966: Fig. 1; Voss 1977: Figs. 4e, 5a), none of which appears as finished or nearly finished as specimen 90074. Deller and Ellis (1992: Fig. 24d, e) illustrate small oval bifaces from Thedford which vaguely resemble the specimen. In some respects (size, bend fracture, evidence for at least brief reuse after fracture, craftsmanship) it matches the description of their alternately beveled tool type (ibid.: Fig. 41; Ellis and Deller 1988:113-14, Figs. 2-3), but its width:thickness ratio is low and beveling is slight and is not alternate, occurring on the same face on the both margins. However, Ellis and Deller (1988:113) note a tendency for beveling to be confined to the tip area on large alternately beveled bifaces, so this Leavitt specimen may fit their type description. Elsewhere, Frison and Bradley (1980:81-82) report similar specimens.

88259 (Fig. 6.3b). From the Moore collection, this specimen is a fairly large intact biface. It appears to be a biface preform, and the margins and base, which bears a thin but well-defined cortex rind, are unabraded. Although bifacial chipping is complete, the base may be a reworked flake platform. Chipping on the base and proximal margin segment is primary, broad and expanding, probably the product of soft hammer percussion. Overlapping facets on each face isolate a series of triangular segments along the margin, a pattern observed in other fluted biface assemblages (Deller and Ellis 1992:32; Tunnell 1977:149), and probably designed to isolate platforms for subsequent flake removals. The margins in this segment are highly sinuous, having been reworked bifacially in a continuous series of very small facets. This may indicate use or wear in a haft. Support for the latter interpretation is found in the well-worked and somewhat reduced nature of the blade segment, which forms approximately the distal half of the specimen. There, a combination of lamellar and expanding facets emanating from the entire margin is found. Margin wear is alternate, formed largely by a

TABLE 6.4
Biface Use-Wear Attributes

	Edge Angle		Tip Angle		LEFT EDGE				RIGHT EDGE			
Spec.	l	r	l	r	curv.	form	type	distr.	curv.	form	type	distr.
FLUTED BIFACES												
90070	40	75	.	.	0	1	2	1	0	1	1	2
90072	45	50	.	.	0	1	1	3	0	1	1	2
88264-5	.	.	.	.	0	1	2	2	.	.	.	.
88264-7	35	45	.	.	0	1	1	2	0	1	1	2
90071	75	.	.	.	0	1	1	2	.	.	.	.
85-27-100	40	45	.	.	.	.	.	.	.	.	.	.
88255	70	60	70	70	0	1	.	.	1	1	.	.
85-27-334-1	35	55	.	.	0	1	1	3	0	1	1	2
NON-FLUTED BIFACES												
90073	45	45	.	.	0	1	1	2	0	1	.	.
90074	35	50	.	.	0	1	1	2	0	1	1	2
85-27-292	50	55	35	30	0	1	2	3	0	1	.	.
85-27-48	75	70	.	.	0	1	.	.	2	1	1	3
88290	55	.	.	.	0	1	1	2	0	.	.	.
85-27-8	.	.	.	.	.	.	.	.	.	.	.	.
85-27-8	60	60	40	40	0	1	1	2	0	1	1	3
88280	.	.	.	.	.	.	.	.	.	.	.	.
85-27-334-4	80	80	30	45	0	1	1	3	0	1	.	.
85-27-334-21	55	55	55	60	0	2	1	2	0	2	1	2
88259	65	60	40	50	0	2	2	2	0	2	2	2
85-27-1-35	.	.	.	.	.	.	.	.	.	.	.	.
88286	45	.	.	.	1	0	1	0	.	.	.	.
85-27-309	.	.	.	.	.	.	.	.	.	.	.	.

Edge angle, tip angle: l = left, r = right
Curvature: 0 = straight; 1 = slight, 2 = pronounced
Form: 0 = concave, 1 = straight, 2 = convex, 3 = irregular
Edge damage type: 1 = scalar, 2 = step
Edge damage distribution: 1 = isolated, 2 = patchy, 3 = continuous

combination of step and feather facets on one margin and abraded feather facets on the other. A single distinct notch in one margin is probably a plow scar. Specimen 88259 is a preform that also was used. With slight reworking, it probably could have been fashioned into a fluted biface. In its overall outline form and primary faceting, it resembles a Barnes specimen illustrated by Wright and Roosa (1966: Fig. 4a).

85-27-292 (Fig. 6.3c). This misshapen specimen evidently is the distal fragment of a large biface that also bears a cavity formed by the weathering of a vein inclusion in the chert matrix, and loss of the central node of the chert nodule. The fragment's proximal margin is formed by a bend fracture. Too little of either face remains for definitive observations, but the specimen apparently was a large, fairly thick, ovoid biface. The remaining original tool margin segment is fairly heavily resharpened. In addition, the tool was reworked following fracture, since the fracture plane and the margin were used as platforms for the removal of flakes. Although this practice documents extensive use and recycling, it effectively obliterates most traces of original use.

88290 (Fig. 6.3d). A fragment of a biface formed on a large flake blank, this specimen has been reworked, probably expediently, as a small flake core. The original piece terminates in a hinge fracture, and flakes then were struck from both margins on opposing faces. They have reworked most traces of original faceting.

90073 (Fig. 6.3e). This Upper Mercer specimen is the distal fragment of an unfinished lanceolate biface that may have been fluted. It bears a bend fracture, and the tip, which is quite thick, is broken in the same fashion. On both faces, faceting is primary and expanding, forming a pattern of partially overlapping facets that isolate projecting triangular areas near the margin. These may have served as platforms for subsequent removals from the opposite face (Deller and Ellis 1992:32; Tunnell 1977:149). One margin is unresharpened, bearing a highly sinuous edge, and the other is slightly reshar-

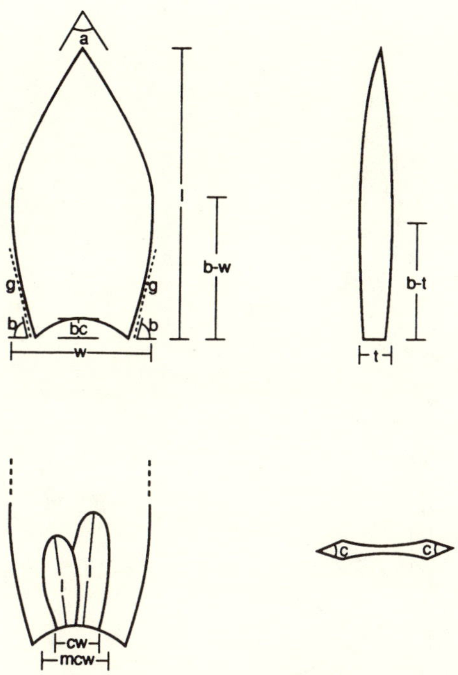

Biface Variables	
a= tip angle	w= maximum width
b= corner angle	b-w= base to max. width
c= edge angle	b-t= base to max. thickness
bc= base concavity	t= maximum thickness
g= haft length	cw= channel width
l= axis length	mcw= max. channel width
	l'= channel length

Figure 6.1. Biface variables.

pened on one face only. These properties suggest that the specimen was broken in a fluting attempt on the reverse face. The obverse face bears a shallow but distinct flute scar with a hinge termination. The tip is steeply and alternately beveled; since no resharpening facets invade the fracture plane at the tip, the bevel apparently preceded fracture.

85-27-100 (Fig. 6.4a). The only fluted biface discovered during the 1984 season, this specimen is a thin preform. Margins are sinuous, produced by broad, expanding primary facets whose partial overlap left remnant ridges between successive facets. This is an often-observed property of Barnes preforms and bifaces, called facial preparation for fluting (Deller and Ellis 1992:32). Presumably, this preparation formed a well-defined central ridge on both faces of the implement where facets from opposite margins intersected, but fluting has transformed both faces. The obverse face bears a single long, relatively narrow and slightly off-center flute. The reverse face was fluted at least twice, one also being a long and slightly off-center removal, the second a feather-terminating finishing flute along the left margin of the large flute. Both large flutes extended past the point of fracture and their termination cannot be determined. The fracture is not a hinge fracture or *outre passe;* rather, it is a bend fracture that probably occurred as stress was placed on the specimen during fluting. Such fracture is common in Parkhill and other Paleo-Indian industries (Deller and Ellis 1992:32-33). The base is beveled for reverse-face fluting and is deeply indented and abraded. The biface exhibits fairly high face angles in comparison to most fluted specimens at Leavitt. The finished tool may have retained this form, or retouch could have made the margins more nearly parallel. Its size clearly places the specimen in the large fluted biface class. The implement exhibits no trace of reworking after fracture and was apparently discarded at once. It thus provides the only direct evidence from Leavitt of the critical final stages of thinning and fluting of bifaces. Deller and Ellis (1992: Figs. 20f-i, 21f, g) illustrate several specimens that resemble 85-27-100, although all are identified as finished products, not preforms broken in the final stages of fluting. In state of completion, fracture type and overall form, this specimen bears strong resemblances to several Barnes site bifaces (Wright and Roosa 1966: Figs. 2d, e, 3d, f). Their presence helps to identify Barnes as a locus where fluted bifaces were completed in anticipation of use. Though less activity of this nature evidently transpired at Leavitt, specimen 85-27-100 documents its occurrence.

90072 (Fig. 6.4b). This is a conjoined specimen from the Sanford collection and the 1978 UMMA collection (bearing a single catalogue number) that still lacks its distal segment. The specimen is an unfinished biface that probably was broken in fluting. Margins are unabraded. Its obverse face bears an exceptionally long and wide flute which either terminated in a double hinge or, less likely, removed all but the distal extremity of an earlier flute. Following this fluting, the base was rebeveled and lightly abraded in preparation for reverse face fluting. A single thin, slightly off-center flute was struck from this face. The operation probably fractured the specimen, although the refitted fracture plane transversely bisects the flute channel. At this point, the base evidently was discarded. Although the medial fragment's margins are unabraded, this segment bears distinct traces of use. Apparently, the distal right margin of the obverse face was reworked unifacially, probably seeing use as an expedient uniface. Since the reworking extends onto the distal fracture surface, both the medial

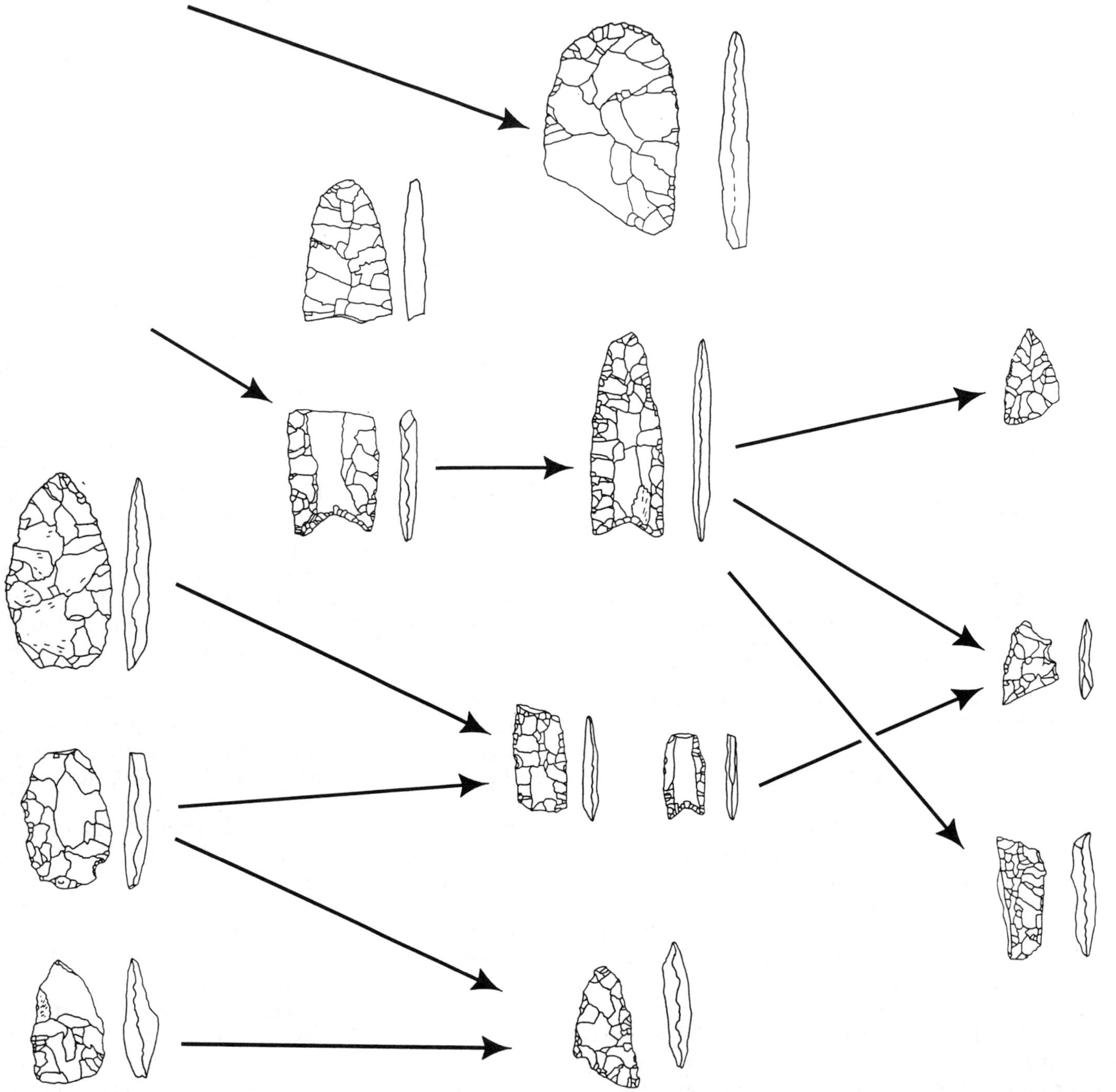

Figure 6.2. Reduction sequence for bifaces. The hypothetical core shown in Figure 5.3 might serve equally well here. Readers might visualize the arrows leading from the upper left corner as originating from such a core.

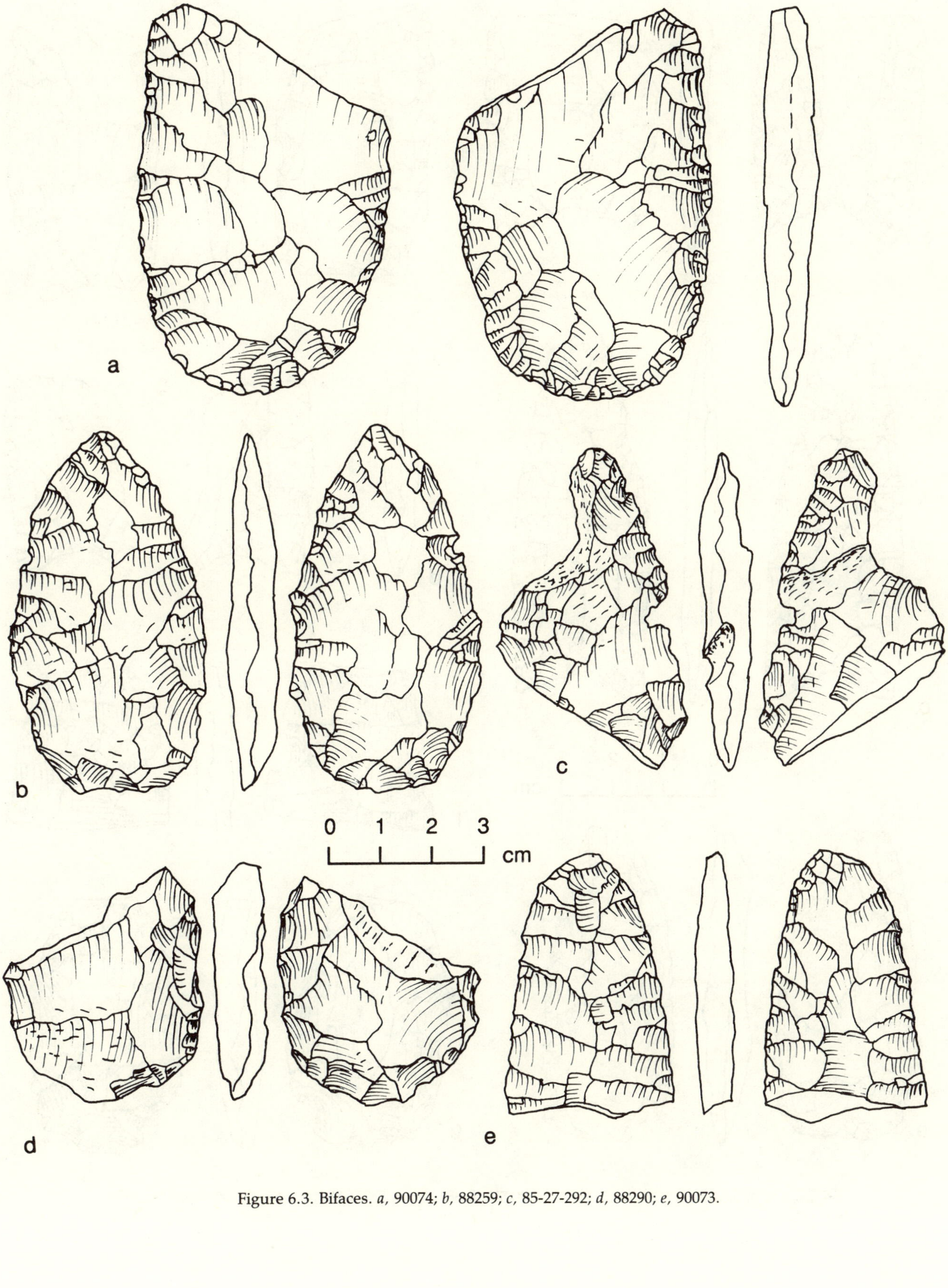

Figure 6.3. Bifaces. *a*, 90074; *b*, 88259; *c*, 85-27-292; *d*, 88290; *e*, 90073.

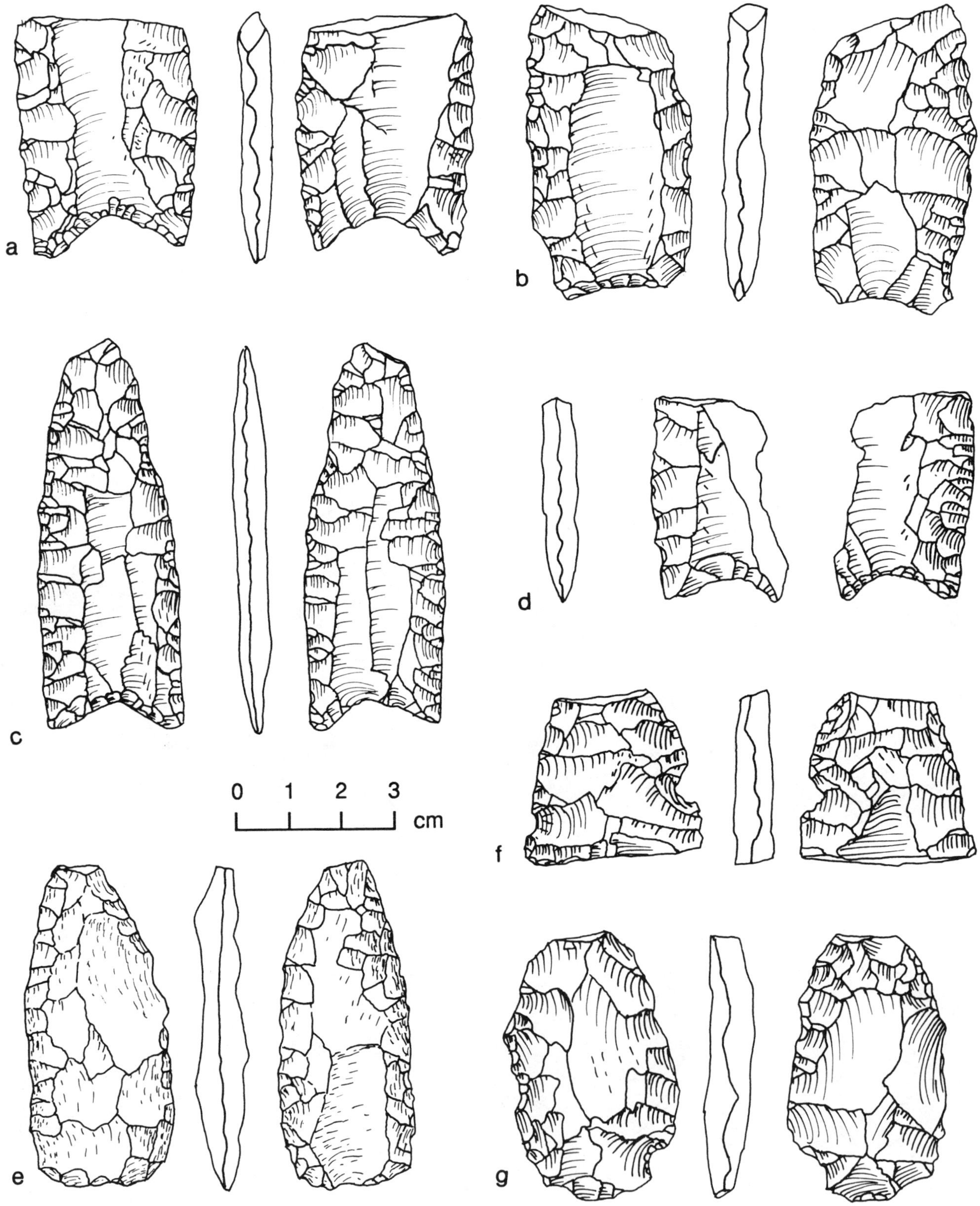

Figure 6.4. Bifaces. *a*, 85-27-100; *b*, 90072; *c*, 90070; *d*, 88264-5; *e*, 88255/88216; *f*, 85-27-334-1; *g*, 85-27-48.

and the unrecovered distal fragment probably were produced in the same episode. The opposite margin bears a series of three well-defined facets, all struck from the reverse face and separated. They thus form what appears to be a denticulate edge. In location and form of fracture, in preform shape, and in fluting, this specimen bears similarities to a fluted biface from Thedford (Deller and Ellis 1992: Fig. 20e).

90070 (Fig. 6.4c). This specimen is a large fluted biface. The obverse face bears three flute scars, including a long flute followed by two shorter fractures, the third terminates normally. The reverse face bears two partly overlapping flute scars, both of which exhibit normal terminations. Although the base is ground, it has not been reworked on the reverse face since fluting. It is also asymmetrically convex. The margins are ground for a length of 28-29 mm above the base, and are virtually parallel. The blade is heavily and asymmetrically resharpened. The right margin bears traces of extensive and steep beveling from the obverse face; the margin outline is irregular, forming two broad, shallow indentations separated by a blunt protuberance. There is no visible resharpening of this margin on the obverse face. Resharpening declines in frequency and obtuseness distally. The left margin is less heavily resharpened and is not beveled. It is, however, dull and may have been deliberately abraded, either by use or as backing from the opposite margin. The tip is fractured obliquely or terminated naturally in this fashion on the original flake blank. Thus, it may simply not have been retouched. Tunnell (1977: Figs. 3.2, 4.5) illustrates several specimens of the latter form. Composed of Bayport cortex, the tip also is abraded. The Parkhill phase practice of grinding the tips of bifaces, probably in preparation for fluting, in order to increase friction between the specimen and its backstop is well documented (Deller and Ellis 1992:32-33; Ellis 1984:164; Storck 1983). Western Folsom-affinity assemblages exhibit similar tip abrasion (Frison and Bradley 1980: Fig. 29b; Tunnell 1977: Wilmsen and Roberts 1978). This may be an example of such deliberate grinding, although the oblique termination relative to the specimen's longitudinal axis renders this interpretation somewhat questionable. Whatever the case, specimen 90070's chief use was as a cutting implement, not a spear point. It is the largest and one of the few intact fluted bifaces found at Leavitt, thus furnishing the best grounds for comparison with kindred assemblages. Surprisingly, however, specimen 90070 does not closely resemble fluted bifaces from Thedford; among other properties, flute length is much greater at Thedford (Deller and Ellis 1992: Figs. 20-21, Tables 9-10).

88264-5 (Fig. 6.4d). This specimen is the proximal fragment of a fluted biface which also lacks one entire margin. The base and remaining margin are lightly abraded. Fluting is complete on both faces, and no margin facets overlap the flute channels. The base is finished by a series of small flake removals on both faces. Above the haft segment on the remaining margin there is an inflection formed by slight retouch and/or use facets, which are unifacial and terminate primarily in step fractures. The transverse fracture appears to have been caused by snapping. Probably after this fracture, one margin was removed either by heat fracture or a combination of heat and bipolar reduction. Several unfinished fluted bifaces from the Barnes site somewhat resemble this specimen (Wright and Roosa 1966: Figs. 2e, f, 3d).

88255/88216 (Fig. 6.4e). This quartzite specimen is a conjoined fluted preform or finished tool. The proximal fragment was found by Sanford and the distal fragment (actually medial, since a small section of the tip still is missing), was recovered in the 1978 surface collection. The latter is noticeably discolored, possibly a result of local soil conditions. Since the proximal fragment was not piece-plotted, the distance between the two fragments at discovery is unknown. The specimen was fashioned from a flake blank excurvate in longitudinal section. Faceting is as difficult to observe as it must have been to produce, and thickness varies irregularly along the section. The biface was fluted a single time, on the incurvate face, and the flute terminated by stepping. The base was not prepared either for additional fluting on the same or the opposite face, is only slightly convex, and does not appear to have been beveled. The unfluted face of the specimen is thickest near the base, so fluting probably would have been attempted here. It is difficult to determine if the specimen was utilized, and it may have been fractured in fluting, if not after discard. Neither fracture plane exhibits traces of reworking, so the favored interpretation is that it was abandoned after fracture. Otherwise, its discard is unaccountable. Wright and Roosa (1966: Fig. 4b) illustrate an unfinished Bayport fluted biface that somewhat resembles this specimen. Fluted and unfluted bifaces of quartzite are not uncommon at eastern North American Paleo-Indian sites. They have been recovered in Ontario (Jackson 1984), Ohio, Pennsylvania, and Wisconsin. Many from Wisconsin are fashioned from Hixton silicified sandstone not, strictly speaking, quartzite.

85-27-334-1 (Fig. 6.4f). The medial fragment of a large fluted biface, this specimen bears bend fractures at both ends. Oxidation of portions of the chert matrix indicate heat treatment. The distal section of a flute is visible on one face, terminating in a hinge fracture. Remaining primary faceting is a combination of expanding and collateral. Reworking is considerable, but the specimen probably was broken during fluting or at least before use as an intact tool. A pattern of partly overlapping marginal flake scars producing a sinuous edge, considered a diagnostic attribute of unfinished Barnes preforms (Deller and Ellis 1992:32), is observable on part of one margin. A notch was formed on each margin, probably after fracture. However, they are not directly opposite one another. That on the right margin of the fluted face is broad and shallow; along with most of this margin, it is abraded. The opposing notch is deeper and more acute, and no part of that margin is abraded. Thus, the notches probably are by-products of use, not deliberately formed to facilitate hafting of the medial fragment or for securing the specimen in a holding device (Deller and Ellis 1992:32, Figs. 20a, 21c, e, 22a, b) before fluting. Significantly, Deller and Ellis make no reference to use after fracture of the Thedford site specimens. Notching for hafting cannot be excluded completely, however; Bradley and Stanford (1987: Figs. A2.4cc and A2.5h) illustrate similar notching on specimens from a western Cody Complex site that they interpret as hafting modifications. The unabraded margin also bears facets from a series of at least three narrow flakes removed from the proximal end of the edge after fracture. It is unknown whether these flakes were struck for use or as incidental by-products of use of the tool. The abraded margin on the fluted face bears a series of facets produced by crushing or step fracture at its intersection with the distal fracture plane. Although they may indicate an attempt to thin the specimen, it is likelier that they are traces of use of the edge, perhaps in wedging. With this slight exception, neither fracture plane is reworked. Obviously, the specimen was reworked considerably after fracture, but the nature and degree of use are unknown.

Two Malkin Collection specimens were inspected in the field but not returned to the laboratory for closer inspection and measurement. For this reason, they cannot reliably be placed in the large-biface reduction sequence, and are instead described here as individual specimens. Like Malkin collection unifaces, these specimens are not included in assemblage counts or subsequent analysis.

Malkin Biface No. 1 (Fig. 6.6a, b). This specimen is a unifacially worked flake blank. Outline form is lanceolate to triangular. The ventral face is unfaceted except for the area of the platform and bulb of percussion, which is perpendicular to the specimen's longitudinal axis near the proximal segment. Thus, the flake proximal segment is reworked, its distal margin forming one margin of the tool, its lateral margin forming the tool's base. The dorsal surface is completely covered by expanding primary facets. This extensive working and secondary flaking have produced a steep beveled edge on the dorsal right margin. Very short (2 mm) facets terminating in step fractures on either face occupy the length of the ventral surface on this margin. The dorsal left margin—the reworked proximal segment of the flake blank—is very thin and is not beveled or extensively retouched on either face. There is no abrasion of base or margins and the tool probably was not hafted. A single short channel flake, which terminated normally, was struck from the dorsal face of the tool. The base is not beveled and does not appear to have been extensively prepared for fluting, nor does it exhibit evidence of preparation for reverse-face fluting. Such fluting may have been unnecessary, since the specimen already is quite thin and the reverse face is the unfaceted ventral surface of the flake blank. The specimen does not closely resemble a recognized fluted biface type, but it is definitely fluted. It is the only known regional example of fluting of flake blanks worked only on one face, and the channel flake dimensions and the absence of extensive basal preparation for fluting all distinguish it from most fluted bifaces.

Malkin Biface No. 2 (Fig. 6.6c, d). A large lanceolate to triangular biface, the specimen bears massive, expanding primary facets and secondary retouch on both faces. Cavities from vein inclusions in the chert matrix are found on one face. The biface is thick, with maximum thickness on a remnant crown located on the longitudinal axis. Retouch on both margins is extensive and produced slight alternate beveling. Margins, tip and base are not abraded, and the specimen probably was not hafted. The tip is blunt. A broad, short flute was struck from one face, terminating normally. The other face bears a series of longer, narrow thinning facets. There is no evidence of basal beveling or other preparation for fluting. Like Malkin Biface No. 1, this specimen does not resemble a recognized Great Lakes fluted biface type.

Small Bifaces

85-27-48 (Fig. 6.4g). This small biface is an unfinished preform. Primary faceting is massive, expanding and somewhat irregular. Although most of it is derived from the margins, some primary flakes were struck from the base. No edge of the specimen is abraded. Incomplete attempts at thinning are marked by the nearly complete bevel of one margin; the other, however, is markedly and irregularly sinuous. This sinuous pattern extends to near the base, where a relatively deep indentation forms a fortuitous notch of the implement. The distal end of the specimen terminates in a plane to both faces, probably a platform remnant of the flake blank. It is abraded at its juncture with the dorsal face of the core from which it was struck. Whatever bulb of percussion may have been present has been removed. The specimen may have been abandoned for failure to remove this platform remnant, or because the unbeveled edge could not be thinned. Alternatively, it may have been lost before continued thinning could take place. Whatever the case, the specimen bears no trace of use. A small, possibly beveled, ovoid biface from the Barnes site (Wright and Roosa 1966: Fig. 1e) somewhat resembles specimen 85-27-48. Several Thedford site unfluted preforms (e.g., Deller and Ellis 1992: Fig. 24b) also resemble this specimen.

85-27-8 (Fig. 6.5a). This small, irregular and extremely thick biface also is an unfinished preform. Although it may have been made from a thick flake blank, it probably is a core blank fashioned from a small chert nodule. Faceting on both faces is massive and irregular, and margins and base are lightly abraded. Markedly plano-convex in cross-section, the tool may have been beveled in preparation for thinning. The flat face is basally thinned, and bears a large facet struck from the tip that has removed the faceted surface along one margin. This may have been a rejuvenation facet designed to rebevel the edge in order to continue thinning on the opposite margin. Thinning facets on the latter terminate in steps against the prominent medial ridge of the face, and indicate that continued thinning was impossible. The specimen probably was abandoned at that point. It bears no trace of use or reworking.

88280 (Fig. 6.5b). This proximal specimen was either a late-stage preform for a small biface (like specimen 85-27-48) or a finished biface. Whatever its original form, it was recycled for use as a small biface core. The specimen was obliquely fractured by bending either before use as a core or during that use. The specimen is also briefly described in Chapter 4.

88286 (Fig. 6.5c). This is a small, irregular fragment of a thin biface. Its proximal margin is formed by an oblique bend fracture. Faceting on both faces is shallow and expanding. The remaining original left margin is steeply beveled to form a slightly concave, serrated or denticulated edge. The opposite margin, which is not the original one, also is steeply beveled and heavily resharpened, consisting of two broad, shallow concavities separated by a blunt spur; a second, more prominent and acute spur is formed between one resharpened concavity and a lunate scar (Keeley 1980: Fig. 10g). The latter and the second spur may be fortuitous. The specimen, in short, is a heavily reworked biface fragment.

85-27-8 (Fig. 6.5d). This proximal fragment probably was a finished biface, judging from the fine secondary retouch it bears on a remaining margin. Broken by bending, it then was used as a bipolar core. Evidence for such use is discussed in Chapter 4.

85-27-309 (Fig. 6.5e). This quartzite specimen is fashioned from a thin flake blank. It is the distal fragment of a small biface that is completely flaked only on the dorsal face. The ventral face is retouched only along the margins.

88264-7 (Fig. 6.5f). Small for a fluted biface, this specimen is a reworked proximal fragment lacking both basal ears. The flake blank is lenticular in cross-section, and margins are nearly parallel, unusual for a Barnes biface (Wright 1981a, 1981b). Margins are abraded, and the base is damaged. A single, comparatively short and narrow channel occupies the center of each face. The blade does not seem to have been extensively resharpened before the tool was fractured, and it is not nearly resharpened to the haft segment. The distal fracture is an oblique bend fracture, but an apparently heat-induced fracture occupies one face just below the distal fracture. The distal corner formed by the bend fracture has been reworked, with retouch along the original tool margin up to the fracture surface. This effort produced an apparent graver bit. The tool margin below this bit is retouched primarily on one face only, and the pattern of retouch forms three successive shallow notches. Although this could indicate use-wear or retouch for functional purposes, it may also have been to facilitate hafting of the reworked specimen. Most fluted bifaces from Thedford are larger than this and the following specimen (Deller and Ellis 1992: Figs. 20-21). A single channel flake biface (ibid.: Fig. 40c) was found there, but neither of the small Leavitt fluted bifaces is fashioned from channel flakes.

90071 (Fig. 6.5g). Formed on a thin flake blank, this item is the smallest fluted biface in the Leavitt assemblage. It bears most of the definitive properties of Barnes bifaces—moderate basal concavity, expanding lateral margins, heavy base and margin abrasion, Folsom fluting—but is much smaller than most recognized Barnes specimens. A single flute nearly the width of the biface occupies each face, although the distal remnant of an earlier channel is visible on one surface. The biface is a proximal fragment missing the tip and one margin down to the haft segment, the latter removed by a

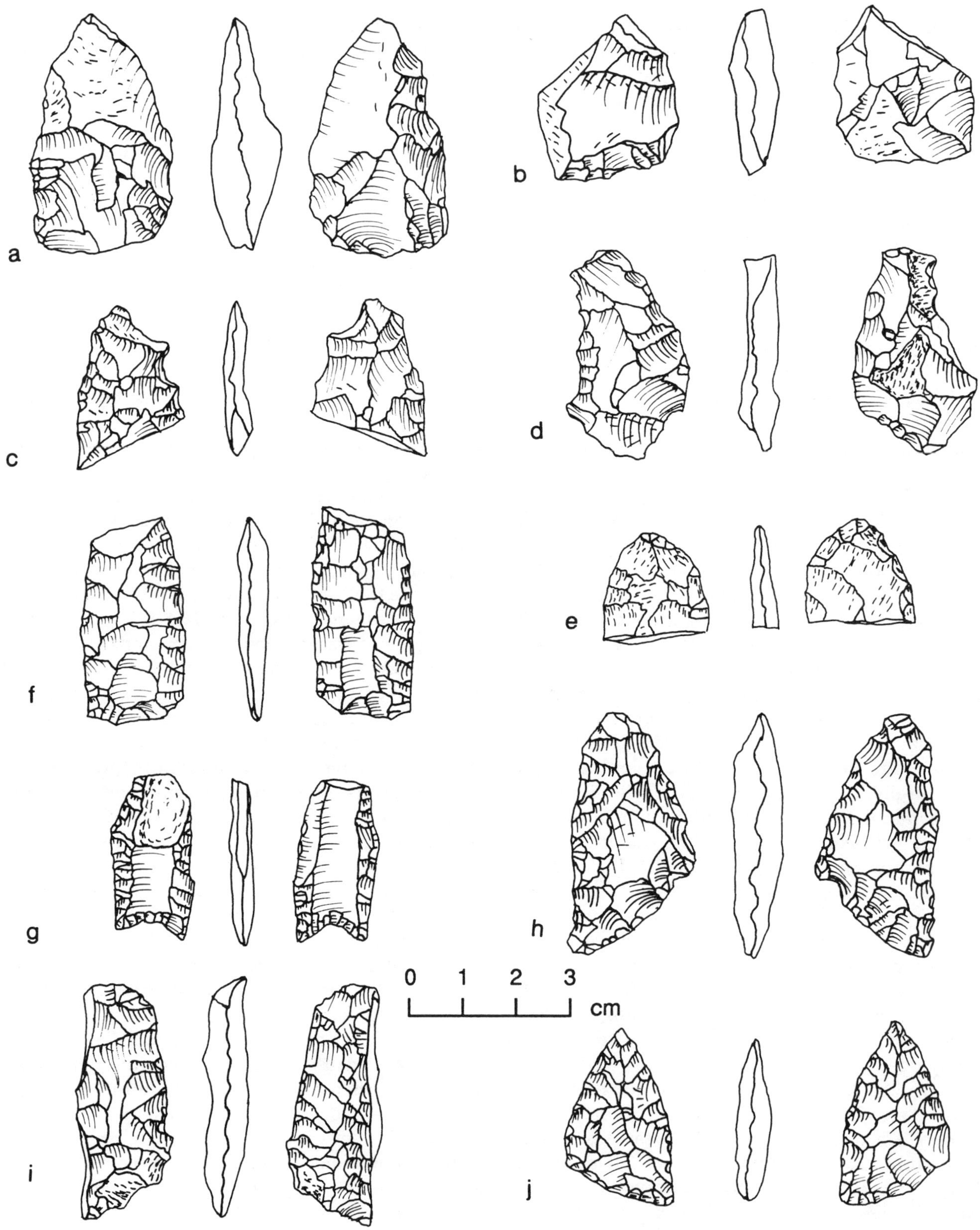

Figure 6.5. Bifaces. *a*, 85-27-8; *b*, 88280; *c*, 88286; *d*, 85-27-8; *e*, 85-27-309; *f*, 88264-7; *g*, 90071; *h*, 85-27-334-4; *i*, 85-27-1-35, *j*, 85-27-334-21.

Figure 6.6. Malkin Bifaces 1 (*a*, obverse; *b*, reverse) and 2 (*c*, obverse; *d*, reverse).

pseudo-burin spall. A large potlid occupies the distal half of the opposite face. The remaining margin bears evidence of heavy wear and resharpening—this was no toy—in the form of abrasion, crushing and step fractures. In addition, that margin is inflected markedly above the haft segment, indicating extensive resharpening. The specimen exhibits no evidence of post-fracture reworking.

85-27-334-4 (Fig. 6.5h). A heavily used tool, this Ten Mile Creek specimen is fashioned from a thick flake blank of a lustrous variety of Ten Mile Creek chert. Original form is difficult to reconstruct owing to heavy use. Nearly plano-convex in transverse cross-section, the base and one margin are formed by broad, short expanding facets; the base has a fairly acute edge angle, but the margin is steep. It is abraded and bears no evidence of resharpening, and is interpreted as the nonfunctional edge of a backed biface. The opposite margin is extensively resharpened, bearing a complex series of steps, feather, and hinge-termination facets. The edge is steep-angled and nearly beveled, with most resharpening facets on the steep-angled face. The tool is intact and probably was discarded because resharpening had exhausted its utility. A backed biface was found at

Thedford (Deller and Ellis 1992: Fig. 42), but specimen 85-27-334-4 does not resemble it in form.

85-27-1-35 (Fig. 6.5i). Still another Ten Mile Creek biface, this heat-treated specimen is the result of a lateral fracture. Its remaining original margin is beveled and heavily worn. Production or use-failure lateral fracture is common at Folsom-affinity sites (Wilmsen and Roberts 1978:105-7, Figs. 102, 103; Frison and Bradley 1980), though most specimens are fragments of fluted bifaces and indicate fluting failure. This specimen bears no evidence of fluting. Ellis and Deller (1988:114-15, Figs. 4-5) include laterally broken specimens in their backed biface type, which is marked by several attributes not found on the present specimen (e.g., thinning flakes struck from the backed section, beveling, basal concavity).

85-27-334-21 (Fig. 6.5j). Another Ten Mile Creek specimen, this is a small, heavily resharpened biface, intact save for one corner. Reddish tinting on one face may indicate heat treatment. Although lanceolate in form, resharpening has produced a triangular final form. Base and margins are abraded, and the base is thinned on both faces. On one, a single narrow, relatively long and asymmetrical flake was removed, but the specimen cannot be considered fluted. Primary facets are shallow and collateral. A subtle but distinct inflection of both margins is evident at the base blade juncture, where blade resharpening has reformed the margin. Resharpening is symmetrical in both dimensions; that is, the edges are not beveled and are equally inflected. Secondary faceting is extremely fine, and both edges are slightly serrated. The specimen is an exhausted or nearly exhausted biface. Whether it was abandoned upon fracture or was fractured subsequently is unknown, although the fractured corner is not reworked.

Broken Bifaces

Several other broken and nondiagnostic bifaces were found at Leavitt. They are treated as part of the Paleo-Indian assemblage for purposes of description, although they are too fragmentary for measurement and therefore do not appear in Tables 6.1-6.4. Some bifaces also were reworked as bipolar cores, and are described with other cores in Chapter 4.

One specimen, 85-27-324, is a fragment of a tool produced by an unsuccessful attempt at biface thinning that culminated in a large overshot. Technically, it may be considered a flake. Slight use-wear is found along one lateral margin of the specimen, which is not a margin of the original biface. Specimen 85-27-243 is a fragment of the edge of an Upper Mercer biface. It does not fit or conjoin with specimen 90073 (Fig. 6.3e), although it is not impossible that the two fragments are parts of the same original tool. For what it is worth, 85-27-243 is a blocky fragment which may have been created by exposure to intense heat or the deliberate shattering or radial fracture (Frison and Bradley 1980:97-99, Fig. 63) of a biface. Unless the two halves of a broken biface are treated and disposed of differently, one half for instance simply being discarded without modification after fracture (e.g., specimen 90073) and the other subsequently altered, the two Upper Mercer specimens probably are from different original specimens. Hence, the "minimum number" of Upper Mercer bifaces at Leavitt probably is two, not one. Specimen 88290 is a proximal fragment of a biface preform that may have been broken in final production. Specimen 85-27-1-41 is the margin fragment of a large Bayport biface; 85-27-243 is a small, badly heat-damaged, fragment of a biface made from an unidentified but lustrous and fine-grained chert.

Later-Period Diagnostic Bifaces

Several bifaces were recovered during the 1984 excavation that cannot be classified as Paleo-Indian in origin. Most, in fact, appear to be Early Archaic diagnostics. They are illustrated in Figure 6.7 and described briefly in this section. Table 6.5 presents metric and other data on this group of implements.

85-27-312 (Fig. 6.7a). This proximal specimen has a slightly expanding stem with ground base and margins. It is formed on a thin flake blank exhibiting a remnant of the flake ventral surface on one face; the stem is formed by expanding primary flake facets. Abrasion extends along the margins from the base, past the shoulder, and approximately 7 cm along the length of the blade. Above this abraded segment, the blade margin is distinctly inflected, indicating resharpening. Blade cross-section is lenticular, and the specimen exhibits a transverse fracture at a flaw in the raw material. It is not reworked.

85-27-178 (Fig. 6.7b). The Ten Mile Creek specimen is a narrow, straight-stemmed biface proximal fragment. It is distinctly reddened, possibly by heat treatment. Base and margins of the stem are not abraded. Although one shoulder blade juncture is partly obscured by retouch, the stem appears to be asymmetrically placed on the blade, suggesting that resharpening and probably use were more extensive on one blade margin. The bend fracture is oblique and intersects a

TABLE 6.5
Attributes of Later-Period Diagnostic Bifaces

				OVERALL			STEM	
Spec.	N E	Matl.	Cond.	len.	wid.	thk.	len.	wid.
85-27-312	513/515	BP	proximal	—	25.3	6.1	10.0	16.6
85-27-178	517/528	?	proximal	—	22.6	5.7	10.4	10.0
85-27-41	522/511	TM	whole	21.9	15.1	4.5	7.9	—
85-27-245	525/530	BP?	whole	24.6	20.9	7.4	7.0	13.4
85-27-261	527/524	TM?	whole	28.7	15.1	4.5	7.0	8.9
85-27-50	537/511	KP	distal	—	—	5.3	—	—
85-27-335	surface	BP	proximal	—	—	—	—	—

Measurements in millimeters; BP = Bayport chert, TM = Ten Mile Creek chert, KP = Kettle Point chert

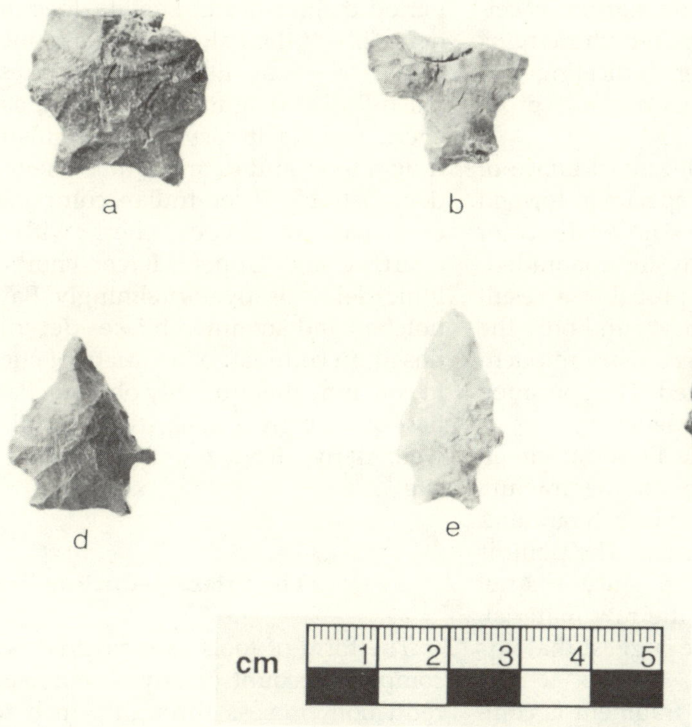

Figure 6.7. Later-period diagnostics. *a*, 85-27-312; *b*, 85-27-178; *c*, 85-27-41; *d*, 85-27-245; *e*, 85-27-261; *f*, 85-27-335.

crystalline inclusion in the chert matrix. The specimen is not reworked.

85-27-41 (Fig. 6.7c). This Ten Mile Creek biface is a small, expanding-stem or bifurcate base form with a partially fractured base. The remaining stem margin is ground. Blade margins are serrated and one margin at the shoulder bears a distinct projection or ear, a remnant of the original blade margin since isolated by resharpening of the rest of the margin. Blade cross-section is plano-convex, and retouch on the convex surface is oblique and lamellar, probably a result of pressure flaking. One margin on the plane surface bears step fracture termination, indicating a different method of resharpening. Since it is fractured, base morphology cannot be determined, but overall form and flaking suggests that the specimen could be a broken bifurcate-base biface, which is a definite Early Archaic diagnostic form. The chert appears to be slightly discolored, and may have been heat-treated.

85-27-245 (Fig. 6.7d). This intact Western Onondaga specimen is a short, straight-stemmed biface. Base and stem margins are ground and the base is thinned on one face by flakes that exceed the short stem in length, amounting to pseudo-fluting. The blade is thick, heavily reworked and irregular in plan. The margins intersect to form a thick, narrow point that may have functioned as a piercing implement; alternatively, the two margins were used and reworked independently, forming the point as an incidental product of resharpening. One margin is irregular and concave, the other is straight; the latter bears a distinct projection at the shoulder, indicating extensive resharpening of the margin. Faceting is secondary, oblique and lamellar on both margins on one face, but primary on the other, indicating that only the former was resharpened. This biface is probably an exhausted, discarded tool.

85-27-261 (Fig. 6.7e). This well-made, intact biface of unknown material is a bifurcate base specimen formed on a thin flake blank. The blank bears no evidence of heat treatment. Base and stem margins are unabraded. Blade margins are slightly irregular, probably a result of resharpening. Most faceting is primary, and only the areas near the blade margins exhibit secondary retouch. The blade is asymmetrically resharpened. The specimen does not seem to be extensively resharpened.

85-27-50 (not illustrated). This Kettle Point specimen is a distal fragment with a large lip on the fracture plane. One face is potlidded, indicating heat treatment. Secondary faceting is oblique and lamellar. The point is rounded, possibly by an impact fracture since it is not retouched. Although not diagnostic, the raw material, flaking pattern and overall appearance suggest that it is an Early Archaic biface.

85-27-335 (Fig. 6.7f). This proximal fragment is composed of extremely fossilferous Bayport chert, and has been heavily damaged by heat. Base is expanding stem in form, but damage makes it impossible to detect abrasion. The flake blank is very thin, and transverse cross-section is lenticular. The extensive damage to this specimen makes further description impossible.

Leavitt is by no means the only Great Lakes Paleo-Indian site to contain later-period diagnostics. Plano-affinity bifaces were recovered at Zander (Stewart 1984: Fig. 5), which may or may not be contemporaneous with the fluted biface assemblage there. A considerable range of non-Paleo-Indian occupations is reflected in the biface assemblage at Thedford (Deller and Ellis 1992: Fig. 3). Elsewhere, Byers (1954:343) reports later-period diagnostics at the Bull Brook site, and Lindenmeier also produced later specimens (Wilmsen and Roberts 1978: Fig. 59). The Gainey site (Simons et al. 1984) contains small Archaic and Woodland components in one portion of the site. Nobles Pond (Gramly and Summers 1986; Seeman 1991) also has produced a number of later-period diagnostics (D.B. Simons, pers. comm.). Eastern North America was occupied, intensively in places, for over eleven millennia before European invasion. This has produced a complex palimpsest of overlapping occupations which, ultimately, can only be separated and studied using distributional approaches (Ebert 1986). There are few purely single-component plow zone sites to be found in the region, and the presence of later-period diagnostics at Leavitt does not alter the context or quality of the Paleo-Indian assemblage there.

As Deller and Ellis (1992:11) stress, few if any non-Paleo-Indian diagnostics are composed of Collingwood chert, making it easy to distinguish them from Paleo-Indian tools and debris. The same is true at Leavitt; the demonstrably Paleo-Indian component consists almost exclusively of Bayport chert, with minor amounts of quartzite and Upper Mercer cherts. As noted above, lithic debris is overwhelmingly Bayport as well. The notched and stemmed bifaces described above are composed, in contrast, of a variety of cherts. It is reasonable to conclude that not only obvious Paleo-Indian diagnostics, but the great majority of nondiagnostic material as well, derive from the Paleo-Indian occupation of the site.

The Biface Reduction Trajectory

The form of tools as recovered is not sufficient for a complete account of any assemblage or industry. The reduction process through which tools pass must be characterized as well in any comprehensive study. Reduction practices are a valid subject in their own right, representing as they do a domain of behavior, if a relatively minor one in broader anthropological perspective. But reduction practices also may be diagnostic of particular cultures or time periods and thereby possess value as a time marker. Certain Paleo-Indian reduction practices in Ontario, for instance, may be diagnostic (Ellis 1984; Deller and Ellis 1992). Finally, reduction practices influence tool size and form, and may in that sense be regarded as a factor that accounts for some variability in stone tool industries. More broadly, reduction practices themselves are influenced by organizational factors that also affect finished tools. Thus, the ways in which artisans transformed raw materials to finished products were influenced at least in part by organizational factors. Not only the form and relative frequency of finished tools, but also the ways in which the tools were made, were subject to nonutilitarian constraints.

Bradley (1975) provided one well-known systematic approach to reduction analysis, as well as a glossary of relevant terms. In his terminology, "blank" denotes a flake struck from a core, before any reduction to a finished product, and "preform" denotes a specimen in nearly completed but not finished form. Bradley also emphasized the value of replication to reduction analysis (1975:7), which Paleo-Indian specialists were quick to attempt. Bradley proposed a four-stage reduction process, from preliminary modification to finished tool through successive or alternate blank and preform stages. His first stage itself is divisible into four substages. By now, however, nearly as many reduction schemes exist as there are archaeologists to implement them.

Biface Production

Bifaces probably were produced from biface-core flake blanks in a manner similar, if not identical, to that described for certain uniface blanks in Chapter 5. The inferred reduction sequence following blank production is presented in Figure 6.2, which allows for a range of blank sizes and corresponding finished tool types, presumably of functional significance. The largest type is represented by specimen 90074, a large but apparently finished proximal fragment. The second size class is a mid-sized one consisting of both unfluted (e.g., Upper Mercer specimen 90073, which is a distal fragment and could conceivably have been fluted) and fluted (e.g., specimens 85-27-100, 90072, 90070-6, 88264-5, 85-27-334-1, perhaps the quartzite specimen 88255/88216) specimens. The late preform stage for this type is represented by specimen 88259. The third type consists, among Bayport specimens, of both fluted (specimens 90071 and 88264-7) and perhaps unfluted (85-27-8 before it was broken and recycled as a bipolar core) varieties. Earlier-stage preforms for this size class include specimens 85-27-48 and 88280 before its bipolar recycling. Earliest-stage preforms for this size class either were produced directly from biface cores or were reduced from preforms of the second size class. Among specimens of other raw materials, the third class includes variable small, unfluted bifaces of Ten Mile Creek chert (specimens 85-27-334-4, 85-27-334-21 and 85-27-1-35) and perhaps quartzite tip specimen 85-27-309. No preforms of Ten Mile Creek chert, quartzite or other non-Bayport materials were recovered, unless quartzite specimen 88254, briefly described among unifaces, could have served as a blank for the production of bifaces.

The Fluted Biface Production Process

The stages of Folsom-affinity fluted biface production were set forth in Crabtree's (1966) seminal work. His detailed and meticulous account techniques identified three procedures as possible ways to produce fluted bifaces (1966:9, 12-15, 17-21): indirect percussion using a rest or anvil; direct pressure with chest crutch, clamp and anvil; and a combination of the two. The main procedures apparently are identical to the stage of preform production; although Crabtree does not discuss these stages in detail (1966:13, 17-18), they involve continuous reduction of a flake or core blank to a size and form suitable for fluting. In this respect, Crabtree's reconstructed fluting procedures broadly resemble those proposed here, as subsequent discussion will show. Although the exact number of stages in Crabtree's scheme is not indicated, his Figure 25, depicting the entire production sequence, includes twelve stages from flake blank to finished form. Crabtree's work has spawned a series of additional studies (Flenniken 1978; Frison and Bradley 1981; Judge 1973; Storck 1983; Tunnell 1977). Rather than dwelling on the details of this research, which documents strong similarities between eastern and western Folsom-affinity industries in fluted biface production, Deller and Ellis's (1992:30-34) approach based on a more general model of biface production is followed. That approach recognizes three stages, which are expanded here to six: (1) flake blank production; (2) margin production; (3) thinning; (4) finishing; (5) facial preparation for fluting; and (6) fluting. Like Thedford (Deller and Ellis 1992:31), the first two stages are not represented by abandoned specimens at Leavitt, although specimen 85-27-48 bears a possible platform remnant indicating its origin as a flake blank. This is not surprising in view of the organization of Paleo-Indian technologies, in particular the staging (Binford 1979) of tool production inferred in several fluted biface industries.

Biface production involves a combination of discrete and continuous processes. Thus, several fluted biface stages involve distinct operations which in turn produce distinct attributes, such as beveled bases and prepared, abraded tips. However, most of the production process is continuous in nature, involving the reduction in all three dimensions of flake or core blanks to the desired form. Thus, although thinning is only one of the three stages defined by Deller and Ellis (1992), it is in fact a process rather than a stage and it describes the majority of the work involved in tool production. The stages may be ordered in a sequence, but the same sequence is not necessarily followed in each case. Thus, a specimen may exhibit attributes of more than one production stage, and not necessarily successive ones.

The thinning stage is represented by specimen 85-27-48, the small Bayport biface found in Unit 317N 522E. The small size of the biface, however, makes it clear that it could have served as a preform only for the small fluted biface class, although it is not clear if the tool was designed for finishing as a fluted biface rather than some other biface form. Specimen 85-27-100 shows both Stage 3 and Stage 4 finishing which exemplifies the continuous rather than discrete nature of biface production.

Facial preparation for fluting refers to the removal of a series of parallel collateral flakes from opposite margins on a single face, producing a medial ridge formed at the intersection of flake facets from the opposing margins. This is thought to have facilitated fluting by guiding the flute along the longitudinal axis of the specimen (Deller and Ellis 1992:32; Storck 1983:83). Possible examples of this practice at Leavitt are found on specimens 90073 and 85-27-334. Tip preparation, in the form of a chisel-like, abraded distal edge, is found at Thedford (Deller and Ellis 1992:32) and Fisher (Storck 1983). This practice is considered a measure designed to increase friction between the biface and the base on which it was placed in the fluting process (Tunnell 1977:150). Specimen 90073, the Upper Mercer distal biface fragment, bears an alternately beveled tip subsequently damaged during the fluting process. Specimen 90070, a finished and utilized fluted biface, bears an abraded distal edge which may represent tip preparation, although that edge is oblique, not perpendicular, to the tool's longitudinal axis (Fig. 6.4c). The specimen bears evidence of considerable use. If the tip indeed indicates preparation for fluting, specimen 90070 demonstrates that fluted bifaces could be used without subsequent modification of the prepared tip.

Basal preparation for fluting is evident in the conjoined proximal fragment 90072, where pronounced beveling was carried out. That tool probably was broken during the fluting process.

Discussion

Three issues bear emphasizing at this juncture. First, not all bifaces are interpreted as specimens in some stage before fluting; rather, some evidently were produced and used without being intended for fluting at any point (e.g., specimens 85-27-334-4 and 85-27-334-21). In effect, not all bifaces in Parkhill industry assemblages were intended for fluting, a truism that nevertheless is worth stressing. Second, it is not certain that all, or any, of the few specimens interpreted as preforms for fluted bifaces were in fact destined for fluting before they were discarded. The attributes they bear are consistent with the reconstructed fluted biface production process set forth above, but it is entirely possible that some or all were designed for a different final form. Third, and related to the second point, preforms probably were functional tools in their own right, designed to be used and gradually transformed into fluted or other bifaces as circumstances required. Thus, at least specimen 88259, a probable biface preform, exhibits signs of utilization. Such tools can only be considered preforms in a limited sense, and one which reflects our strong emphasis on a single, albeit definitive, property of Paleo-Indian industries.

In effect, the process described here is a general production and use process with fluted bifaces as one, but not necessarily the only, outcome. It accomodates Ellis's (1984) staged production model, in which general bifaces or preforms of relatively standard dimensions are the only original outcome, with fluted bifaces and other tool classes as more specialized final forms. Although Ellis (1984:167-74) describes some other final forms, it is notable that none of these is found in the Leavitt assemblage. This is explained on one of three grounds: (1) all such tools were carried away from the site upon its abandonment; (2) none were imported to it or produced there; or (3) simple sampling error. The probability of the third is impossible to estimate while the other two cannot be distinguished on present evidence. As will be shown, a relatively high curation rate characterized the Leavitt assemblage, making the first possibility plausible. However, it also is possible that the production process, at least at Leavitt if not for Michigan Parkhill phase sites in general, is more specialized than the comparable process at Ontario Parkhill sites. If so, this difference in technological organization may indicate systematic differences in other organizational properties as well.

Whatever the case, the Leavitt assemblage provides imperfect evidence for the fluted biface production process. Early production stages are not represented at all, and later stages are represented imperfectly at best, by very few specimens. In fact, finished and utilized fluted bifaces outnumber those interpreted as preforms. And specimens in the latter category could only have served as preforms for the small class of fluted bifaces; no preforms suitable for conversion to the large class were

TABLE 6.6
Rates of Failure in Fluted Biface Production

Assemblage	Broken in Production	Total	Rate (%)	Source
WESTERN FOLSOM				
Middle Park	21	53	39.6	Naze 1986:18
Rio Grande	—	—	25	Judge 1973:170
Experimental	—	—	37	Flenniken 1978:474
PARKHILL PHASE				
Barnes	10	28?	35.7	Voss 1977; Wright and Roosa 1966
Fisher	80	156	51.3	Storck 1983
Leavitt	2	8	25.0	this report

Totals include the production failures. Leavitt figures are for all fluted bifaces, including quartzite specimen 88216 and 88255.

recovered. This should occasion no surprise in view of the highly curated nature of Paleo-Indian industries and the practice of staged production (Binford 1979) which Ellis (1984) infers for Ontario Parkhill assemblages. In effect, these assemblages were designed for the production of preforms at or near chert sources, and subsequent high curation of the specimens. Under these circumstances, most tools should be discarded only when broken or exhausted, not at a comparatively early stage of their use-life.

Failure Rates in Fluting

This discussion of fluted biface production has been qualitative in nature, in contrast to the continuous nature of the actual process. At this juncture, the quantitative properties of the process are considered. Since Leavitt itself yielded fragmentary evidence, it is necessary to employ suitable data from other Parkhill phase sites in the region. Without doubt, Great Lakes Paleo-Indian industries are characterized by high rates of tool curation. In fact, this often-cited view has assumed the status of a virtual article of faith among Paleo-Indian researchers in the region. Analysis of the Leavitt assemblage supports the view in large measure. In one respect, however—the production of fluted bifaces—Paleo-Indian industries were exceptionally wasteful. At Barnes, Thedford and other Great Lakes Parkhill phase sites, the discarded assemblage reflects a surprisingly high rate of failure in fluting, usually by fracture. Thus breakage in production ("discard process 2" discussed in Chapter 7; see also Shott 1989a), occurs at high frequency in Great Lakes Paleo-Indian industries, an observation which indicates a low curation rate. Along with Leavitt, data from selected sites are compiled in Table 6.6. All fluted bifaces from Leavitt are included in the table; although quartzite specimen 88216/88255 is broken, it is unknown if the fracture occurred during production or use. Conservatively, the latter is assumed here. If the fracture was instead during production, failure rate at Leavitt would be higher. Since two unfinished Leavitt specimens were fractured in production and discarded, the rate there is 25.0%.

The figures shown in Table 6.6 must be qualified to an unknown degree by noting that some fragments of unfinished fluted bifaces at some sites may have been from a single original specimen which was not conjoined or no longer was conjoinable. In effect, the figures are inflated to this degree by double counting of the fragments of intact original specimens. In addition, broken fluted bifaces often are reworked for subsequent use or refluting in many Paleo-Indian assemblages (Deller and Ellis 1992:32; Roosa 1977a, 1977b; Simons et al. 1984; Storck 1983:85), which also mitigates the high breakage rate to some degree. Nevertheless, the data show that biface fluting was a risky enterprise characterized by high failure rates, and the conclusion applies to the comparatively small Leavitt assemblages as well.

Storck (1983:84) defined several types of fluted biface fracture based on Fisher site specimens. Hinge, or *outre passe*, fractures dominate that assemblage (Table 6.6), followed by minor fractures at the distal section. Although longitudinal fractures are common in western Folsom-affinity assemblages (Frison and Bradley 1980: Fig. 34; Wilmsen and Roberts 1978: Fig. 102), they are relatively uncommon at Fisher. Finally, lateral bend fractures do not occur at Fisher despite their high frequency elsewhere (Deller and Ellis 1992; Frison and Bradley 1980: Fig. 31; Roosa 1977a; Wilmsen and Roberts 1978). Both unfinished specimens at Leavitt were fractured by bending. The significance of these distinct patterns of fracture frequency are unclear, and will remain so until they are linked to organizational models of tool production.

Small Fluted Bifaces

The Leavitt fluted biface assemblage is characterized by two relatively distinct size classes (Figs. 6.4-6.5). Specimens in the large class (Figs. 6.4a-f) compare closely to other Parkhill phase Great Lakes assemblages. The two specimens that form the small class (Figs. 6.5f, 6.5g) also have counterparts in the region. Several specimens, including unfinished ones, occur at Barnes (Voss 1977: Fig. 4a,b; Wright and Roosa 1966: Fig. 3e), at Parkhill (Roosa and Deller 1982) and at Thedford (Deller and Ellis 1992: Fig. 21e, f, i). Although a considerable

TABLE 6.7
Metric Data on Small Fluted Bifaces from Leavitt, Thedford and Middle Park

Site	Length	Width	Thickness	Concavity	Source
Middle Park	30.	17.	—	—	Naze 1986
Leavitt 88264-7	—	19.3	6.2	2.3	this report
Leavitt 90071	—	15.6	4.6	3.6	this report
Thedford	40.1	22.1	5.1	2.5	Deller & Ellis 1992: Fig.21e
Thedford	32.1	16.7	3.6	1.8	Deller & Ellis 1992: Fig.21i

Measurements in millimeters.
Middle Park data are estimated from Naze's (1986) Figure 4a.

number of small fluted bifaces was found at Fisher (P. Storck, pers. comm.), full documentation and the comparison it permits awaits publication of the Fisher site report. These specimens are not to be confused with fluted points made from channel flakes or other kinds of flakes, which are found at Parkhill (Roosa and Deller 1982:8) and elsewhere in eastern North America (Moeller 1980:52-53, Pl. 7a, c).

Table 6.7 compares metric attributes of the small Leavitt specimens with bifaces from Thedford, from Middle Park, Colorado (Naze 1986) and from the Agate Basin site (Frison and Stanford 1982). In addition, Tunnell (1977: Figs. 2, 6) illustrates small fluted biface specimens from Adair-Steadman in central Texas, although no metric data are furnished. Figure 2.41a from Frison and Stanford (1982) evidently is the specimen illustrated by Agogino and Frankforter (1964; cited in Naze 1986:24) from the Brewster site, now considered a part of the Agate Basin site. Because measurements of the western Folsom specimens were taken from illustrations, they may not be exact. Assuming that they are reasonably accurate, Table 6.7 shows that metric attributes of the Leavitt and western Folson specimens are similar. Note in particular the close agreement in width, which is not affected by resharpening as much as is length. At Thedford, small fluted bifaces are made exclusively of Collingwood chert; Bayport, of secondary importance there, is confined to large bifaces (Deller and Ellis 1992). In contrast, Bayport is used for both size classes at Leavitt.

Apparently, a small fluted biface is a component of Folsom-affinity Paleo-Indian industries, although a secondary one judging from the observed abundance of specimens. The functional significance of the class is unknown, although Deller (1982:4) suggests that it may indicate specialized hunting of small game. In contrast, Tunnell (1977:143) suggests that it represents a recycling strategy, in which specimens broken in fluting are reworked into smaller finished forms. Whatever the case, both Leavitt specimens clearly are functional, although an additional magical or religious significance (Bonnichsen and Keyser 1982) cannot be discounted. As theory is developed to interpret biface size classes, the processual meaning of these data may be revealed (Shott 1990).

Estimating the Size of Blanks Imported to Leavitt

As at Thedford, only advanced preforms were imported to Leavitt, making it impossible to determine directly the size, form and origin (i.e., core or flake blank) of earlier-stage preforms in the Parkhill phase reduction trajectory. As Crabtree (1966:18) notes anyway, the extensive modification that bifaces undergo in the production process generally makes it difficult, if not impossible, to identify the trajectory's starting point. What can be inferred (admittedly on somewhat tenuous grounds) is the "stage" or point at which preforms stood upon importation to the site. The stages are broadly consistent with the biface reduction stages discussed above. Stages can be identified first by comparing metric attributes of recovered preforms to finished bifaces and then by comparing the resulting differences to those found at other Paleo-Indian sites. However, sample sizes in this comparison range from one to three, and the statistical validity of the results should not be overstated.

Concerning large fluted bifaces and the preforms from which they originated, Table 6.8 shows progressive reduction in width, a great reduction in thickness from unfluted to fluted preform stages and, surprisingly, longer finished than unfinished specimens. The latter observation might ordinarily be attributed to sample-size vagaries or the fact that the sole large unfluted preform—specimen 88259—also was used, but similar and more abundant data from Thedford (Table 6.8) show that there too, finished specimens are longer than unfinished ones. Not surprisingly, weight also declines considerably and basal concavity increases as production is completed.

TABLE 6.8
Comparative Metric Data on Stages in Fluted Biface Production

Stage	Length	Width	Thickness	Weight	Concavity
LEAVITT-Large Biface					
1. unfluted preform	70.7	37.4	9.5	28.2	0.0
2. fluted preform	—	32.5	6.7	—	7.8
3. finished fluted	72.7	28.5	6.6	13.2	5.2
LEAVITT-Small Biface					
1. unfluted preform	50.2	30.4	8.6	15.3	—
3. finished fluted	—	17.4	5.4	—	2.9
THEDFORD					
1. unfluted preform	67.1	30.2	11.1	—	—
3. finished fluted	94.5	25.5	6.1	—	—
BARNES[a]					
1. unfluted preform	92.0	42.0	11.0	—	—
2. fluted preform	63.7	27.0	6.9	—	—
3. finished fluted	60.5	24.0	5.0	—	—
LINDENMEIER					
1. fluted preform	48.6	24.8	4.3	—	—
3. finished fluted	34.6	18.6	3.7	—	—
EXPERIMENTAL[b]					
1. unfluted preform	93.	45.	8.	—	—
3. finished fluted	81.	33.	9.	—	—

Sources: Deller and Ellis 1992 for Thedford; Wright and Roosa 1966 for Barnes; Wilmsen and Roberts 1978 for Lindenmeier; and Callahan 1978 for experimental data. Data in millimeters and grams.
[a]The three stages used here correspond to Wright and Roosa's (1966) Stages 2–4. Length and width values for Barnes include several estimated values, as described in Wright and Roosa 1966.
[b]The two stages presented here correspond to Callahan's (1978) Stages 4 and 9.

Percentage reduction by "stage" in the Leavitt assemblage also appears in Table 6.9. Comparison in the small-biface class treats specimen 85-27-48 (Fig. 6.4g) as representative of the preform stage. Comparison is hampered by the fragmentary condition of finished specimens and the absence of fluted preforms, but the degree of thickness reduction from unfluted preform to finished tool closely resembles the large-biface value (Table 6.9).

Comparative data from Thedford and elsewhere are presented in Tables 6.8 and 6.9. As noted above, finished Thedford specimens are longer than preforms recovered there, but other dimensions exhibit the expected reduction from preform to finished tool. Width reduction is similar to the Leavitt value, but thickness reduction is greater at Thedford, reflecting both thicker preforms and thinner finished products. Weight reduction during finishing at Thedford apparently is achieved primarily by thinning.

This finding could be attributed to raw material differences, varying functional requirements at the sites, different degrees of reduction at quarries or elsewhere before importation to the site, or nothing more significant than sampling error. At face value, however, Leavitt preforms were somewhat more extensively reduced before introduction to the site than were Thedford specimens, either because Leavitt was occupied a longer time after obtaining quarry supplies or because of systematic fluted-biface design differences between adjacent Parkhill phase groups. Whatever the case, reduction in thickness consistently exceeds other metric attributes. These findings also establish conclusively that thinning, not reductions in length or width, forms the final stages of fluted biface production, consistent with most existing models of the process.

Perhaps the most appropriate comparison of Leavitt bifaces is to Barnes (Wright and Roosa 1966; Voss 1977), which is not only closer to it than is Thedford but shares a predominance of Bayport chert. Again, provisos concerning sample size apply, but Tables 6.8 and 6.9 sug-

TABLE 6.9
Comparative Degree of Reduction in the Fluted Biface Production Process

Stages	Length	Width	Thickness	Wt.	Concavity
LEAVITT—Large Biface					
1-2	—	0.87	0.70	—	—
2-3	—	0.88	0.98	—	0.67
1-3	1.03	0.76	0.69	0.47	—
LEAVITT—Small Biface					
1-3	—	0.57	0.63	—	—
THEDFORD					
1-3	1.41	0.84	0.55	—	—
BARNES					
1-2	0.69	0.64	0.63	—	—
2-3	0.95	0.89	0.72	—	—
1-3	0.66	0.57	0.45	—	—
LINDENMEIER					
1-3	0.74	0.75	0.86	—	—
EXPERIMENTAL					
1-3	0.87	0.73	1.12	—	—

Read the lefthand column as "from Stage 1 to 2," etc. Figures are higher-stage values divided by lower-stage ones.

gest that considerably smaller unfluted preforms were imported to Leavitt than to Barnes, befitting Leavitt's greater distance from quarry supplies and the carrying costs (Shott 1986a, 1986b) that this implies. Moreover, Leavitt values consistently, though not in all cases, exceed Barnes' and Table 6.9 values indicate less reduction. The conclusion is inescapable: less reduction overall probably occurred at Leavitt than at Barnes and, correspondingly, specimens were imported to Leavitt nearer to their finished form.

Compared to Great Lakes assemblages, Lindenmeier fluted bifaces were reduced a similar degree in width but more in length and less in thickness (Table 6.9). Callahan's (1978) reduction sequence also is summarized in Table 6.9, even though it is intended to replicate Clovis, not Folsom, reduction. Again, width reduction is similar to the Great Lakes cases, but length and thickness do not behave as they do at Leavitt, Barnes and Thedford.

Other metric attributes deserve brief mention in this comparison. Not surprisingly, large-biface preforms lack basal concavities while fluted specimens possess them, but the deeper concavities of finished specimens than unfinished fluted ones is contrary to expectations (Table 6.8). That is, attributes of size like length, width and thickness should decline in the production process, and generally do in the archaeological assemblages. Basal concavity, however, is an attribute of finished products that should increase. A possible explanation for this counterintuitive finding lies in a comparison of fluted preform 85-27-100 (Fig. 6.4a) and finished specimen 90070 (Fig. 6.4c). The former has sharp, projecting basal ears while the latter's are blunted and abraded, a process that could easily reduce basal concavity.

Fluting attributes are, to say the least, important properties of fluted bifaces. Comparison of channel length (combining all measurable flute scars, obverse and reverse) of Leavitt preforms and finished specimens is confined to preform 90072 (Fig. 6.4b) and finished biface 90070 (Fig. 6.4c), since other specimens are too fragmentary to measure. Expected equality in values more or less is found (Table 6.3), since channel length should not decline in the final production steps. However, the specimen 90072 value is the mean of two disparate values, and the lower of them reflects the somewhat atypical fluting found on that specimen's reverse face, which may have contributed to its failure. At any rate, maximum channel length probably mattered less to Paleo-Indian artisans than did the minimum length necessary to facilitate hafting. As Table 6.3 shows, the minimum of preform and finished channel lengths are similar. Likewise, channel width values are similar. Again, Paleo-Indians probably sought a minimum channel width, scarcely caring if results slightly exceeded the necessary threshold. Here again, the finished value is slightly greater than the preform one, though the two are similar (Table 6.3). On balance and in view of the sparse available data, fluting attributes are best considered to differ minimally between preforms and finished specimens.

Fluted preforms lack hafts (Table 6.2) and so cannot be compared to finished specimens in haft attributes. Interestingly, functional margin or edge angles of preform 90072 fall well within the range of angles found among finished specimens (Table 6.4); several of the latter exceed the preform's values, suggesting at least some steepening of functional margins during use and resharpening. Finally, margin use attributes of curvature (principally none), morphology (principally straight) and damage type (principally scalar) differ little among fluted bifaces, but damage distribution exhibits considerable variation (Table 6.4). Fluted bifaces at Leavitt were somewhat versatile functionally (sensu Shott 1986b) and were used to varying degrees of intensity.

Non-fluted bifaces cover a wide range in size, form and use attributes (Tables 6.1-6.4). A range of production practices and functional task applications is suggested.

Continuous Variation in Fluted Bifaces

Introduction

If much of the meaning behind variation in size and form of Paleo-Indian tools, especially fluted bifaces, remains to be revealed, at least provisional interpretations of this meaning can be attempted. Detailed morphological analyses of Great Lakes fluted biface types (Roosa 1966; Roosa and Deller 1982; Wright 1981a) have identified a set of reasonably distinct types, from Gainey to Crowfield. Moreover, these and other studies of site distributions and ages (Deller and Ellis 1988; Shott 1986a; Storck 1982) have established the chronological parameters of the types. Thus, Great Lakes fluted biface forms encompass not merely a set of types, but a time series of them.

These studies also have demonstrated what Deller and Ellis (1992:36) aptly describe as the polythetic nature of the types. That is, specimens fall into one or another type based not on the presence or absence of individual critical attributes, but on the general pattern of attribute association. Specimens must possess most, not all, attributes definitive of a type and few, not necessarily none, definitive of others. Because many of these attributes are in fact continuous metric variables, types are defined in part by characteristic ranges and distributions of values. Bifaces are tools and differences between biface types in metric variables represent changing functional performance requirements of tools. If metric changes occur abruptly in time, comparable change in performance requirements may be adduced. More gradual change presumably reflects similarly gradual changes in performance requirements. The meaning to attach to observed time-dependent variation is a separate matter that requires appropriate general theory linking stone tool size and form directly to performance requirements and ultimately to culture change (Schiffer and Skibo 1987; Shott n.d.).

Most North American hafted biface types are time markers, but the definition of types renders time as a series of discrete segments and the culture process that operates through it as a series of episodic changes. Culture process, however, can be continuous. Recently, archaeologists have begun to explore relatively fine variation in continuous attributes of material remains and to attribute it to continuous culture change (Braun 1987; Plog and Hantman 1990), revealing kinds and rates of culture change not otherwise observable. Although chronological control and theory with which to attach meaning to continuous variation both are poorly developed in the case of Great Lakes Paleo-Indian studies, at least a preliminary assay of the nature and meaning of variation in fluted bifaces is justified.

Deller and Ellis (1992: Tables 12-16) lay the foundation for this work in the data they compile on metric variation in successive Gainey, Parkhill and Crowfield assemblages. Leavitt is compared to that body of data here. The comparison must be qualified by the extremely limited nature of metric data from Leavitt (in some cases $n = 1$). Therefore, comparison will necessarily be confined to central tendencies as measured by the mean, ignoring equally important measures of distribution and dispersion. Similarly, raw material differences can complicate the comparison of assemblages. Although most specialists acknowledge few differences between, say, Parkhill assemblages dominated by Bayport or Collingwood cherts, such differences may nevertheless exist. Especially in fluted bifaces, social dimensions of variation can also complicate time-space metric patterning (Voss 1977; Wilmsen and Roberts 1978). Finally, sample selection may influence results; in the following comparison, the quartzite specimen 88216/88255 is omitted, since quartzite differs qualitatively from Bayport, Collingwood and all other cherts. However, small fluted bifaces 88264 and 90071 are included as were, apparently, small Thedford specimens in Deller and Ellis's tables. Also following those authors (1992:41), finished specimens were included but preforms were omitted.

Data and Results

Table 6.10, largely based on Deller and Ellis's (1992) Tables 12-16, presents mean values for selected metric and angular variables from several Great Lakes Paleo-Indian assemblages. Gainey-affinity assemblages from Ontario are included, but data from the much larger type site (Simons et al. 1984) await completion of the analysis there. Crowfield site data (Deller and Ellis 1984) also are omitted. Data from Barnes (Voss 1977; Wright and Roosa 1966) are available only in limited form and therefore are used for only limited purposes.

It is gratifying to note that Table 6.10 reveals general similarity between Leavitt and other Parkhill-affinity assemblages in most respects. (Small samples for length and the sensitivity of this variable to resharpening reduce its value in the comparison.) Consistent with the polythetic nature of established types and with previous typological judgment (Roosa 1966; Wright 1981a), the

TABLE 6.10
Metric Trends in Great Lakes Fluted Biface Assemblages

Site	Length N	Length x̄	Max. Width N	Max. Width x̄	Thickness N	Thickness x̄	Base Wid. N	Base Wid. x̄	Concavity N	Concavity x̄	Face Angle N	Face Angle x̄
Gainey[a]	8	59.8	14	26.1	13	7.2	14	25.2	13	5.5	27	90.7
Leavitt	1	72.7	3	25.5[b]	5	6.1[b]	3	18.5[b]	3	5.3	3	93.5
Thedford	3	94.5	5	25.5	6	6.1	4	18.5	5	3.6	8	96.9
Parkhill	5	45.6	21	20.4	26	5.6	25	17.0	40	3.8	53	97.2
Fisher	4	43.0	18	17.0	16	5.3	20	15.1	20	3.2	30	96.0

All measurements in millimeters. Leavitt data supplied in this report; all other data taken from Deller and Ellis 1992: Tables 12-16.
[a]Gainey-affinity assemblages in Ontario, not the Gainey site.
[b]Rounding obscures the slightly higher Leavitt value compared to Thedford.

TABLE 6.11
Assemblage Rank and Total Rank by Attribute

Assemblage	Length	Width	Thickness	Base Width	Concavity	Face Angle	Total
Ontario Gainey	3	1	1	1	1	1	8
Leavitt	2	2	2	2	2	2	12
Thedford	1	3	3	3	4	4	18
Parkhill	4	4	4	4	3	5	24
Fisher	5	5	5	5	5	3	28

Leavitt material can be securely placed in the Barnes type of Parkhill affinity. Equally consistent with this property of the types, Parkhill-affinity assemblages vary considerably in mean values, reflecting perhaps time-dependent continuous change in functional performance requirements. Most regional specialists agree that fluted biface metric attributes generally decline and that face angle increases through time.

Ranking assemblages in increasing order in metric attributes (*1* for highest values) and decreasing order in face angle (*1* for lowest value) should give Gainey-affinity values the lowest cumulative value of ranks. Table 6.11 shows this to be true; other assemblages are ordered there by rank, with Leavitt occupying the next position, first among Parkhill-affinity assemblages. With respect to these variables, therefore, Leavitt exhibits the greatest similarity to the Gainey phase. Assuming variation to be time-dependent (and effectively ignoring, in consequence, possible complicating factors such as raw material and social conditions), Leavitt emerges as the earliest Parkhill phase assemblage under study.

This ordering treats all variables as equally important. As noted above, however, length of recovered specimens probably reflects resharpening and therefore curation rate as much as it does original design. In contrast, width variables are identified in studies of later prehistoric projectiles as especially sensitive to functional performance standards because they are the most closely constrained by hafting requirements (Shott n.d.; Thomas 1978). If the same requirements constrained Paleo-Indian technologies, then chronological trends in maximum width and base width form the most sensitive reflections of changing performance requirements and the broader culture changes that underlie them. As Table 6.11 shows, assemblages under study exhibit the same ordering in base width and maximum width, and Leavitt again is first among Parkhill-affinity assemblage, though the Thedford maximum width value is nearly identical to Leavitt's. It may also be significant that maximum width values are more evenly distributed than are base width values. With respect to the latter, Gainey-affinity assemblages clearly emerge as an outlier. This pattern suggests that base width reduction occurred at a higher rate than did corresponding reduction in maximum width of specimens. As a partial corollary, face angle rose simultaneously, as it must when mean values for base and maximum width diverge. It is possible, then, that face angle is not itself a design attribute of Great Lakes fluted bifaces, but merely the necessary product of different rates of reduction in width variables.

The limited data available from Barnes exclude it from full comparison here, though Deller and Ellis

(1992: Tables 12-16) include thickness and base-width data from that site. In thickness, Barnes lies at the opposite end of the Parkhill phase range from Leavitt but in base width—perhaps one of the most important time-dependent and, therefore, diagnostic attributes—it is nearly identical, falling between Leavitt and Thedford.

As noted above, documenting and explaining metric trends are two distinct things. Provisionally, the observed trend may be explained by a need for greater range in projectiles, or by changes in diet breadth or subsistence diversity, or both (Shott 1990). It scarcely requires emphasizing, however, that far more data and far closer chronological control are required to validate these suggestions, and alternatives that may exist.

Wilmsen and Roberts (1978:176-77) suggest that fluting is a practice that aids hafting by maximizing the contact and therefore the friction between stone point and shaft or, more likely, foreshaft. They explain its prevalence in the Paleo-Indian period by the general paucity of resins and other natural adhesives in the early Holocene habitats of the continent. Whatever the merits of this argument—and the prevalence of fluting in the North American Southeast, where such adhesives probably were common even at the time, casts some doubt on it—few question the association of fluting with hafting requirements. Because stone points must articulate with other components of the larger tool of which they form a part, their size and form may reveal, even if obliquely, the size of the original composite (Christenson 1986; Shott n.d.; Thomas 1978). It is reasonable to suggest that the length and especially width of fluted biface channel scars reflect in some way the size of the foreshafts used to haft them. As noted above, projectile point width is more closely constrained by hafting requirements than is length, so emphasis here is placed on the former attribute.

Table 6.3 shows data on channel-scar width at Leavitt, suggesting that foreshafts were 14-15 mm in diameter. Data on Parkhill phase foreshafts do not exist, and data on roughly comparable Folsom foreshafts did not turn up in an admittedly brief search of relevant literature. Lindenmeier, for instance, features a sizeable bone industry but no illustrated items there resemble foreshafts (Wilmsen and Roberts 1978:126-34). However, Clovis bone tools reasonably interpreted as foreshafts are reported. From Blackwater Draw, Hester (1972: Figs. 100e, 105a-c) provides data on probable bone foreshafts, which average approximately 17.3 mm in diameter or width. A remarkably similar value of 17.9 mm is found for channel width of Anzick Cache specimens (Lahren and Bonnichsen 1974: Table 1). However, the proximal ends of the beveled sections of these specimens would have directly articulated with the bases of fluted bifaces (ibid: Figs. 1-3), and mean width in this region is 11.4 mm. As Table 6.3 shows, Leavitt channel width values fall between these extremes.

Channel width of Clovis bifaces generally exceeds that of Folsom bifaces, suggesting that the former were hafted to wider and probably longer foreshafts and shafts. If so, Clovis foreshafts should be wider than Folsom channel widths, and the Clovis foreshaft data support this prediction. Mean channel width of Parkhill phase Barnes fluted bifaces, as well as their overall size, suggests that they share closer affinity with Folsom specimens.

Conclusion

The Leavitt biface assemblage is neither exceptionally large nor unique. However, a collection's research potential is not measured by its size. Leavitt bifaces reveal stages or points of fluted biface production, rates of failure in production, and size modes of possible functional significance. Possible chronological trends in biface dimensions suggest that the Leavitt site lies at the early end of the continuum of change marking Parkhill phase occupation of the Great Lakes region.

CHAPTER 7

Assemblage Formation Processes

Introduction

To this point, the collection of artifacts from the Leavitt site has been considered, individually and collectively, as a set of tool types and classes. Description and analysis have concerned how tools were made, why specific tool-production choices were made, and how and how much tools were used. In this brief chapter, we speculate on how the Leavitt assemblage, as a collection of tools, came into being (Ammerman and Feldman 1974)—the formation processes (Schiffer 1975, 1976) that characterize the Leavitt assemblage.

Most Paleo-Indian specialists still hew to the doctrine of archaeological behavioralism (Shott 1989a:283-84), which regards assemblages as simple and direct reflections of the nature and frequency of activities in which they were used. Clearly, the substantive behavior at any site makes an important contribution to the composition of its assemblage, but in any cultural system characterized by organizational factors like high curation rates and functional versatility in tools, behavior is refracted—complicated by other factors—not simply reflected in the material record.

In addition to substantive behavior, different tool-class use-lives, degrees of functional versatility (Shott 1986b:19) or "mapping relations" (Ammerman and Feldman 1974:611), occupation span, the related quantity of assemblage size, and other factors determine the composition of assemblages (Schiffer 1975; Shott 1989b). Thus, our talk of Paleo-Indian kill sites and base camps stands at the level of unevaluated assumption, not established proposition. Size effects on the composition of Parkhill Phase and other Paleo-Indian assemblages have been demonstrated in earlier studies (Shott 1986a:159-68; 1990), and Leavitt conforms to the general pattern. This means that the site cannot be interpreted in any straightforward way as a base camp, kill site or any other particular type of site. Paleo-Indian assemblage formation processes are too complex, too complicated by organizational factors, to permit such facile interpretations.

Formation processes affect the composition of assemblages independently of substantive activities. Even if they did not, however, archaeologists could not simplistically read substantive behavior from the composition of assemblages, because tool form does not directly reflect function and the associated behavior. Form:function identities were once considered axiomatic, but underwent serious challenges more recently on the strength of ethnographic (Hayden 1978) and archaeological (Odell 1981; Wendorf 1968) studies. Ellis and Deller (1988:126-29) correctly stake out an intermediate position that neither denies nor assumes such identities. They rightly note the great functional specificity of ethnographic Arctic material cultures, although it is perilous to draw a simple analogy between nineteenth century Inuit and early Holocene Paleo-Indians. The tool types they define in Ontario Paleo-Indian assemblages may be functionally specific tools, but systematic analysis of Leavitt and other Paleo-Indian assemblages documents a considerable degree of functional versatility (Marshall 1985; Shott 1986a, 1989d). Similarly, a substantial body of cross-cultural data, drawn from many groups in a variety of habitats, documents a considerable range of variation in versatility and also identifies strong mobility constraints on the size and composition of material-culture inventories (Shott 1986b). Based on these findings, it is only reasonable to suggest that Paleo-Indian tool inventories included both versatile and functionally specific tools. Nevertheless, it is questionable to assume that the size and composition of a single site's assemblage accurately reflects the kinds and frequencies of activities that occurred at the site, even if it were occupied only once.

Discard Processes

Stone tools, as well as other artifacts, can enter the archaeological record in a number of ways. This observation has a number of important implications which merit careful consideration and extended treatment. These implications include: systematic biases inherent in the relative frequency of different tool types in the archaeological record; the form of the tools comprising those types; and the nature of organization characterizing different technologies and larger cultural systems. Consideration of these implications is best preceded by discussion of the various processes by which tools enter the archaeological record; these will be termed discard processes. The following major types of discard processes may be identified (Shott 1989a:17-21):

1) *Breakage in production.* This means the tool has been accidentally fractured before reaching finished form. Breakage can occur either by accident unrelated to production, such as dropping the tool on a hard surface or, more likely, as an unintended result of the production process itself. This is especially likely to occur in a production process which involves numerous stages, such as the fluting of bifaces. Callahan (1979:84-88, 108-16, 145-53) presents an extensive catalog of such production errors. This condition, obviously, is indicated by the presence of a break on a tool, but tools can be used after a fracture often for purposes unrelated to their original objective as discussed below. Distinguishing breaks which occur during production or use from those occurring after use has begun can be difficult at times; often, the origin of a fracture cannot be identified with complete certainty. At North American sites, however, most post-occupational fractures probably occurred quite recently relative to the date of occupation, as a consequence of plowing and related modern activities (Mallouf 1982; Roper 1976). Frequently, such fractures can be distinguished from old or original breaks, since they expose a fresher, unweathered surface of the specimen. In this connection, it is worth noting that all conjoinable items at the Leavitt site exhibiting what was classified as recent fracture were from the same or adjacent excavation units. Conversely, virtually all joins formed on what were classified as original fractures involved specimens from widely scattered units. When a fracture is considered original, it still remains to distinguish unfinished from finished specimens. Most broken specimens at Leavitt are bifaces. Unfinished bifaces may be distinguished from finished ones by such properties as the absence of marginal and basal abrasion, visible use-wear, and resharpening flakes. Fluted bifaces are especially easy to distinguish since a series of discrete and observable steps is involved in their production, and the order of those steps is fairly well known. The absence of final production stage attributes constitutes strong evidence for the identification of unfinished implements.

2) *Abandonment during or after production.* Tools may be abandoned, even if intact, if they prove unsuitable for their intended purpose. The presence of flaws in the raw material, for example, or ridges which cannot be removed during thinning can produce this outcome. Such tools are whole and may appear serviceable. The absence of evidence of use and maintenance, in the form of edge wear and resharpening flakes, indicates that such items were abandoned without use. It is conceivable that functional but unused tools may be cached for future use, but be mistaken for abandoned tools. Caches, however, usually are unmistakable in appearance; they include many items and are found in rather unique archaeological contexts. No caches were found at Leavitt, although Parkhill Phase caches have been found elsewhere (Deller and Ellis 1992; Wright and Roosa 1966; Shott 1986a:199-207 discusses possible caches). All specimens placed in the category of abandoned tools posed insurmountable technical obstacles to continued production or use, usually in the form of remnant or other areas on the tool surface which could not be reduced.

3) *Breakage in use.* Following completion and some use, many tools are broken in the course of normal use. Tools discarded by this process obviously exhibit fracture, but also possess attributes, such as extensive use-wear and marginal resharpening, which indicated that they underwent at least one cycle of use and maintenance. This process shares with the first the problem of distinguishing original from recent fractures.

4) *Loss or abandonment.* Tools may simply be lost or abandoned while still serviceable. Loss is a straightforward concept, although its frequency can vary with a number of factors (Ebert 1979). Abandonment occurs when a still-functional item is deliberately rejected, and not retained for future use. In concept, abandonment is the opposite of curation (Binford 1979), and entails the conscious discard of tools which retain utility. This process probably occurs most often upon site abandonment, as size, weight, or absence of immediate need cause people to leave serviceable items behind (Gould 1978; Hayden 1978). Heavy, bulky items, or quickly fashioned expedient tools are most likely candidates for abandonment. Abandonment may occur at rates which also vary according to a number of factors. In many cases, abandonment is unrelated to intrinsic properties of tools. Instead, it may vary with prosaic factors such

as the completion of tasks in which expedient tools are used (Gould et al. 1971). In such circumstances, abandonment may vary directly with the rate of task performance (Schiffer 1975). Loss may appear to be a negligible discard process, best viewed as a virtually random factor of little importance. In other instances, however, it may vary with objective properties of items such as their size. Like most discard processes, little ethnographic data exists on the frequency with which loss occurs. Furthermore, available data do not always agree, although most sources indicate that loss is an uncommon occurrence. Binford (1977:33) records a loss rate of approximately one item per 186 episodes of use and curation. Similarly, Yellen (1977:196) reports a single occurrence of loss of a curated item in what must have been at least several hundred such episodes. In contrast, Ebert (1979:63) indicates that loss is a frequent occurrence and is an important contributor to archaeological assemblages. Yellen and Ebert studied the same forager group at approximately the same time. The reason for the divergence of their accounts is unclear.

5) *Depletion.* Tools which escape production failures, breakage and loss finally are depleted or exhausted through numerous use and maintenance cycles. The outcome of the process is a depleted tool. Such tools may be considered drained of all of their utility, and the outcome may be viewed as the normal result of tool use, although relatively few tools may be deposited archaeologically by this process, depending on the nature of the technological system in which they are employed. Depletion is evidenced by heavy resharpening and, perhaps, steep edge angles. Tools bearing recognizable and distinct haft and functional segments should exhibit a high ratio of those segments. It is important to stress, however, that different specimens of the same tool class, defined by haft segment attributes or other criteria, may appear different upon depletion. If their manner of use varied during their use-lives, their depleted form may differ. Some may retain little more than a stub of the original functional segment, the only remnant left after repeated resharpening. Others, in contrast, may retain much of one original margin and none of the other. In these cases, length and morphology of the depleted specimens differ a great deal, but both are depleted nonetheless (Miller 1980: Fig. 53) (Fig. 8.6).

6) *Recycling.* Defined by Schiffer (1976:38), this process refers to the use of a tool for different purposes and in a distinct use context from its original, intended use. Recycling is not to be confused with versatility, the use of tools in a variety of task applications. In the latter, the specimen is maintained and used for purposes at least broadly consistent with its intended functional applications. If the specimen was designed for hafting, for instance, it remains hafted. Recycling, in contrast, is the appropriation of a specimen for entirely different and unforeseen purposes. It necessarily follows the completion of other processes, such as breakage or depletion, and is designed to modify the tool, perhaps extending its utility in the process. The use of broken or depleted tools as bipolar cores, sources of small flakes used expediently and discarded after short periods of use, is a good example of recycling, as well as a common practice carried out by North American Paleo-Indian groups (Gramly 1983; Goodyear 1993; MacDonald 1968).

Implications of Discard Processes

The foregoing discussion carries important implications for the character of archaeological assemblages and the nature of technological organization in forager societies. Two implications are considered here; one concerns the difference between tool use rates and discard rates and the consequences this difference has for archaeological assemblages, and the other concerns within-class variability in metric attributes.

Preservation and sampling problems aside, the archaeological frequency of tool types is determined by their characteristic discard rates. Theoretical treatments (Ammerman and Feldman 1974) have underscored the important point that use rates and discard rates do not necessarily correspond between tool classes. That is, tool classes used at equal rates may not be discarded and deposited archaeologically at the same rate. Instead, differences may exist in mean use-lives of items in the respective classes, with the result that tool classes with lower mean use-lives values are discarded at higher rates. In this fashion, they are overrepresented archaeologically relative to their use rate in the systemic context (Schiffer 1975).

Differences in discard rates between tool classes may be attributed to differences in the discard processes which characterize them. Given their intrinsic properties and their manner of use, some classes are susceptible to breakage before they reach depletion, while others are less vulnerable to this process. The latter should be discarded more often upon depletion. Similarly, certain classes may be more likely than others to undergo recycling, thereby extending their utility and use-life. Breakage, obviously, has the effect of reducing mean use-life of specimens in a tool class. Consequently, those classes characterized by high breakage rates will be discarded and deposited archaeologically at higher rates than others relative to their potential maximum use-life. Thus, those classes will be overrepresented archaeologically relative to their systemic frequency.

The second implication of discard processes concerns within-class variability in tool metric attributes. All tool classes are subject to loss, abandonment and depletion; no tool can last indefinitely. However, items from those classes subject to a considerable degree to breakage have an additional route into the archaeological record. All else, including metric attributes, equal, the greater the number of discard processes to which tool classes are subject, the more variability in those attributes they should exhibit.

A hypothetical example may illustrate the point. Assume two distinct tool classes characterized by the same degree of variability—not necessarily the same mean values—in the metric attributes of original unused specimens. To the extent that attribute variability defines standardization or lack thereof, the two classes may be regarded as equally standardized. Assume further that depletion is the only discard process to which the classes are subject. In the course of normal use and maintenance, all specimens in each class will undergo a characteristic sequence or continuum of reduction to their final, depleted form. Only at that point will any of them be discarded to enter the archaeological record. In this example, the two classes should exhibit roughly equal variability in metric attributes of the depleted specimens.

Relaxing the second assumption, however, and subjecting one class to breakage as well as depletion while the other undergoes only the latter, produces different results. In this instance, some specimens are discarded at intermediate points on the use-life and reduction continuum, while others are discarded only upon depletion. The outcome is more variable, less standardized metric attributes for the class subject to breakage. This discussion, of course, omits from consideration those attributes, such as length, for which complete measurements cannot be made due to breakage. Obviously, such attributes also will be highly variable. Wilmsen and Roberts (1978:162) have observed such a process at Lindenmeier.

Analysis

Since discard processes may have important effects on the character of archaeological assemblages, their role in the formation of the Leavitt assemblage warrants investigation. For this purpose, tools were coded by suspected discard type. The criteria described previously guided this effort. It is worth noting that a number of tool fragments, both bifaces and unifaces, were excluded from analysis because they simply are too small to warrant detailed treatment. Generally, they consist of small edge or bit fragments just large enough to identify as fragments of tools. It is unknown if the specimens were broken in manufacture or use, but it is likely that many were fractured following occupation of the sites, perhaps by plowing. Their exclusion will underestimate tool breakage rates, since some specimens may have broken during production or use.

Results of the analyses are summarized in Table 7.1. One minor point of clarification is in order before considering the results. Inspection of the table shows that marginal totals for the assemblages can exceed the actual assemblage size. This is because specimens subject to recycling were coded for original and final discard process, where observable, as well as recycling. That is, a specimen which was broken in use and then recycled would be coded for both processes. In this manner, recycled specimens could be coded for more than one discard process, with the result that the number of occurrences of all processes combined can, and usually does, exceed assemblage size. It is clear that bifaces and unifaces are subject to different discard processes. Bifaces are discarded chiefly upon breakage; recycling of broken bifaces also occurs frequently. Unifaces, in contrast, are discarded primarily as a result of depletion. Relatively few are broken, fewer still recycled upon breakage.

TABLE 7.1
Discard Processes in the Leavitt and Barnes Assemblages

	Discard Process						
Site	1	2	3	4	5	6	*N*
BIFACE							
Leavitt	3	2	13	6	6	6	28
Barnes	10	1	9	0	1	1	22
UNIFACE							
Leavitt	0	1	7	2	19	18	47
Barnes	1	0	0	0	5	2	8

1 = breakage in production; 2 = abandonment in production; 3 = breakage in use; 4 = recycling; 5 = loss/abandonment; 6 = depletion

For comparative purposes, a similar classification of the original Barnes site specimens (Wright and Roosa 1966) was performed (Table 7.1). Voss' (1977) data from the later excavations at that site are not sufficiently detailed for similar treatment. Figures 7.1 and 7.2 summarize the results graphically. The discard process values are converted to relative frequencies. Viewing the order of processes from failure in production to depletion as

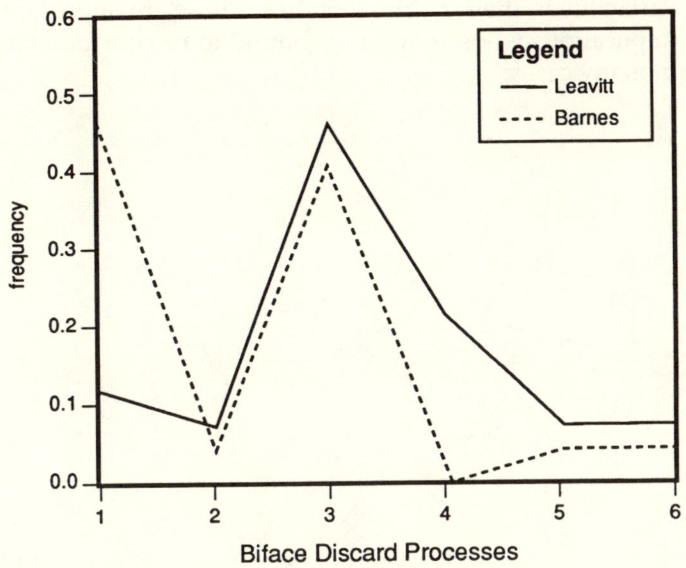

Figure 7.1. Biface discard processes in the Leavitt and Barnes assemblages.

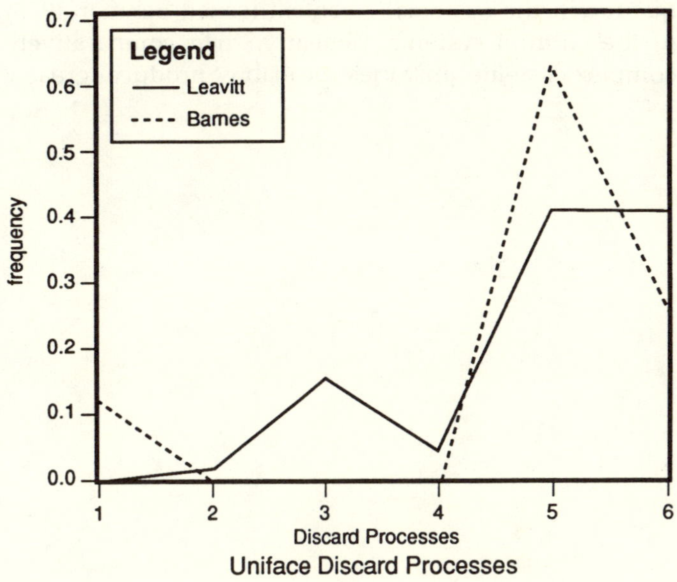

Figure 7.2. Uniface discard processes in the Leavitt and Barnes assemblages.

a life cycle sequence for tools, the figures may be considered density functions expressing the probability that stone tools will exit the systemic context and be discarded at a given point. Breakage in use and, to a lesser extent, in production, are the likeliest outcomes for bifaces; unifacial implements, in contrast, are far likelier to be abandoned through depletion.

The only major difference between Leavitt and Barnes appears in the comparison of bifaces. The Leavitt distribution is clearly unimodal; breakage in use is by far the most common discard process. Barnes, in contrast, exhibits a bimodal distribution. In effect, it is similar to Leavitt except for a distinct mode representing breakage in production. At any rate, both distributions clearly underscore the importance of breakage rather than depletion in biface discard at the sites. No major differences characterize the uniface distributions at Leavitt and Barnes, although the small sample size, especially for the latter, produces minor, and probably statistically insignificant interclass variability.

In comparing the biface and uniface distributions in the Leavitt assemblage, a maximum likelihood test of independence yields highly significant differences (L = 34.18, df = 5, p = .00). Similar conclusions apply to the Barnes assemblage (L = 18.87, df = 4, p = .00), although in that case breakage in production also is an important discard process structuring the biface assemblage. Cell count deficiencies, a problem endemic to many tests performed on archaeological data from small assemblages, are especially acute in this instance and caution is advised in the use of these findings.

Comparing frequency distributions between biface assemblages at the two sites also yields significant results (L = 13.3, df = 5, p = .02), which probably are attributable to the greater production breakage rates which characterize the Barnes assemblage. Comparison of uniface assemblages produces more equivocal results (L = 8.05, df = 5, p = .15); by most conventional standards, it cannot be concluded that different discard processes characterized the Leavitt and Barnes uniface assemblages. Nevertheless, these findings support the conclusion that distinct discard processes characterized the biface components of the two assemblages.

Conclusion

To summarize the findings, it is apparent that biface and uniface components of the Leavitt assemblage are conditioned by distinct discard processes. Bifaces break, both in production and use, at far higher rates than unifaces, which tend to enter the archaeological record only upon depletion. Bifaces, in short, exhibit more complex use-life histories.

The implications discussed previously bear heeding in this connection. The relative frequency of bifaces in archaeological assemblages overrepresents their frequency in the systematic context (sensu Schiffer 1976) of the cultural systems. Similarly, their comparatively complex use-life histories probably produce greater variability in their metric attributes. These are important implications whose effects are bound to be considerable in many cases.

Chapter 8

Spatial Analysis

Artifacts are recovered in spatial context, and a full account of any site considers its spatial structure. Relevant properties of structure include the areal extent and patterns of distribution of remains, and patterns of association between artifact classes. In this chapter, the spatial structure of Leavitt is described and analyzed, and comparisons to other Great Lakes Paleo-Indian sites are made.

Spatial Structure in Forager Sites

Patterns of tool class distribution and association commonly identified or inferred at Paleo-Indian sites are consistent with primary discard of imperishable debris. These patterns, in effect, are considered to represent the places at which tools were both used and discarded. Yellen (1977) documents at length such patterns of use and discard among Kalahari foragers. Murray (1980) suggests that primary discard of tools and debris is characteristic of forager societies in general.

Foragers, however, also are known to practice secondary disposal of debris, which can significantly increase the complexity of resulting distribution patterns and produce patterns of associated tools that may not have been used together. Examples of such practices may be found among both logistically (Binford 1978a, 1978b; Janes 1983) and residentially (Fisher 1986; O'Connell 1987) organized forager groups (sensu Binford 1980). O'Connell, in fact, assays considerable variability in discard behavior among foragers, and indicates that secondary disposal of items greater than 5 cm in maximum dimension is the norm among the Alyawara (1987:82). For other groups, he suggests that patterns of space use and debris discard vary by season, by the nature and scale of activities, and by the span and organizational context of occupations. Considerable variability and complexity in the spatial structure of archaeological sites should be observed under these circumstances, and secondary discard probably characterized some sites. At a minimum, then, primary discard and clear spatial patterning revealing the nature and location of activities cannot be assumed.

To generalize from these observations, the spatial properties of archaeological sites—artifact density and distribution, degree and kind of associations between artifact classes, areal extent of debris—are related to factors like occupation span, the rate and amount of resource procurement, and rates of tool production, use, and discard (Binford 1978b:359; O'Connell 1987; Whallon 1984). Variability in the last three rates produces corresponding variability in archaeological spatial patterns. Forager cultural systems (sensu Binford 1980) are characterized by relatively constant rates of resource procurement and, probably, tool production and use. Although occupation span may vary between sites, the range of such variability is modest (Shott 1986b). The Parkhill phase groups of the upper Great Lakes region may have fallen more toward Binford's forager than collector pole, suggesting that variability among Parkhill phase sites should be relatively modest. In addition, it may directly reflect the occupational factors proposed by Binford: span and rates of food and tool production.

Secondary discard may be viewed as a process that distorts the true or original patterning of activities in space at sites or, alternatively, as a part of that patterning itself because discard, like other activities, is distributed spatially in some fashion (Binford 1987:463). In either case, patterning in the distribution of artifact classes reveals the nature of space use at the site. Like most eastern North American sites, however, Leavitt has been repeatedly plowed, a process that truly distorts original patterning. Seminal but limited studies assayed surprisingly modest effects of plowing (Lewarch and O'Brien 1981; Roper 1976), but more recent studies suggest that this modern practice severely disturbs archaeological remains (Odell and Cowan 1987; Yorston et al. 1990). In one study, item dispersal was found to be cumulative, not asymptotic (Odell and Cowan 1987:467). Under controlled conditions, original site size was doubled in twelve plowing episodes with mean item dispersal per episode of nearly 2 m. Although plow dispersal can increase the apparent size of sites, its effects cannot be indefinitely cumulative. If they were, the extensive plowing that has occurred in many areas would have produced broad, diffuse artifact scatters and few recognizable concentrations. Some degree of scale and structure must resist dispersal effects. Fortunately, no size effects were recognized in dispersal (Odell and Cowan 1987:473-74), and plowing apparently acts uniformly to disperse or expand the size—but not necessarily alter the patterning—of original deposits. Most dispersal occurs in the direction of plowing.

These findings identify details of land use history as important information in the analysis and interpretation of archaeological spatial patterning. Unfortunately, the details for Leavitt are unknown, though the site has been plowed often, if not annually, for at least fifty years and perhaps considerably longer. Direction of plowing in 1984 was north to south, but it is unknown if other directions were ever taken. Lacking detailed information, it is possible only to conclude that artifacts at Leavitt probably are considerably dispersed from their original locations, and that the distribution's areal extent after plowing is considerably larger than it was originally. However, nothing in Odell and Cowan's (1987) results suggest that patterns of association between artifact classes or the actual form of spatial distributions—as opposed to their scale—are significantly altered from original conditions.

Spatial Analysis in Great Lakes Paleo-Indian Sites

Two other Great Lakes Parkhill phase sites, Barnes and Thedford, have been the subjects of detailed spatial analysis. Differences in size and form of the areas excavated, definitions of tool classes used in analysis, the analytical methods used, and in the underlying spatial structure of each site have all contributed to important differences in results at those sites.

Four major clusters are defined at Thedford (Deller and Ellis 1992:101, Fig. 72), and several other unexcavated ones may exist. Three are considered peripheral work and/or habitation areas distributed around a central communal area. Most clusters contain at least one feature. At Barnes, four to six clusters are identified (Voss and Shott 1981: Figs. 3-4) depending on the results preferred. In either case, two functionally distinct work areas—one involving biface production and perhaps use, the other involving unifaces—are located on the margins of a tool-poor flake debris cluster. (This latter is subdivided into three density classes that differ little in composition when smoothed item frequencies are used in analysis.) A third, smaller, tool cluster lies on the opposite side of the central debris cluster. All tool clusters contain a feature (Voss 1977: Fig. 2).

Spatial structure at Thedford is interpreted as the product of brief occupation by a number of family or work parties sharing a common central area and engaging in a considerable range of activities (Deller and Ellis 1992:121). In contrast, Barnes is considered a smaller occupation by a group of unspecified size and composition, but who engaged in a considerable, if more limited, range of activities (Voss 1977:263-64; Voss and Shott 1981:4-5). In both cases, relatively clear patterning is seen by analysts, but the scale of patterning differs considerably. Cluster or activity areas at Barnes cover 16-48 m^2, while Thedford clusters are approximately three times larger, at 80-164 m^2.

However, patterning appears somewhat less ambiguous at Thedford than at Barnes. Although both sites—like Leavitt—have been repeatedly plowed, Barnes may have been somewhat more intensively surface-collected before excavation (Deller and Ellis 1992:4; Wright and Roosa 1966:850). The nonsystematic nature of earlier collections at both sites—a quality they share with the pre-1978 work at Leavitt—makes it somewhat difficult, however, to compare them rigorously in this respect.

Spatial Distributions and Structure at Leavitt

Surface Distributions

The distribution of piece-plotted material from 1984 surface collections at Leavitt is shown in Figure 8.1. Three bifaces, however, were found too far from the center of the site to appear in the figure. Specimen 85-27-334-1, the fluted biface medial fragment (Fig. 6.4f) was found northeast of the mapped area at approximately 558N 565E. Specimen 85-27-334-21 (Fig. 6.5j) was found at approximately 497N 480E, southwest of the excavation blocks. Biface 85-27-334-25 was found at approximately 502N 410E. These specimens are spatial outliers to a distribution that clearly centers on the excavation blocks and adjacent areas.

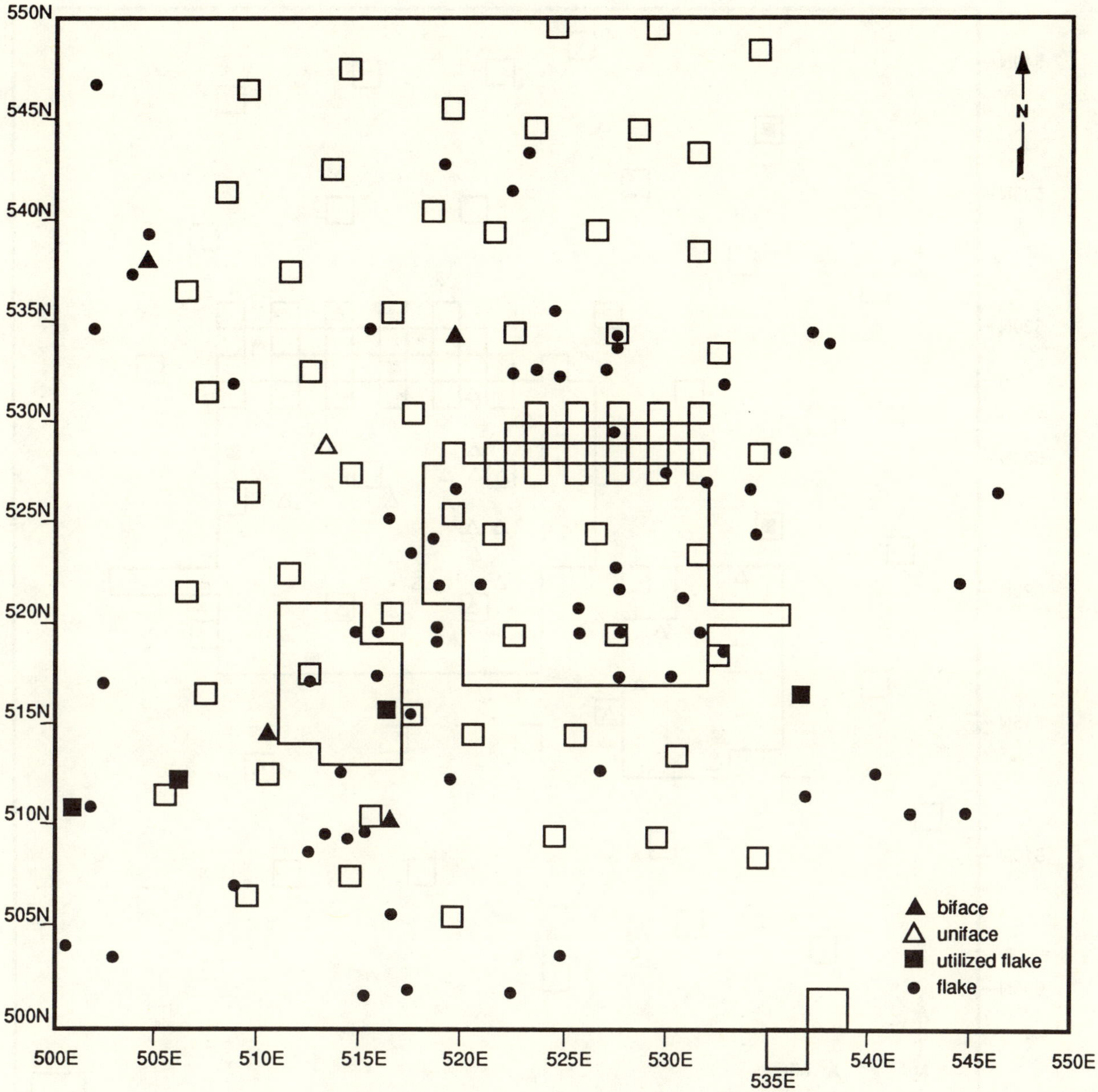

Figure 8.1. Distribution of piece-plots from the 1984 surface collection.

Tool Distributions

As discussed in Chapter 1, block excavations at Leavitt largely covered the peaks in the artifact density distribution. Distribution of tools in excavation units is shown in Figure 8.2. Many tools, especially bifaces, were found in earlier investigations at Leavitt and others were recovered during the 1984 season. Consequently, only a fraction of all tools are shown in Figure 8.2. The previous collections from the site not only reduce the number of tools found in excavation, but they alter the site's overall spatial structure in unknown ways. Some tools found in previous visits to Leavitt probably fell within the excavated area and their selective removal may obscure patterning and weaken the degree of association between tools and debris classes.

Too few tools were found in Block 2 to reach any meaningful conclusions, but unifaces apparently are clustered in the western portions of Block 1 (Fig. 8.2). This distribution is somewhat complementary to the

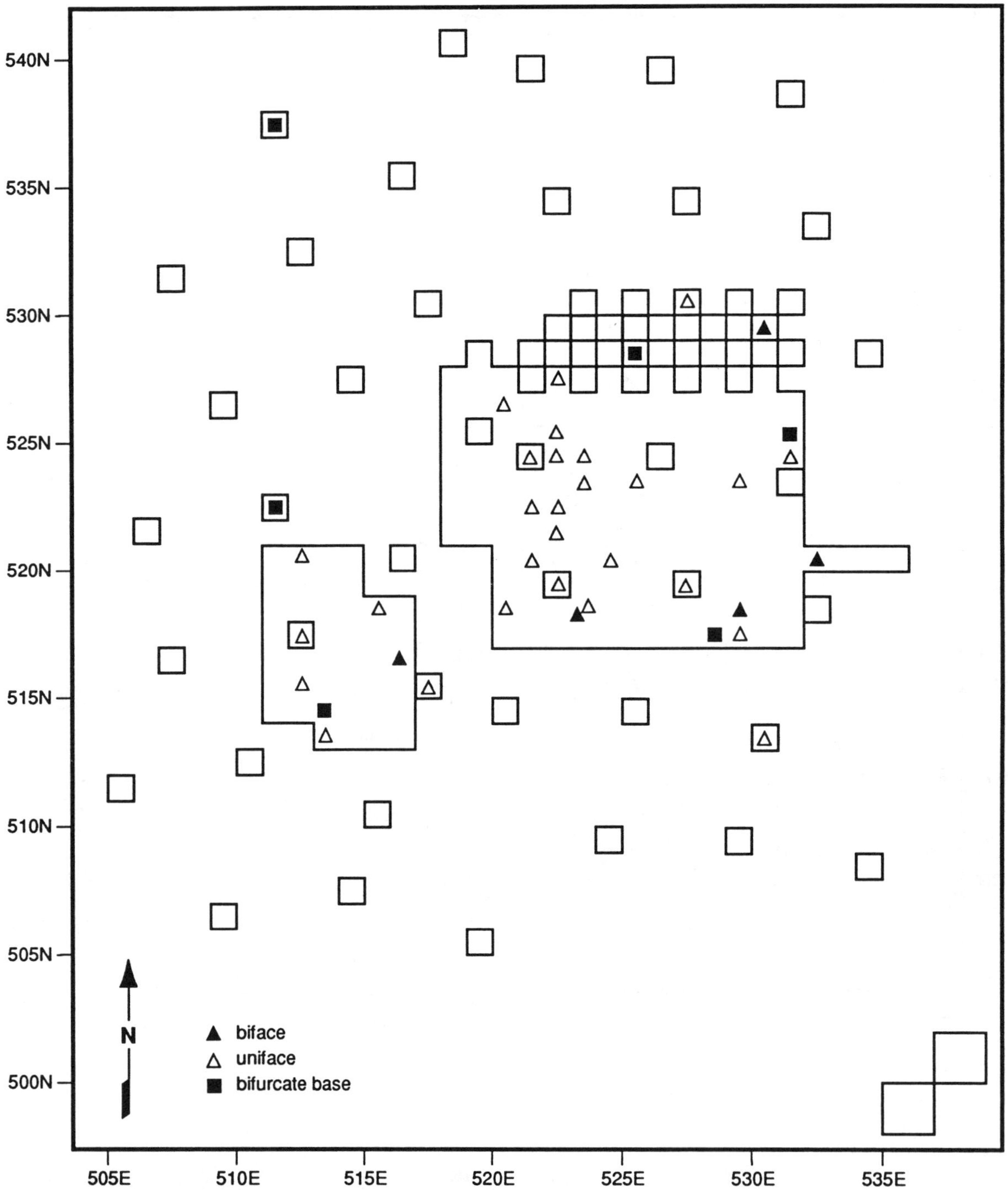

Figure 8.2. Distribution of tools in excavation units.

overall distribution of flake debris in that block (Figs. 8.3-8.8), although it coincides somewhat more closely with the distribution of uniface retouch flakes. The apparent clustering in unifaces is belied when the distribution is tested for randomness by comparison to the Poisson model. At either the original unit size (chi square = .09, df = 1, $p \simeq .75$) or at an aggregated scale of 2 × 2 m^2 units (chi square = 1.46, df = 1, $.50 < p < .75$), the frequency distribution of unifacial specimens per unit does not depart significantly from randomness. (At the aggregated scale, analysis was confined to the rectangular section of Block 1 between 517-527N and 520-

532E, consisting of 120 of the 162 original units in the block.) There is, in sum, no significant pattern or clustering in the overall distribution of tools at the site.

Patterns of association between tool classes and their diagnostic flake debris (i.e., bifaces and biface retouch flakes, unifaces and uniface retouch flakes) are difficult to measure because of the extremely low tool frequencies, especially bifaces, in the excavation units. Most units contained at most a single tool (Fig. 8.2), making tool frequencies effectively ordinal in nature. To match this scale and to investigate more closely the possible association of unifaces and their diagnostic debris noted above, flake debris was reduced to the same scale by calculating *z*-scores or standard normal deviates for both biface and uniface retouch flakes. In each class, values less than zero were assigned a value of *0*, and values of zero and greater a value of *1*. With data in this form, association between tools and their diagnostic debris was measured using *tau*, a nonparametric statistic (Siegel 1956). In no case were significant associations found (for bifaces and biface retouch flakes, $tau = -.07$ and $p = .37$ in Block 1, $tau = .16$ and $p = .28$ in Block 2; for unifaces and uniface retouch flakes, $tau = .01$ and $p = .85$ in Block 1, $tau = -.02$ and $p = .89$ in Block 2).

Distribution of Flake Debris Classes

Block 1. Distributions by Bayport debris classes are shown in Figures 8.3-8.7. The biface retouch flake class displays a distinct peak at 520N 529E, an artifact of Feature 4 which lies partly within it. Another peak occurs at 520N 521E and the general pattern is for highest frequencies to occur across the entire block approximately between 520N and 525N. Uniface retouch flakes are fewer, but a distinct peak in their distribution lies at 525N 522E to 523E (Fig. 8.4). Otherwise, frequencies in this class rise to the south and do not fall off at the limit of the block. Faceted-platform flakes (Fig. 8.5) are widely but sparsely distributed, with a peak circa 521N to 523N and 521E to 524E. This peak overlaps but does not coincide perfectly with the smaller of the two biface retouch flake peaks (Fig. 8.3). Flat-platform flake debris has a distribution similar to biface retouch and faceted-platform classes (Fig. 8.6). Channel flakes, though not common, form two apparent clusters separated by approximately 6 m (Fig. 8.7). The eastern cluster, formed by only three specimens, is situated near Feature 4, but does not coincide with a cluster of bifaces or any other tools (Fig. 8.2). The western cluster lies in the same area as the uniface tool cluster (Fig. 8.2).

The distribution of aggregated non-Bayport debris classes does not resemble the Bayport distribution, forming instead two apparent clusters at the northeast and southwest corners of the excavation block (Fig. 8.8).

Block 2. Bayport biface retouch flakes are numerous in Block 2 and clustered to some degree in the eastern half of the block (Fig. 8.9). Uniface retouch flakes display stronger clustering, especially in the center of the area (Fig. 8.10). Faceted-platform flakes are distributed in peaks at the east and west margins (Fig. 8.11), a pattern which coincides somewhat with the biface retouch flake distribution. Flat-platform flakes are distributed in a manner similar to uniface retouch flakes (Fig. 8.12). On balance, Bayport debris distributions in Block 2 form a relatively well defined east-west trending peak. Although the north and south margins of the debris distribution are reasonably well defined, the east and west margins apparently are not.

Debris Class Correlations

Correlation of flake debris classes by excavation block is summarized in Table 8.1, which shows Pearson's *r* coefficients for all pairs of classes. (Nonparametric correlation measured by Kendall's *tau* produced nearly identical results and therefore is not presented.) Comparatively low frequencies of tools precluded their inclusion in this analysis. Most debris classes co-vary significantly, the only consistent exception being low-frequency classes, notably channel flakes and non-Bayport debris. All significant correlations are positive and none of the few negative values is significant. Correlations are exaggerated to some degree, since some classes in Table 8.1 are the sums of other classes and are therefore not independent; thus, they are extremely likely to covary with their constituents. Nevertheless, even independent classes tend to co-vary strongly across the site. No subsets of classes are distinguished in this analysis; instead, a single global pattern of co-variation is indicated, probably corresponding to overall density.

This conclusion is somewhat surprising. In undisturbed point-provenience data, Whallon (1984) found little site-wide or global correlation of artifact classes. Co-variation of classes in that case is found only within the smaller clusters that compose the overall distribution. Following Whallon's reasoning, the global patterns of co-variation observed at Leavitt imply a relatively simple or perhaps degraded spatial structure.

Conjoinable Fragments

Many tools and flakes recovered at Leavitt were fragmentary. In the analysis, a systematic effort was made to match and conjoin tool fragments, and it yielded a

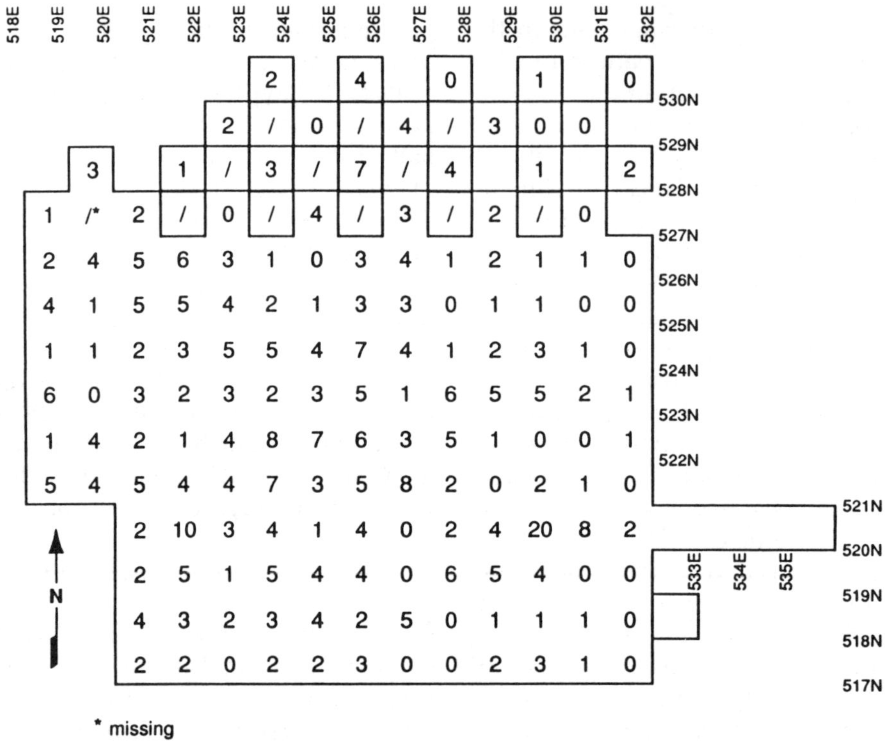

Figure 8.3. Distribution of biface retouch flakes in Excavation Block 1.

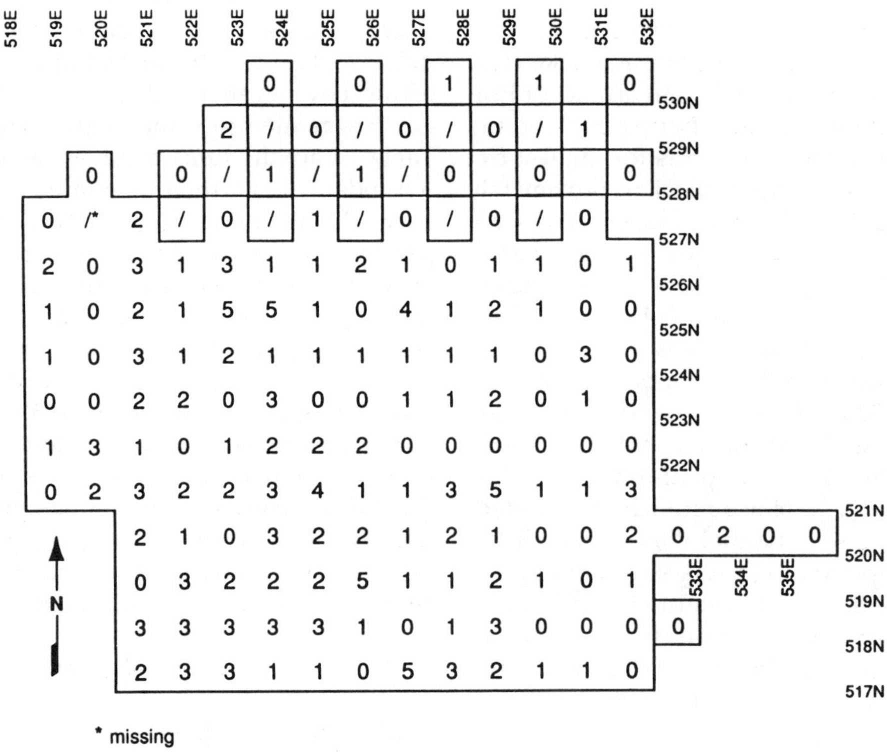

Figure 8.4. Distribution of uniface retouch in Excavation Block 1.

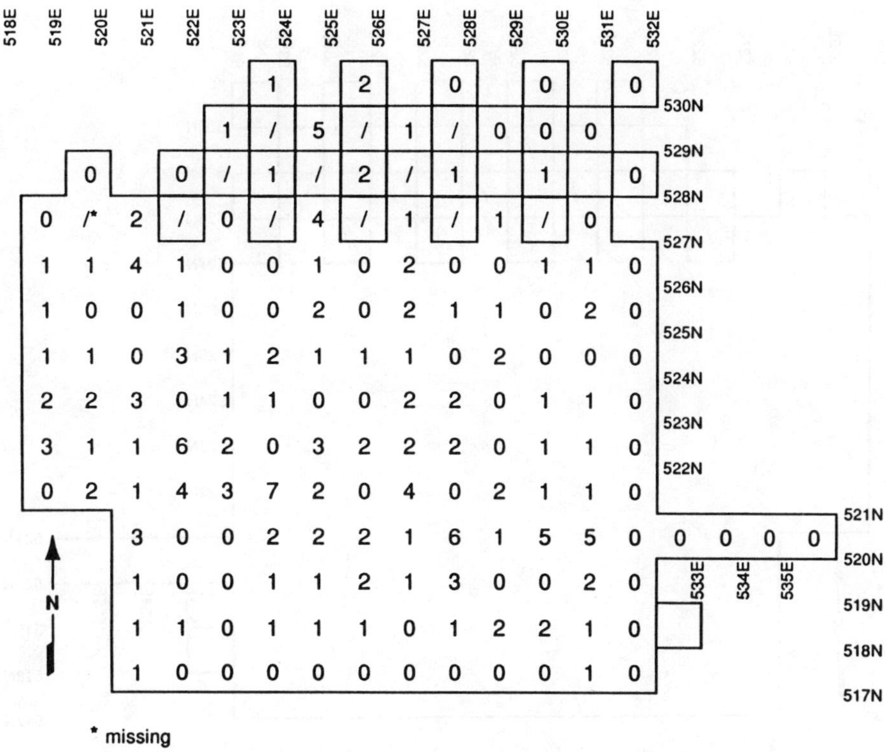

Figure 8.5. Distribution of faceted platform flakes in Excavation Block 1.

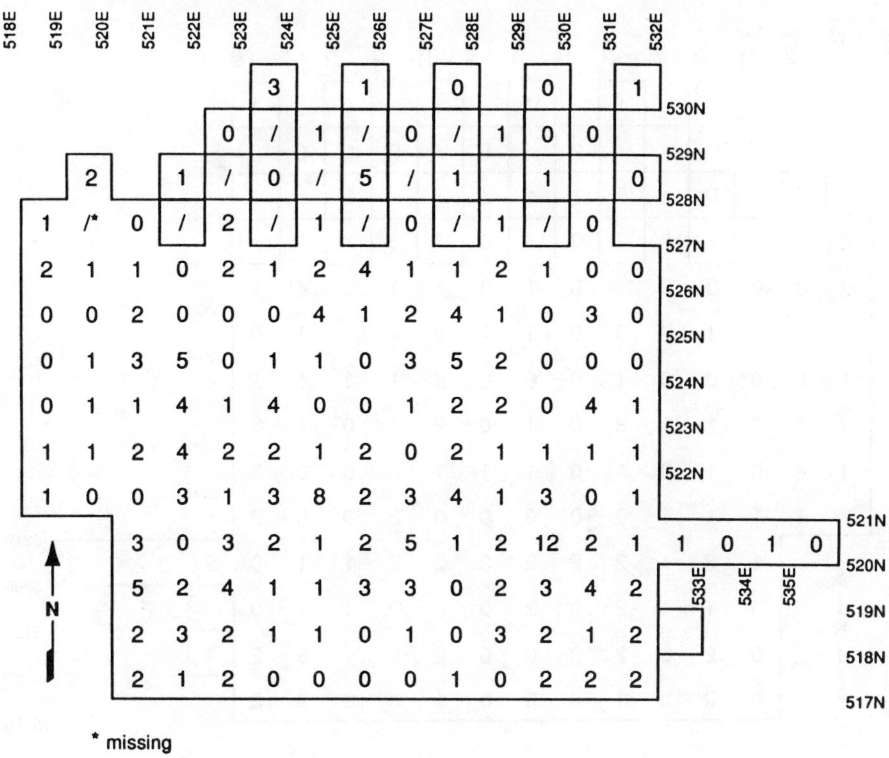

Figure 8.6. Distribution of flat platform flakes in Excavation Block 1.

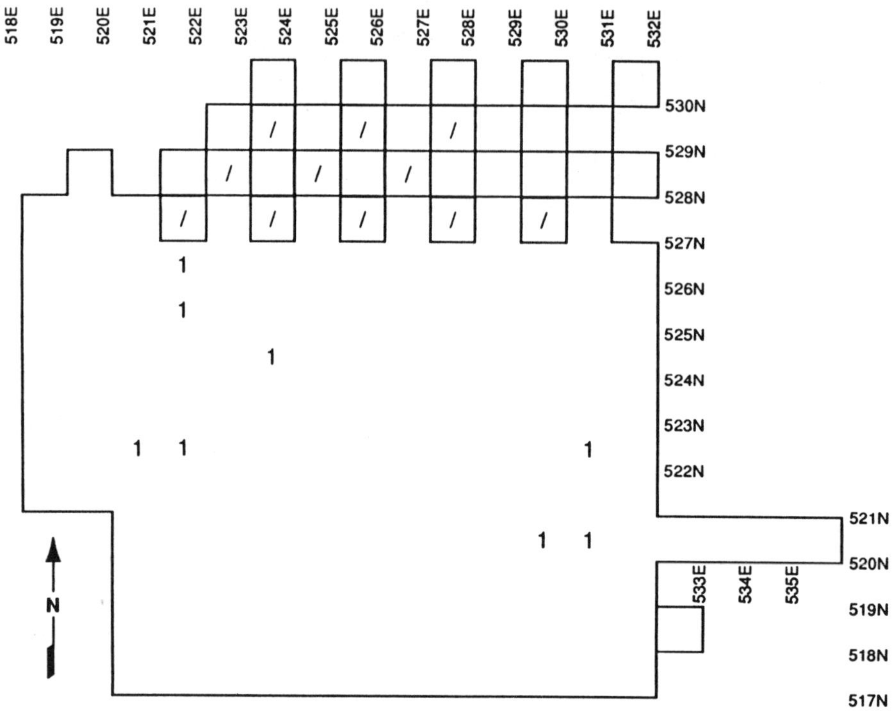

Figure 8.7. Distribution of channel flakes in Excavation Block 1.

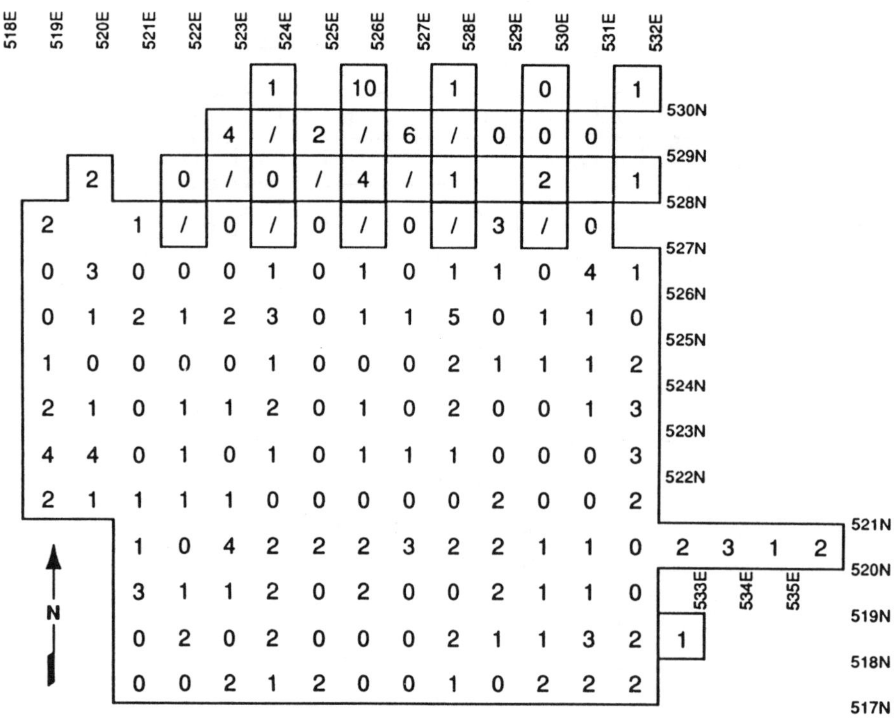

Figure 8.8. Distribution of non-Bayport flake debris in Excavation Block 1.

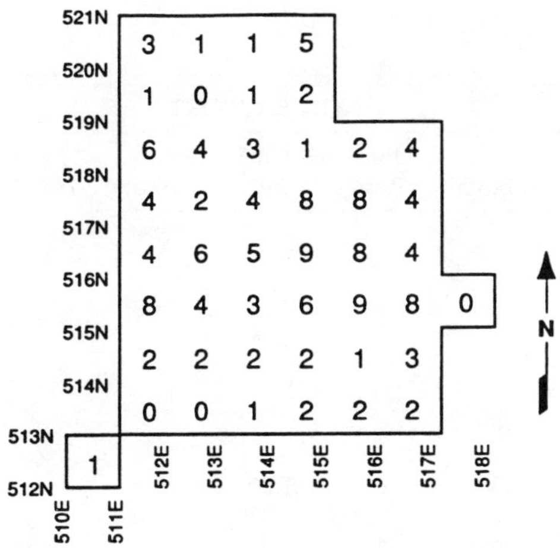

Figure 8.9. Distribution of Bayport biface retouch flakes in Excavation Block 2.

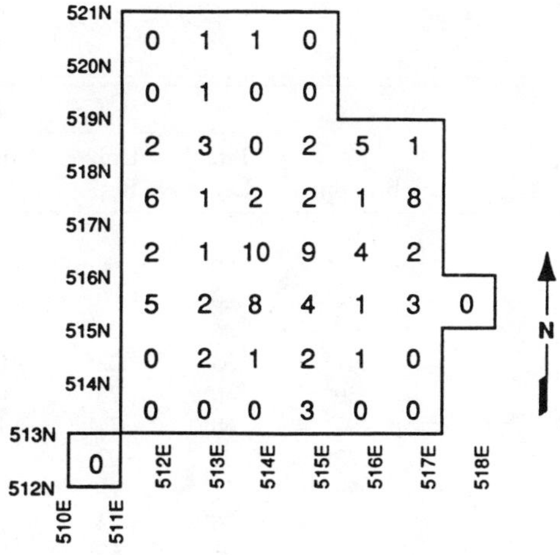

Figure 8.10. Distribution of Bayport uniface retouch flakes in Excavation Block 2.

TABLE 8.1a
Correlation of Debris Classes in Block 1

		BAYPORT						NON-BAYPORT				
	Broken	Bif. Ret.	Uni. Ret.	Chan. Fl.	Faceted	Flat	Subtotal	Bif. Ret.	Uni. Ret.	Subtotal	TOTAL	Weight
Broken	1.00											
Bif. ret.	.65*	1.00										
Uni. ret.	.14	.07	1.00									
Chan. fl.	.28*	.29*	-.14	1.00								
Faceted	.43*	.36*	.03	.28*	1.00							
Flat	.50*	.29*	.11	.17*	.29*	1.00						
Subtotal	.96*	.75*	.23*	.31*	.54*	.59*	1.00					
Bif. ret.	.04	.03	-.09	-.04	-.01	-.03	.02	1.00				
Uni. ret.	.14	-.02	.06	-.07	.01	.20*	.13	.01	1.00			
Subtotal	-.04	-.09	-.03	-.11	-.04	.01	-.06	.26*	.20*	1.00		
Total	.96*	.74*	.22*	.30*	.53*	.59*	.99*	.05	.15*	.05	1.00	
Weight	.66*	.59*	.16*	.16*	.44*	.50*	.72*	.15*	.03	.08	.74*	1.00

*Significant at .05.

number of joins or cross-mends. The distribution of the 19 conjoining fragments found in the 1984 excavation is plotted in Figure 8.13. All cross-mended artifacts are placed at the center of the excavation unit in which they were found, and distances between cross-mends are calculated from those points. Both biface cross-mends are fluted bifaces (specimens 90072 and 88216/88259); in both instances, at least one of the matching fragments was recovered in the initial collections from the site and exact or unit provenience is unknown. Several other cross-mends also were made between tool fragments found in the earlier surface collections and between those and fragments recovered during the 1984 project. All of the former lack precise provenience, of course, and cannot be plotted. The latter are characterized by incompatible provenience information, since even fragments found in the 1978 surface collection can be placed only within the large units used then.

Inspection of Figure 8.13 shows that most cross-mends occur within the two excavation clusters. One, however, links the clusters, which suggests that they were occupied simultaneously rather than successively. Of course, successive occupation still is a possibility, since later occupants could have retrieved and used specimens discarded earlier.

The fracture planes of all conjoinable fragments were

TABLE 8.1b
Correlation of Debris Classes in Block 2

		BAYPORT						NON-BAYPORT				
	Broken	Bif. Ret.	Uni. Ret.	Chan. Fl.	Faceted	Flat	Subtotal	Bif. Ret.	Uni. Ret.	Subtotal	TOTAL	Weight
Broken	1.00											
Bif. ret.	.56*	1.00										
Uni. ret.	.62*	.40*	1.00									
Chan. fl.	.07	.06	.24	1.00								
Faceted	.41*	.33*	.22	-.03	1.00							
Flat	.50*	.40*	.26	.03	.44*	1.00						
Subtotal	.94*	.68*	.74*	.10*	.53*	.53*	1.00					
Bif. ret.	.23	.02	.03	-.07	.37*	.18	.16	1.00				
Uni. ret.	.29	.23	.25	.20	.08	-.07	.30	.03	1.00			
*Subtotal	.48*	.36*	.24	-.07	.31*	.23	.44*	.56*	.33*	1.00		
*Total	.96*	.68*	.69*	.08	.52*	.60*	.98*	.26	.29	.54*	1.00	
Weight	.70*	.56*	.37*	.11	.38*	.47*	.69*	.31*	.30	.51*	.73*	1.00

*Significant at .05.

TABLE 8.2
Distance between Conjoinable Fragments at Crowfield and Leavitt

	Distance (m) $\bar{x}$	s.d.
Crowfield[a]	3.00	1.72
Crowfield[b]	2.95	1.83
Leavitt (ancient)	6.13	2.28
Leavitt (recent)	0.28	0.63

[a]One member within feature (Deller and Ellis 1984: Fig.10).
[b]Both members outside feature (Deller and Ellis 1984: Fig. 11).

TABLE 8.3
Mean Class Frequencies by Cluster in Blocks 1 and 2

	Broken		Bif. Ret.		Uni. Ret.		Faceted		Flat		Non-BP		Tool		
Cluster	$\bar{x}$	s.d.	$\bar{x}$	s.d.	$\bar{x}$	s.d.	$\bar{x}$	s.d.	$\bar{x}$	s.d.	$\bar{x}$	s.d.	$\bar{x}$	s.d.	Total
BLOCK 1															
1	5.5	2.1	1.1	0.8	0.6	0.5	0.4	0.3	0.9	0.7	1.1	0.8	0.2	0.2	9.8
2	10.8	1.7	2.7	1.2	1.2	0.8	1.1	0.7	1.3	0.8	1.2	1.3	0.2	0.2	18.5
3	16.3	1.9	3.7	1.1	1.5	0.7	1.8	0.8	1.9	0.9	1.1	0.7	0.2	0.2	26.5
4	30.7	1.2	7.6	0.8	0.9	0.7	2.4	0.7	4.7	0.4	1.1	0.4	0.0	0.0	47.4
BLOCK 2															
1	7.7	2.5	1.8	0.6	0.9	0.5	0.9	0.4	1.4	0.6	1.3	0.6	0.1	0.1	14.1
2	14.3	2.5	4.0	0.8	2.3	0.9	2.1	1.0	2.2	1.0	1.7	1.0	0.1	0.1	26.7
3	25.5	2.9	5.9	1.5	4.2	1.6	2.3	1.0	3.6	1.2	2.7	0.7	0.2	0.1	44.4

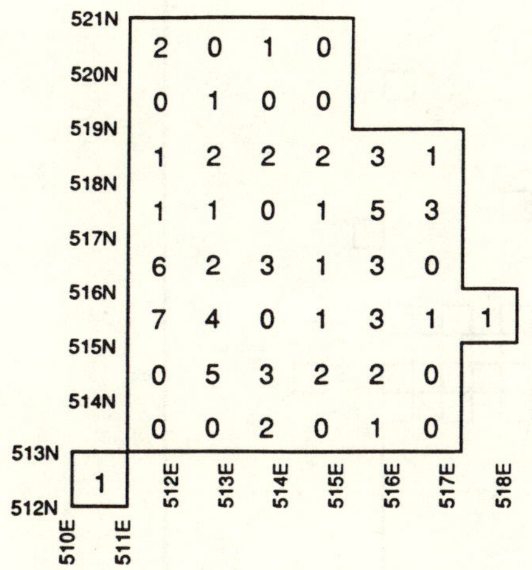

Figure 8.11. Distribution of Bayport faceted platform flakes in Excavation Block 2.

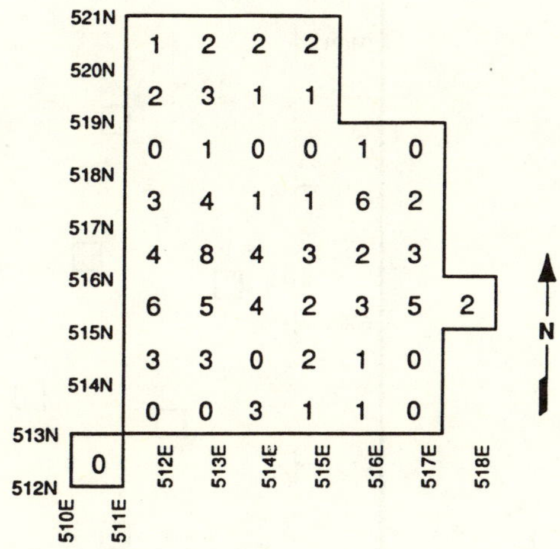

Figure 8.12. Distribution of Bayport flat platform flakes in Excavation Block 2.

inspected for evidence of weathering, in an effort to distinguish recent, presumably plow-induced fractures from those which occurred during the site's occupation. Admittedly, plow-induced fractures several decades old may be difficult to distinguish from legitimately ancient ones. However, unmistakeable evidence of re-use and sometimes retouching is visible on fracture planes of many specimens, evidence which is distinguishable from plow damage (Mallouf 1982). A major difference between recent plow-induced and presumably ancient fractures is shown in Figure 8.13. Almost without exception, cross-mends formed on recent fractures are between fragments in the same or adjacent units. Giving cross-mends within units a distance value of 0.0, the mean of five such joins is 0.28. In contrast, cross-mends formed on ancient fractures cover a much wider range of distances ($\bar{x}$ = 6.13), and are distinctly bimodal (Fig. 8.14). Were plowing the dispersal agent, the distribution of distances would be unimodal and perhaps skewed. The difference in mean distances is statistically significant (t = 6.53, df = 4.94, p = .00).

These results can be compared to an exceptionally well-documented case of artifact dispersal by plow, from the Crowfield-Willaeys site in southwestern Ontario. That site, itself a late Paleo-Indian occupation (Deller and Ellis 1984), consists of a probable burial cache of over 200 stone tools. Almost all are heat-fractured in situ, but plowing also has disturbed the site's integrity and probably produced more fractures. However, it definitely has dispersed artifacts from the presumed burial feature (Deller and Ellis 1984: Figs.10, 11), and no other dispersal agent can be identified. Thus, all artifact dispersal at Crowfield-Willaeys can be attributed to the plow. For some conjoined pairs, one piece was found in the feature; in other cases, however, both (or all, where more than two were involved) were displaced from the feature. The mean distances for both categories of conjoined specimens are shown in Table 8.2. Again, these mean values differs significantly from the value for presumably ancient cross-mends at Leavitt (for joins with one piece in the feature, t = 3.60, df = 10.98, p = .004; for joins outside the feature, t = 3.55, df = 12.29, p = .004).

These findings suggest that plow dispersal probably cannot account for the distribution of presumably ancient cross-mends at the Leavitt site, and implicates instead deliberate or incidental transport by the site's occupants. However, a different pattern in the frequency distribution of cross-mends is found at the Thedford site (Deller and Ellis 1986: Fig.70), where recent or at least post-occupational joins both outnumber original ones and appear to exceed them in the mean distance linking conjoinable fragments.

Unconstrained Clustering

Spatial structure at a number of midcontinental Paleo-Indian sites has been analyzed using variants of unconstrained clustering (Whallon 1984). These include Gainey (Simons et al. 1984; Voss and Shott 1981), Barnes and Holcombe (Voss and Shott 1981) in Michigan; further east, Potts in New York has received similar treatment (Lothrop 1986). Unconstrained clustering operates on a set of points characterized by the relative frequen-

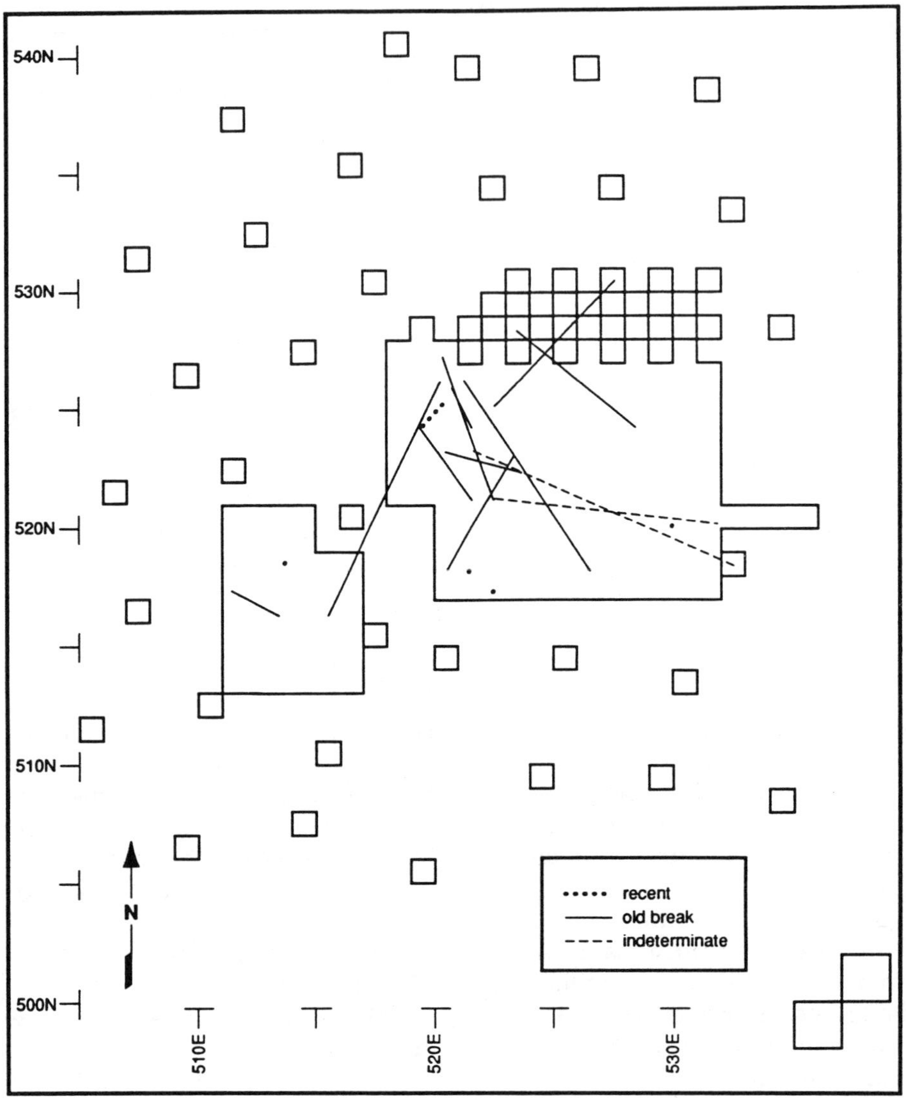

Figure 8.13. Distribution of conjoinable fragments

cies of artifact classes at each point. It can be used on point-provenience data or the unit-provenience data far more common in eastern North America (Whallon 1984). Typically—though not necessarily—raw frequencies of classes in unit-provenience data are smoothed by two-dimensional running averages (Whallon 1984). Clustering by any of a variety of algorithms (Kintigh and Ammerman 1982; Whallon 1984) then proceeds on the data matrix of relative frequencies, and clusters are defined by internal homogeneity in artifact composition (Whallon 1984).

Unconstrained clustering possesses several virtues. It is replicable, it avoids the sometimes spurious findings of simple visual inspection (Kintigh and Ammerman 1984), it does not assume global patterns of variability, it allows defined clusters to vary in size, shape, density and composition, and it groups units or points whether or not they are contiguous. In short, it is not overly constrained by assumptions concerning the structure and pattern of spatial distributions. However, unconstrained clustering also tends to define clusters by artifact-class density, and the results sometimes resist straightforward interpretation (Simons et al. 1984:270). Moreover, it produces discrete clusters that ignore or obscure the effects of overlapping activity areas (Whallon 1984).

Unconstrained clustering was used in the following manner at Leavitt. Because previous collections have

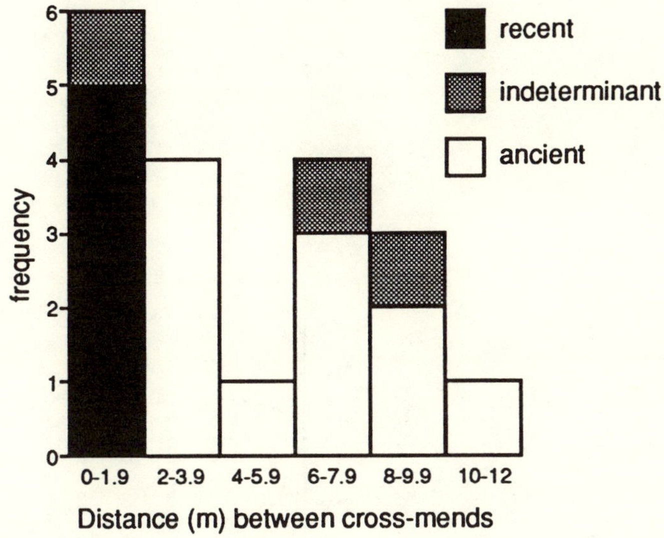

Figure 8.14. Frequency distribution of distance between conjoinable fragments.

removed an unknown number of tools from the excavation blocks, unit-provenience tool frequencies are very low. Consequently, all bifaces and unifaces, regardless of class or type, were grouped into a single undifferentiated class of tools. Among the predominantly Bayport debris, the platform classes discussed in Chapter 4—broken, biface retouch, uniface retouch, faceted and flat—were used. Channel flakes were omitted owing to their extremely low frequencies. Debris of other cherts was pooled to form a single class—non-Bayport debris—regardless of chert type or platform class.

The resulting classes were tabulated, and smoothed frequencies of each class were calculated separately for each excavation block. Smoothed data then were clustered in SPSS using squared Euclidean distance and the variance minimization algorithm (SPSS 1986:779), again separately for each block. Significant cluster solutions were identified by inspection of distance coefficients (Norusis 1985:174).

Data were analyzed in several forms, including relative frequencies of all artifact classes, and *z*-scores of those frequencies (Lothrop 1988:481). Broken flakes are far more abundant than other classes (Chapter 4), forming more than half of all material in each block. To remove its possible swamping effects, analysis also was conducted on relative frequencies but without broken flakes. In none of these cases, however, were clear clustering results found. Distance coefficients rose modestly at each stage, failing to identify significant clustering at any stage. The data's resistance to these measures may indicate the loss or degradation of original spatial structure at Leavitt by plowing (Yorston et al. 1990; Whallon 1984), possibly compounded by extensive secondary deposition during the site's occupation. As a reluctant alternative, smoothed absolute frequencies were studied. Although density tends to dominate spatial patterning in absolute data (Whallon 1984), relatively clear clustering results (Fig. 8.15) justifies the approach.

A four-cluster solution was identified in Block 1, and a three-cluster solution was identified in Block 2. Results are fairly straightforward in both areas. In Block 1, Clusters 1 and 2 identify relatively low-density parts of the block, found chiefly on the eastern margin and in the north-central area (Fig. 8.15). Cluster 3 occupies part of the center and the southwestern portion of the block; a distinct set of Cluster 3 units is found between 527N to 529N and 524E to 528E. Finally, Cluster 4 is an extremely high-density zone centered on Feature 4 at 520N-521N and 529E-530E.

Density is the major axis of variability in these results, as shown by mean artifact-class frequencies by cluster (Table 8.3). For Clusters 1 through 3, broken flakes increase by intervals of approximately 5, biface retouch flakes by intervals of approximately 1-1.5, faceted-platform flakes by intervals of approximately 0.7, and flat-platform flakes by intervals of approximately 0.5. The frequency of uniface retouch flakes also rises, but at a slight rate. There are no significant differences in the frequencies of non-Bayport debris or tools. Overall, there exists a clear pattern of increasing artifact frequency and hence density from Cluster 1 to Cluster 3, such that total frequencies rise by multiples of approximately 9 (Table 8.3). Moreover, rate of increase seems to vary with density or absolute frequency of artifact classes. Broken flakes are the most common class, and they display the highest rate of increase. Flat-platform flakes occur at modest frequencies and increase at a considerably lower rate.

Because it displays higher frequencies in virtually every class, Cluster 4 conforms to the general trend (Table 8.3). However, mean frequencies there are roughly twice the value of comparable Cluster 3 frequencies in the most abundant classes. Thus, the trend to increasing density is accelerated between Clusters 3 and 4. (Debris recovered from Feature 4 itself—as opposed to the plow zone and 5 cm sub-plow zone level—was not included in spatial analysis and so does not affect the results.) There are, however, several important exceptions to the general pattern. Uniface retouch flakes are comparatively rare in Cluster 4, and non-Bayport debris is no more abundant there than in other clusters. In fact,

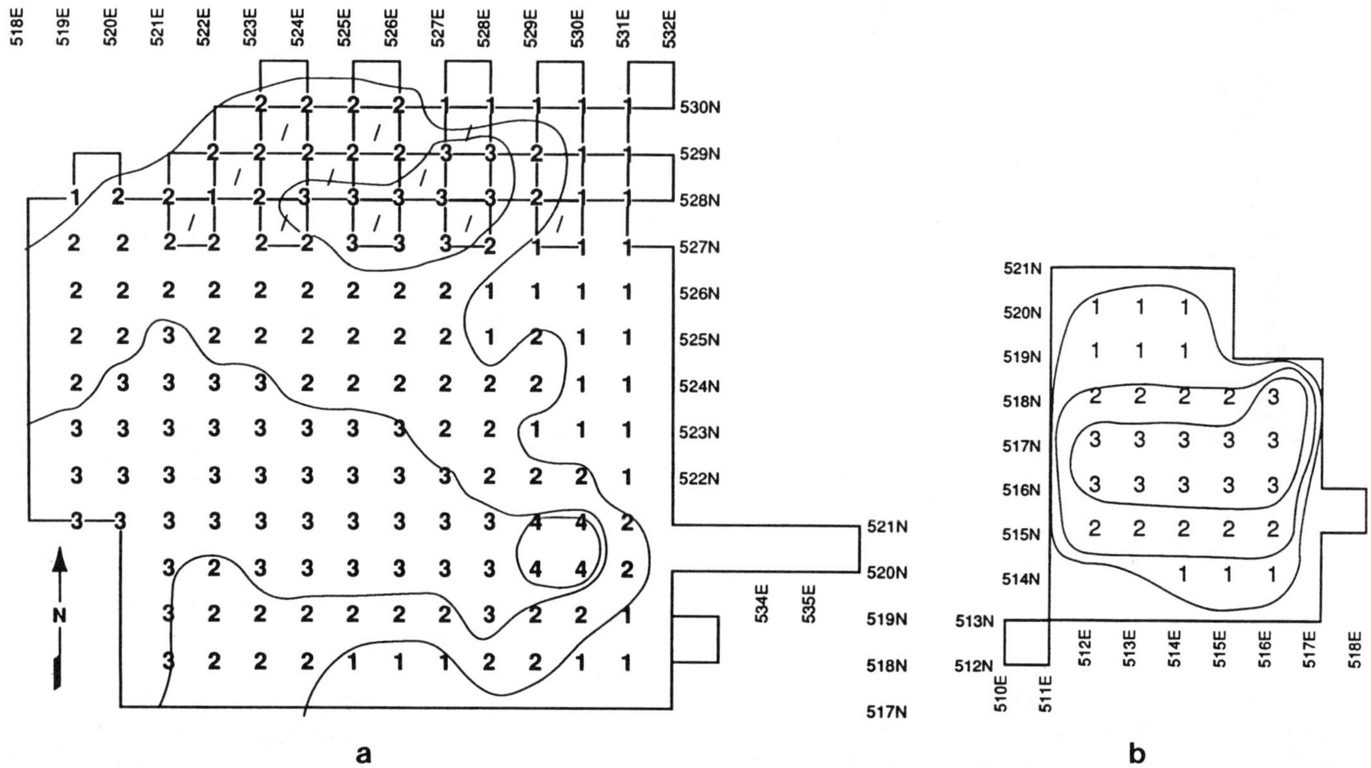

Figure 8.15. Running mean results of cluster analysis. *a*, Block 1; *b*, Block 2.

non-Bayport debris contributes little to overall spatial patterning at Leavitt, varying little in mean density by cluster. Although tool frequencies are low in general, there are no tools at all in Cluster 4, which may be partly explained by the fact that it consists of only four data points.

On balance, artifact density dominates spatial patterning. Most clusters are formed by a single contiguous, if amorphous, set of points, with a few isolated exceptions. Only Cluster 3 forms two distinct spatial units, although the smaller of these includes only ten points.

Spatial patterning in Block 2 is relatively simple. A high-density cluster trends east-west there, flanked by lower-density clusters to the north and south (Fig. 8.15). Mean artifact-class frequencies consistently rise from Cluster 1 to Cluster 3 (Table 8.3), although the rate of increase varies by class. As in Block 1, the rate of increase generally is greatest for the most abundant classes. In Block 2, however, there are no major exceptions to the general pattern; even uniface retouch flakes and tools increase substantially from Cluster 1 to Cluster 3.

It may be noteworthy that artifact densities by cluster are very similar when Block 2 and Clusters 2-4 in Block 1 are compared. In both areas, the densest cluster contains approximately 45 artifacts per unit, the second cluster approximately 27 per unit, and the third 14-18 per unit. Moreover, Clusters 3 and 4 in Block 1 and the Block 2 clusters form a single larger, linear distribution of material that trends east-west (Fig. 8.15).

Conclusion

Spatial patterning at Leavitt resists simple explication, and density emerges as its only major dimension. This conclusion is not an artifact of the analytical method used, which has been applied successfully in other cases (Kintigh and Ammerman 1982; Whallon 1984), sometimes with unit-provenience data. Spatial patterning is not as clear as it is at other Great Lakes

Paleo-Indian sites. The distinct tool clusters evident at Thedford, for instance, do not appear at Leavitt, although clusters may have existed before the long and varied history of collection began at the site. It is possible, for instance, that a clear pattern like Thedford's would emerge in more extensive excavation at Leavitt. Several artifacts were found a considerable distance from the excavation blocks and may have formed part of distinct clusters like the peripheral ones at Thedford. This possibility, however, is conjectural; outlying specimens did not form definable clusters and this proposed explanation fails to explain the significant differences in debris distribution and density found between Leavitt and Thedford.

Two factors in combination might explain Leavitt's spatial structure. First, the high density of material, especially flake debris, suggests relatively long and/or intensive occupation, which probably led to considerable secondary disposal of material (Binford 1980), probably in features. Feature 4, in this scenario, is the only one to survive plowing. Secondary deposition tends to obscure or destroy clear patterning of the type evident at Thedford, which probably reflects primary deposition there. Second, persistent plowing dispersed material to a considerable extent (Odell and Cowan 1987; Yorston et al. 1990), producing an overall pattern of artifact class co-variation in which density alone is the major axis of variability. Admittedly, spatial patterning evidently survived plowing at sites like Thedford, but not at Leavitt.

If nothing else, a major difference between Leavitt and sites such as Barnes and Thedford is revealed. Leavitt is a dense but dispersed distribution of secondary deposits, Barnes and Thedford primary deposits that somehow escaped substantial dispersal despite plowing. Although plow dispersal was judged considerable at Thedford (Deller and Ellis 1992:101), it apparently had relatively minor effects. Prior collection occurred at Barnes (Voss 1977:264) but did not destroy patterning there.

The entire excavated area at Leavitt covered a smaller area than at Thedford, and about the same area as at Barnes. Block 1 is essentially the size of Thedford's central cluster, but Block 2 is little more than half the area of Thedford's peripheral ones. Yet the size of the flake debris assemblage at Leavitt is roughly four times that of Thedford's, and considerably greater than Barnes'. Despite their differences, Leavitt and Barnes are similar in one respect. At both sites, the flake debris distribution forms a relatively simple pattern consisting of two modes or density peaks (Fig. 8.15; Voss 1977: Fig. 3), rather than a series of well defined clusters. Most of the patterning revealed at Barnes is produced by tools. The four-cluster solution presented there (Voss and Shott 1981: Fig. 3) essentially defines clusters by the presence-absence of tools, or the particular tool type present. Cluster 1 includes all units that contain bifaces, all but one of which contain a single specimen. Cluster 2 includes almost all other units having a single tool of any other type. The remaining clusters are defined largely by high and low frequencies of flake debris.

Patterning at Leavitt is problematic, but it is not unreasonable to conclude that, whatever its nature, occupation was characterized by extensive secondary disposal of refuse. Although Deller and Ellis (1992:121) detect similarities in spatial patterning at Thedford and Holcombe (Fitting et al. 1966), considerable variability probably characterized Great Lakes Paleo-Indian site structure. Varying significantly and in complex ways in settlement size and organization, residential population size and occupation span, and probably disposal practices, those sites should be expected to vary in spatial structure in consequence. Only when many more Paleo-Indian sites in the region are excavated will more significant and exact similarities in spatial structure be revealed.

Chapter 9

Conclusion

Introduction

It is customary at this point in site reports to identify the subject as a residential base camp, hunting camp, or some other type of site. Barnes, for instance, is conventionally identified as a hunting camp or rearmament site. Leavitt might be regarded, using the same logic, as some sort of more general residential site. This practice, however, does not consider the effects of organizational factors on assemblage formation, factors discussed in Chapter 7. It also privileges the hunting behavior or other material components of Paleo-Indian cultures at the expense of other classes of behavior. Many more sites must be documented and our understanding of formation processes must improve considerably before the substantive behavior (Shott 1989b) that occurred at Leavitt is identified. And that behavior may prove more complex and diverse than the traditional emphasis on food-getting and simple typologies of sites can encompass. For these reasons, no attempt is made to identify Leavitt as a particular type of Paleo-Indian site. Instead, several distinct but related themes will be discussed, including the emphasis on materialist to the nearly total exclusion of other kinds of interpretation, and the scale of the Paleo-Indian material record and the scale of data recovery efforts appropriate to it.

Cultural Approaches in Paleo-Indian Studies

Burdened with an impoverished material record, it is no surprise that our various syntheses of Paleo-Indian cultures and behavior tend to emphasize small populations in the simplest of social forms, absorbed in exigencies of the subsistence quest. This materialist cast of Paleo-Indian anthropology privileges the role of external environmental conditions in determining the nature of forager cultures. The approach has undeniable advantages, especially in producing sophisticated and ecologically informed models of past habitats. Thanks to it, we know far more than we once did about the biotic composition of early Holocene habitats and the causes and dimensions of their time-space variation.

As worthwhile as this approach is, most would acknowledge its limitations. All archaeological inference is limited in some way, so this quality of materialism is not a unique drawback. However, critics of materialism have long argued that it is not merely limited but inherently flawed, because all cultural behavior is set in some social context whose structure is not always even influenced, let alone determined, by the character of the environment in which it is found. This view is, of course, not a new one, but this may be the first time it has been expressed in a Paleo-Indian context.

Perhaps in response to criticism of traditional materialist methods, the archaeological study of Pleistocene and early Holocene cultures elsewhere in the world has in recent years increasingly emphasized the less derivative, more problematic, social dimensions of those cultures. Complexity in its several guises is adduced from the material remains of various forager societies (Price and Brown 1985). In large measure, such complexity is seen where an abundant and diverse material record is preserved, an observation that suggests the pervasive influence of preservation conditions on our reconstructions of the past.

Measuring this complexity from the Paleo-Indian archaeological record alone is a problematic undertaking. It is only natural, therefore, to consult the ethnographic record in order to gauge the social dimensions of Paleo-Indian cultural complexity. Until recently, that record has been dominated by a general model informed chiefly by research in southern Africa. It is premised on the belief that foragers enjoy a high standard of living at relatively little expense, and that a flexible egalitarian collective closely adapted to ecological constraints is the cornerstone of forager societies (e.g., Lee 1979). This general model has special appeal to archaeologists, since it portrays ethnographic foragers as Paleolithic relicts preserved by virtue of their remoteness. Few seriously propose a facile extension of the model to ancient foragers, but its general properties as described by Lee and other researchers are accepted by many, giving Kalahari groups a "unique exemplary status" (Wilmsen and Denbow 1990:503) in forager studies.

Revisionist critiques of recent years regard this model not merely as simplistic but as fundamentally incorrect. Many of the ethnographic groups whose documentation contributed to the prevailing orthodoxy may not be the pristine isolates that they are portrayed as; instead, centuries of intensive contact with tribal and other societies have transformed them (Headland and Reid 1989). By itself, this observation attacks only their historical isolation. Much more damaging to the orthodox model is the argument that many ethnographic groups are merely exploited and marginalized strata of larger societies, not culturally or ecologically autonomous groups and that, even when isolated for purposes of description and analysis, they are themselves internally stratified (e.g., Wilmsen 1989). In sum, revisionists see class structure and economic dependency, not equality and autonomy, as inherent properties of such foraging groups.

If the existential nature of Kalahari forager society is in dispute, no less can be said of foragers elsewhere. It can also be said, for instance, of high-latitude foragers, who provide the chief ethnographic inspiration for archaeological reconstructions of Paleo-Indian cultures of North America. Although some see fundamental continuity between prehistory and history, celebrating the resourcefulness of these cultures (e.g., Francis and Morantz 1983:14-15, 96-97), others see far-reaching transformations attendant on integration into the fur trade (Leacock 1954, 1982).

A revisionist critique might be in order for Paleo-Indian studies. We deal routinely with extremely sparse material remains and we have a strong tendency to see in them the properties of the forager model developed to a significant extent from Kalahari and North American high-latitude ethnographic data. No one seriously argues, of course, for identity in particulars—Paleo-Indian groups, for instance, consuming mongongo nuts or behaving exactly like the Mistassini Cree—but we adduce the general properties of the model: an egalitarian collective with simple, flexible sociopolitical organization. In view of the current debate over this model, we should carefully examine its limitations. We should consider the social context of Paleo-Indian subsistence, the social conflicts, if any, of Paleo-Indian cultures and how they may have influenced subsistence practices, and the trajectory of the internal dynamics of those cultures.

Scale of the Paleo-Indian Record

If complexity in Paleo-Indian social relations can reside in the material record, it remains a widely held view that such a record is sparse. The view is reinforced by the observation that Paleo-Indian artifacts hold, for a variety of reasons, a special fascination for archaeologists and collectors alike. Despite the interest this fascination excites, little Paleo-Indian material is recovered in typical surveys. By conventional accounts, Paleo-Indian remains are sparser than Archaic remains, which are sparser still than Woodland and later ones. A gradual population increase is often adduced from such evidence.

While few would doubt that Paleo-Indian populations were smaller than those of the late prehistoric period, the differences may not be as great as often supposed. It also is uncertain that earlier Archaic material densities, if not populations, were higher. Close inspection of several midcontinental landscapes has revealed a surprisingly dense and diverse distribution of Paleo-Indian materials. Our attention is understandably attracted to large sites, and these form an extremely important component of the Paleo-Indian record worthy of detailed scrutiny. So, however, do the lower-density components of Paleo-Indian distributions. The complexities of artifact recovery on cultivated surfaces requires repeated collections of the same locations. Using this approach, Jackson and McKillop (1991) document a regional distribution of surprising abundance and diversity; by their estimate, perhaps several hundred Paleo-Indian sites and artifacts may exist in an 80 km^2 area of eastern Ontario. Similarly, an estimate of as many as 67 Paleo-Indian sites may be generated for a single small river basin in southeastern Michigan (Peebles and Shott 1981), not even considering portions of the basin now inundated by Lake Erie. More intensive and selective survey by avocational archaeologists suggests that this figure may itself be relatively low.

But if Paleo-Indian distributions are denser than previously supposed, they still appear sparser than those of subsequent periods. Even in this respect, however, differences shrink on close inspection. Early Archaic diagnostics typically are found in substantially higher frequencies than are Paleo-Indian ones. But most regional syntheses in the Great Lakes postulate a longer span for the Early Archaic than the Paleo-Indian period. Current understanding of regional culture history in southwestern Ontario posits a 600-year span for the Paleo-Indian period and a 2,000-year span for the Early Archaic (Ellis and Deller 1990; Ellis et al. 1990) By admittedly crude reasoning, the smaller size of Early Archaic bifaces suggests a considerably shorter use-life and therefore higher discard rate than Paleo-Indian bifaces (Shott 1989a), though discard rate cannot be calibrated to artifact size in any simple way. Nevertheless, the apparent disparity between Paleo-Indian and Early Archaic diagnostics, and the differences in population they are presumed to reflect, must be qualified by this reasoning.

Scales of Data Recovery

Paleo-Indian sites and artifacts possess a certain cachet associated with rarity. They are apparently less abundant than are later-period remains but, as noted above, the Paleo-Indian material record probably is much larger than many specialists believe. As long as we continue to regard them as rare and to focus our efforts on their aesthetic properties or determining how they were made, the anthropological potential of Paleo-Indian remains will be slight. To increase our knowledge of Paleo-Indian cultures and their transformations requires a commensurate transformation in data collection practices congruent with the probable scale of the material record.

The vast majority of midcontinental Paleo-Indian sites lie in plow zone context. We should stop apologizing for this situation, although undisturbed contexts obviously would be preferable. Sites here are disturbed, but many are thereby exposed. Where circumstances or the appropriate institutional context exist, Paleo-Indian sites have been encountered in surprisingly large numbers (Jackson and McKillop 1991; Munson 1991). Yet standard labor-intensive excavation techniques continue to be used. These techniques are suitable in undisturbed primary contexts but are of questionable value in plow-dispersed ones, where artifacts are scattered and typical artifact recovery rates per excavation unit are much less than one. Under these circumstances, the time and expense invested in recovery rapidly becomes prohibitive. The 1984 Leavitt excavation, for instance, engaged a six-person crew for six weeks to recover several dozen artifacts and some thousands of flakes. Well controlled mechanical excavation might have yielded similar results in several person-days of work.

If we accept the proposition that hundreds of Paleo-Indian sites remain to be discovered and excavated just in Michigan, reliance on conventional excavation methods will make this the work of several lifetimes. Large-scale mechanical techniques are available on a practical basis and are appropriate for many archaeological contexts (Van Horn 1988). Admittedly expensive, they nevertheless will require no more than several field seasons for the recovery of sizeable collections from dozens of sites. Such an approach to data recovery, however, requires a degree of institutional support—a permanent commitment of labor and laboratory facilities as well as project-specific research support—that is not merely rare but practically nonexistent.

In fact, such an arrangement probably would be extremely economical in the long term, although expensive upon initiation. Combined with an organizational approach to the material record, it would provide us with data on an unparalleled scale, data with which to vastly expand our understanding of Paleo-Indian societies not merely as adaptive systems—no matter how important this perspective is—but as cultures with their own histories and systems of meaning. In this way, the anthropological potential of North American Paleo-Indian cultures will be realized far sooner than by following conventional standards of data collection and interpretation.

An Organizational Approach

Viewed in a new light, diversity and abundance may be properties of the Paleo-Indian archaeological record, and corresponding diversity and complexity may have been properties of their cultures. In principle, it should be as possible to infer and explicate patterns of inequality and structural constraints on food-getting as it is to infer patterns of settlement mobility. At present, this view is a conviction more than an established fact, and it is likely to generate a good deal of skepticism. It is justified if only by the certainty that we will never learn to read social processes from sparse remains if we do not try, or if we are unconvinced that they are important.

Like all other prehistoric and modern cultures, Paleo-Indians existed in a real, material world. The challenge is not to deny the existence or the force of material constraints, but to give appropriate weight to both exogenous material conditions and internal social ones. For reasons not immediately obvious, archaeologists tend to assume extreme positions on this issue, denying a role either for material or social conditions. What we require instead is the sensible and anthropologically informed integration of materialist analyses in broader cultural studies.

Conclusion

This report has been no more successful than any other in inferring the social structure and organization of Paleo-Indian cultures, or the social context in which tool-using activities occurred at Leavitt. Its far more modest goals have been, first, to document the assemblage and the data generated from it and, second, to suggest and illustrate several potentially useful lines of inquiry not often pursued in Paleo-Indian studies. As that work continues in the Great Lakes, we will require not only many more basic documentary records like this one, but also an approach to the data they contain that regards Paleo-Indian cultures as not merely sets of adaptive strategies, but the systems of meaning, belief and order in which those adaptations occurred.

Appendix

Archaeobotanical Remains from the Leavitt Site

Kathryn Egan
Michigan State University

Excavation of the Leavitt site resulted in the recovery of a small quantity of carbonized wood from a single feature. This material is significant because it may provide cultural and ecological information relevant to the Paleo-Indian period. Radiocarbon dating of a portion of the sample gives chronometric assays of the Paleo-Indian context of these materials and, if confirmed, the lithic seriation for this period. In addition, these dates will complement the generalized chronologic scheme of paleoenvironmental dynamics in the area.

The sample was collected in its soil matrix and the carbonized wood was extracted in the lab using a binocular microscope with variable 7× to 30× magnification. The sample was initially sorted into two gross categories: "carmelized" wood and wood charcoal. Each of these categories was then examined further and classified into specific taxa.

Unfortunately, a large percentage (95%) of the sample was composed of carmelized wood. The anatomical structure of this material is fused and pores have expanded so that only gross morphology can be used for identification. While the remainder of the charcoal retained its anatomical identity through carbonization, aggradation by environmental and taphonomic forces muted the appearance of some of the anatomical cell structure. This problem was exacerbated by the small size (<0.5 cm) of the specimens. Consequently, the charcoal was identified using both binocular (7× to 30× magnification) and metallurgical (60× to 400× magnification) microscopes. Richard I. Ford made the genus identifications on the basis of specific anatomical cell structures, using the key in *Identification of North American Commercial Pulpwoods and Pulp Fibres* (Strelis and Kennedy 1967) and 400× magnification. In those cases where structural modification precluded positive identification to genus, the closest possible genus or taxon was noted.

Weights only were reported for each category. Counts for each category would be meaningless since identification at the grossest level required dissection of most specimens, thus altering their numbers.

All of the carmelized wood was deciduous and, as noted above, vitrification of the pores precluded more specific identification. The charcoal included three genera: spruce (*Picea*), basswood (*Tilia*), and oak (*Quercus*). (See Table A.1 for weights of each category.)

The diversity of wood genera was interesting in light of the ecological setting and Paleo-Indian activities. On the basis of the tool assemblage the site dates to around 10,500 B.P. which is coeval with the ecological transition from spruce to hardwood forests in Michigan (Luke and Beld 1977; Kapp 1977; Kerfoot 1974; Shott and Welch 1984). Pollen profiles from Demont Lake (Isabella County, Michigan), Frains Lake (Washtenaw County, Michigan), and Crystal Marsh (Montcalm County, Michigan) indicate that the forest composition was a mosaic of spruce and hardwood species (cf., Dent and Kauffman 1985; Webb 1981). The Delcourts (1983) argue that shifting climatic regions were instrumental in the rapid forestation and dramatic changes in forest composition which followed the glacial retreat (ca. 14,000 B.P. in southern Michigan). The pine (*Pinus banksiana*) and hardwood (*Fraxinus; Ostrya* or *Carpinus*) forest surrounding Demont Lake was invaded by spruce and fir at about 11,000 B.P. and was followed by decidous species including birch (*Betula*), elm (*Ulmus*), oak (*Quercus*), and tamarack (*Larix*). Other deciduous species continued to be added to the inventory and the pollen profile

TABLE A.1
Weights of Carbonized Wood from the Leavitt Site (20CL81)

	Feature 4, Section 3	Feature 4, Section 4	Total
"Carmelized" wood	0.006	6.135	6.141
Deteriorated charcoal	0.100	0.115	0.215
Semi-ring porous charcoal		0.001	0.001
Picea		0.010	0.010
cf., *Picea*		0.016	0.016
Tilia		0.038	0.038
cf., *Tilia*		0.012	0.012
Quercus		0.010	0.010
			6.443

In grams.

from Demont Lake indicates that basswood did not enter the area until 7,000 B.P. (Delcourt and Delcourt 1983:286). This paleoecological scheme is repeated at Frains Lake (Kerfoot 1974). Though the pollen core from Crystal Marsh presents a similar overall scheme, it varies in species composition. Significantly, for this analysis, it shows basswood appearing as early as 10,000 B.P. and increasing in occurrence with other deciduous species as spruce declined (Luke and Beld 1977). The pollen profiles, therefore, present a picture of dynamic transition.

The forest surrounding the Leavitt site may well have contained spruce, oak and basswood simultaneously (cf. Crystal Marsh) at the time of Paleo-Indian occupation. In fact, the combination of these species at the Leavitt site supports propositions regarding the mosaic composition of forests at 10,500 B.P. and highlights the necessity for additional pollen and wood charcoal samples from this period.

Interpretation of the cultural significance of this assemblage is more difficult. Use of poor burning spruce in combination with deciduous species may represent collection of locally available deadfall limbs for fuel. This proposition is partially supported by the high percentage of carmelized wood which often results from the burning of green wood at high temperatures or using damp wood (R. Ford, pers. comm.). On the other hand, there is the possibility that the genera represented served several different cultural functions and their combined inclusion in this feature was accidental. At present the archaeobotanical record from Paleo-Indian contexts is not sufficient to evaluate the behavioral analogs appropriate to this assemblage.

In conclusion, while the assemblage does not provide substantive information regarding Paleo-Indian exploitative patterns, it does suggest that floral remains of Paleo-Indian origin can be preserved in eastern North America. Further, it represents a necessary step toward understanding of the environmental context 10,500 years ago.

Bibliography

Adovasio, J.M., J.D. Gunn, J. Donahue, and R. Stuckenrath
1978 Meadowcraft rockshelter, 1977: an overview. American Antiquity 43:632–51.

Agogino, G., and W. Frankforter
1964 The Brewster site: a Paleo-Indian site in eastern Wyoming. Wyoming Archaeologist 7(4):7–11.

Ahearn, P.J., and R.E. Bailey
1980 Pollen record from Chippewa Bog, Lapeer County, Michigan. Michigan Academician 12:297–308.

Ahler, S.A.
1971 Projectile point form and function at Rodgers shelter, Missouri. Missouri Archaeological Society Research Series, 8. Columbia.
1989 Mass analysis of flaking debris: studying the forest rather than the tree. In: Alternative Approaches to Lithic Analysis, D. Henry and G. Odell, eds., pp. 85–118. Archeological Papers of the American Anthropological Association, 1.

Albert, D.A., S.R. Denton, and B.V. Barnes
1986 Regional Landscape Ecosystems of Michigan. University of Michigan School of Natural Resources. Ann Arbor.

Ammerman, A., and M. Feldman
1974 On the "making" of an assemblage of stone tools. American Antiquity 39:610–16.

Amundsen, D., and H.E. Wright
1979 Forest changes in Minnesota at the end of the Pleistocene. Ecological Monographs 49:1–16.

Arundale, W.H., and E. Jones
1989 Historic land use process in Alaska's Koyukuk River area. Arctic 42:148–62.

Bamforth, D.B.
1985 The technological organization of Paleo-Indian small-group bison hunting on the Llano Estacado. Plains Anthropologist 30:243–58.

Beld, S.G., and J.T. Luke
1985 Radiocarbon Dating in Gratiot County-S84–194. Archaeological Survey Completion Report. Alma College. Alma, Michigan.

Belovsky, G.E.
1987 Hunter-gatherer foraging: a linear programming approach. Journal of Anthropological Archaeology 6:29-76.

Benninghoff, W., and D.E. Southworth
1963 Unpublished Pollen Diagrams for Third Sister Lake, Washtenaw County, Michigan. Department of Botany, University of Michigan. Ann Arbor.

Bernabo, J.C., and T. Webb III
1977 Changing patterns in the Holocene pollen record of northeastern North America: a mapped summary. Quaternary Research 8:64–96.

Beyries, S.
1984 Approche fonctionelle de la variabilite des facies du Mousterien. These de troisieme cycle, Université de Paris.
1988 Functional variability of lithic sets in the Middle Paleo-lithic. In: Upper Pleistocene Prehistory of Western Eurasia, H.Dibble and A. Montet-White, eds., pp. 213–23. University Museum, Philadelphia.

Binford, L.R.
1973 Interassemblage variability: the Mousterian and the "functional" argument. In: The Explanation of Culture Change, C.Renfrew, ed., pp. 227–54. London: Duckworth.
1977 Forty-seven trips: a case study in the character of archaeological formation processes. In: Stone Tools as Cultural Markers: Change, Evolution and Complexity, R. Wright, ed., pp.24–36. Atlantic Highlands:Humanities.
1978a Nunamiut Ethnoarchaeology. Academic:New York.
1978b Dimensional analysis of behavior and site structure: learning from an Eskimo hunting stand. American Antiquity 43:330–61.
1979 Organization and formation processes: looking at curated technologies. Journal of Anthropological Research 35:255–73.
1980 Willow smoke and dog's tails: hunter-gatherer settlement systems and archaeological site formation. American Antiquity 45:4–20.
1982 The archaeology of place. Journal of Anthropological Archaeology 1:5–31.

Binford, L.R., and S. Binford
1966 A preliminary analysis of functional variability in the Mousterian of Levallois Facies. American Anthropologist 68:238–95.

Binford, L.R., and G.I. Quimby
1963 Indian sites and chipped stone materials in the northern Lake Michigan area. Fieldiana Anthropology 36:277–307.

Bonnichsen, R., B. Borque, and D. Young
1983 The Moosehorn fluted point discovery, northern Maine. Archaeology of Eastern North America 11:36–48.

Boylan, J.
1977 An analysis of a fluted point from Macomb County, Michigan. Michigan Archaeologist 23:4–10.

Bradley, B.
1975 Lithic reduction sequences: a glossary and discussion. In: Lithic Technology: Making and Using Stone Tools, E.Swanson, ed., pp. 5–13. The Hague: Mouton.

Bradley, B., and D. Stanford
1987 The Claypool study. In: The Horner Site: The Type Site of the Cody Complex, G. Frison and L. Todd, eds., pp. 405–34. Orlando: Academic.

Braun, D.
1987 Coevolution of sedentism, pottery technology, and horticulture in the central Midwest, 200 B.C.-A.D. 600. In: Emergent Horticultural Economies of the Eastern Woodlands, W. Keegan, ed., pp. 153–81. Center for Archaeological Investigations Occasional Paper No. 7. Southern Illinois University, Carbondale.

Brennan, L.A.
1982 A compilation of fluted points of eastern North America by count and distribution: an AENA project. Archaeology of Eastern North America 10:27–46.

Brink, J.W.
1978 An Experimental Study of Microwear Formation on End-Scrapers. Archaeological Survey of Canada Paper, 83. National Museum of Man, Ottawa.

Brunett, F.V.
1966 An archaeological survey of the Manistee River Basin: Sharon, Michigan to Sherman, Michigan. Michigan Archaeologist 12:169–82.

Burch, E.S.
1972 The caribou/wild reindeer as a human resource. American Antiquity 37:339–68.

Butler, B.R.
1963 An Early Man site at Big Camas Prairie, south-central Idaho. Tebiwa 6:22–23.

Byers, D.S.
1954 Bull Brook: a fluted point site in Ipswich, Massachusetts. American Antiquity 19:343–51.
1959 Radiocarbon dates for the Bull Brook site, Massachusetts. American Antiquity 24:427–29.

Callahan, E.
1979 The basics of biface knapping in the Eastern Fluted Point Tradition: a manual for flintknappers and lithic analysts. Archaeology of Eastern North America 7:1-179.

Canby, T.Y.
1979 The search for the first Americans. National Geographic Magazine 156:330–63.

Carr, C.
1985 Getting into data: philosophy and tactics for the analysis of complex data structures. In: For Concordance in Archaeological Analysis: Bridging Data Structure, Quantitative Techniques, and Theory, C. Carr, ed., pp. 18–44. Kansas City: Westport.

Cashdan, E.A.
1984 The effects of food production on mobility in the central Kalahari. In: From Hunters to Farmers: The Causes and Consequences of Food Production in Africa, J. Clark and S. Brandt, eds., pp.311–27. Berkeley: Univ. of California.

Cauvin, M-C., G. Deraprahamian, and D. Helmer
1987 Grattoirs a pans coupes convergents de Mureybet (Syrie) du 8e millenaire: definition, essais de fabrication et emmanchement. In: La Main et L'Outil: Manches et Emmanchements Prehistoriques, D. Stordeur, ed., pp. 257-68. Paris: CNRS.

Christenson, A.
1986 Projectile point size and projectile aerodynamics: an exploratory study. Plains Anthropologist 31:109-18.

Clark, J.D., and H. Kurashina
1981 A study of the work of a modern tanner in Ethiopia and its relevance for archaeological interpretations. In: Modern Material Culture: The Archaeology of Us, R. Gould and M. Schiffer, eds., pp. 303–21. New York: Academic.

Clark, J.E.
1986 Another look at small debitage and microdebitage. Lithic Technology 15:21–33.

Cleland, C.E.
1965 Barren ground caribou (*Rangifer arcticus*) from an Early Man site in southeastern Michigan. American Antiquity 30:350–51.

Coe, M.J., D.H. Cumming, and J. Phillipson
1976 Biomass and production of large African herbivores in relation to rainfall and primary production. Oecologia 22:341–54.

Crabtree, D.E.
1966 A stoneworker's approach to analyzing and replicating the Lindenmeier Folsom. Tebiwa 9:3–39.
1972 An Introduction to Flintworking. Idaho State University Museum Occasional Paper, 28. Pocatello.

Crabtree, D.E., and B.R. Butler
1964 Notes on experiments in flint knapping, I: heat treatment of silica material. Tebiwa 7:1–16.

Crabtree, D.E., and E.L. Davis
1968 Experimental manufacture of wooden implements with tools of flaked stone. Science 159:426–28.

Cross, J.R.
1983 Twigs, branches, trees, and forests: problems of scale in lithic analysis. In: Archaeological Hammers and Theories, J. Moore and A. Keene, eds., pp.207–22. Academic: New York.

Curran, M.L.
1984 The Whipple site and Paleoindian tool assemblage variation: a comparison of intrasite structuring. Archaeology of Eastern North America 12:5–40.

Dansereau, Pierre
1953 The postglacial pine period. Royal Society of Canada Transactions 47:23–38.

Davis, M.B.
1983 Holocene vegetational history of the eastern United States. In: Late-Quaternary Environments of the United States (Vol. 2, The Holocene), H.E. Wright, ed., pp.166–81. Minneapolis.

Dekin, A.A.
1966 A fluted point from Grand Traverse County. Michigan Archaeologist 12:35–36.

Delcourt, P., and H. Delcourt
1983 Late-Quaternary vegetational dynamics and community stability reconsidered. Quaternary Research 19:265-71.

Deller, D.B.
1982 Some Paleo-Indian Cultures and Their Suggested Evolution in Southern Ontario and Michigan. Unpublished ms. on file, McGill University. Montreal.

Deller, D.B., and C.J. Ellis
1984 Crowfield: a preliminary report on a probable Paleo-Indian cremation in southwestern Ontario. Archaeology of Eastern North America 12:41–71.
1988 Early Paleo-Indian complexes in southwestern Ontario. In: Late Pleistocene and Early Holocene Paleoecology and Archaeology of the Eastern Great Lakes Region, R. Laub, N. Miller and D. Steadman, eds., pp. 251–63. Bulletin of the Buffalo Society of Natural Sciences, 33.
1992 Thedford II: A Paleo-Indian Site in the Ausable River Watershed of Southwestern Ontario. University of Michigan Museum of Anthropology, Memoir 24. Ann Arbor.

Dent, R., and B. Kauffman
1985 Aboriginal subsistence and site ecology as interpreted from microfloral and faunal remains. In: Shawnee Minisink: A Stratified Paleoindian-Archaic Site in the Upper Delaware Valley of Pennsylvania, C. McNett, ed., pp. 55–79. Orlando: Academic.

Dibble, H.L.
1984 Interpreting typological variation of Middle Paleolithic lithic scrapers: function, style, or sequence of reduction? Journal of Field Archaeology 11:431–36.
1987 The interpretation of Middle Paleolithic scraper morphology. American Antiquity 52:109–17.

Dibble, H.L., and J. Whittaker
1981 New experimental evidence on the relation between percussion flaking and flake variation. Journal of Archaeological Science 6:283–96.

Dincauze, D.F.
1981 Paleoenvironmental reconstruction in the Northeast: the art of multidisciplinary science. In: Foundations of Northeast Archaeology, D. Snow, ed., pp.51–96. New York: Academic.
1986 Review of "Des elephants, des caribous...et des hommes: la periode Paleoindienne," Recherches Amerindiennes au Quebec 25(2), 1985. Man in the Northeast 32:127–31.

Douglass, C.C.
1928 Report of C.C. Douglass, Assistant Geologist. Third Annual Report of the State Geologist (1849), by D. Houghton. In: Geological Reports of Douglass Houghton, G.N. Fuller, ed., pp.416–38. Michigan Historical Commission, Lansing.

Dragoo, D.
1973 Wells Creek: an Early Man site in Stewart County, Tennessee. Archaeology of Eastern North America 1:1-56.

Dunning, R.W.
1959 Social and Economic Change Among the Northern Ojibwa. University of Toronto Press.

Dustin, F.
1935 A study of the Bayport chert. Papers of the Michigan Academy of Science, Arts and Letters 20:465–76.

Ebert, J.I.
1979 An ethnoarchaeological approach to reassessing the meaning of variability in stone tool assemblages. In: Ethnoarchaeology: Implications of Ethnography for Archaeology, C. Kramer, ed., pp. 59–74. New York: Columbia.

Ehlers, G.M., and W.E. Humphrey
1944 Revision of E.A. Strong's species from the Mississippian Point au Gres limestone of Grand Rapids, Michigan. Contributions from the Museum of Paleontology 6(6):113–30. University of Michigan. Ann Arbor, Michigan.

Eisenberg, L.
1984 Paleo-Indian Settlement Pattern in the Hudson and Delaware Drainages. Occasional Publications in Northeastern Anthropology, 4. Franklin Pierce College. Rindge, N.H.

Eley, B., and P. von Bitter
1989 Cherts of Southern Ontario. Royal Ontario Museum. Toronto.

Ellis, C.J.
1984 Paleo-Indian Lithic Technological Structure and Organization in the Lower Great Lakes Area: A First Approximation. Unpublished Ph.D dissertation, Simon Fraser University. Burnaby, B.C.
1989 The explanation of northeastern Paleoindian lithic procurement patterns. In: Eastern Paleoindian Lithic Resource Use, C. Ellis and J. Lothrop, eds., pp. 139–64. Boulder: Westview.

Ellis, C.J., and D.B. Deller
1988 Some distinctive Paleo-Indian tool types from the lower Great Lakes region. Midcontinental Journal of Archaeology 13:111–58.
1990 Paleo-Indians. In: The Archaeology of Southern Ontario to A.D. 1650, C. Ellis and N. Ferris, eds., pp. 37–63. Ontario Archaeological Society. London, Ontario.

Ellis, C.J., I.T. Kenyon, and M. Spence
1990 The Archaic. In: The Archaeology of Southern Ontario to A.D. 1650, C.Ellis and N.Ferris, eds., pp. 65–124. Ontario Archaeological Society. London, Ontario.

Eschman, D., and P. Karrow
1985 Huron basin glacial lakes: a review. In: Quaternary Evolution of the Great Lakes, P. Karrow and P. Calkin, eds., pp. 79–93. Geological Association of Canada Special Paper No. 30.

Farrand, W.R.
1977 Revision of the two rivers "Valders" drift border and the age of fluted points in Michigan. In: For the Director: Research Essays in Honor of James B. Griffin, C. Cleland, ed., pp. 74–84. Anthropological Papers, University of Michigan Museum of Anthropology, 61. Ann Arbor.

Farrand, W.R., and D.C. Bell
1982 Quaternary Geology of Southern Michigan. Michigan Department of Natural Resources. Lansing.

Farrand, W.R., and D.F. Eschman
1974 Glaciation of the southern peninsula of Michigan: a review. Michigan Academican 7:31–56.

Fisher, D.C.
1984 Taphonomic analysis of late Pleistocene mastadon occurrences: evidence of butchery by North American Paleo-Indians. Paleobiology 10:338–57.
1987 Mastodont procurement by Paleoindians of the Great Lakes region: Hunting or scavenging? In: The Evolution of Human Hunting, M. Nitecki and D. Nitecki, eds., pp. 309–421. New York: Plenum.

Fisher, J.
1986 Shadows in the Forest: Ethnoarchaeology among the Efe Pygmies. Unpublished Ph.D. dissertation, University of California, Berkeley.

Fitting, J., D. DeVisscher, and E. Wahla
1966 The Paleo Indian Occupation of the Holcombe Beach. Anthropological Papers, University of Michigan Museum of Anthropology, 27. Ann Arbor.

Flenniken, J.J.
1978 Reevaluation of the Lindermeier Folsom: a replication experiment in lithic technology. American Antiquity 43:473–80.
1981 Replicative Systems Analysis: A Model Applied to the Vein Quartz Artifacts from the Hoko River Site. Washington State University Laboratory of Anthropology, Report of Investigation, 59. Pullman.

Fox, W.
1989 Review of "Cherts of southern Ontario," by B.Eley and P. von Bitter. Arch Notes 89–6:24–28.

Francis, D., and T. Morantz
1983 Partners in Fur. Montreal: McGill-Queen's University.

Frison, G.C.
1968 A functional analysis of certain chipped stone tools. American Antiquity 33:149–55.
1978 Prehistoric Hunters of the High Plains. New York: Academic.
1979 Observations on the use of stone tools: dulling of working edges of some chipped stone tools in bison butchering. In: Lithic Use-Wear Analysis, B. Hayden, ed., pp. 259–68. New York: Academic.

Frison, G., and B.A. Bradley
1980 Folsom Tools and Technology at the Hanson Site, Wyoming. Albuquerque: University of New Mexico.

Frison, G., and D. Stanford
1982 The Agate Basin Site: A Record of the Paleo-Indian Occupation of the High Plains. New York: Academic.

Frison, G., and L.C. Todd
1987 The Horner Site: The Type Site of the Cody Cultural Complex. Orlando: Academic.

Funk, R.E.
1976 Recent Contributions to Hudson Valley Prehistory. New York State Museum Memoir 22. Albany.

Funk, R.E., D.W. Fisher, and E.M. Reilly
1969 Caribou and Paleoindian in New York state: a presumed association. American Journal of Science 268:181-86.

Gallagher, J.P.
1977 Contemporary stone tools in Ethiopia: implications for archaeology. Journal of Field Archaeology 4:407–14.

Gardner, W.M.
1983 Stop me if you've heard this one before: the Flint Run Paleoindian complex. Archaeology of Eastern North America 11:49–64.

Gardner, W., and R. Verrey
1979 Typology and chronology of fluted points from the Flint Run area. Pennsylvania Archaeologist 49:13–46.

Gifford-Gonzalez, D., D. Damrosch, D. Damrosch, J. Pryor, and R. Thunen
1985 The third dimension in site structure: an experiment in trampling and vertical dispersal. American Antiquity 50:803–18.

Gilliam, J., R. Knapp, and R. Bogue
1967 A post-Wisconsin pollen sequence from Vestaburg Bog. Montcalm County, Michigan. Papers of the Michigan Academy of Science, Arts and Letters 52:3–17.

Goodyear, A.C.
1989 A hypothesis for the use of cryptocrystalline raw materials among Paleoindian groups of North America. In: Eastern Paleoindian Lithic Resource Use, C.J. Ellis and J.C. Lothrop, eds., pp.1–9. Boulder: Westview.
1993 Toolkit entropy and bipolar reduction: a study of interassemblage lithic variability among Paleo-Indian sites in the northeastern United States. North American Archaeologist 14:1–23.

Gould, R.A.
1978 The anthropology of residues. American Anthropologist 80:815–35.

Gould, R.A., D. Koster, and H.Sontz
1971 The lithic assemblage of the Western Desert aborigines. American Antiquity 36:149–69.

Graham, R., and E. Lundelius
1984 Coevolutionary disequilibrium and Pleistocene extinctions. In: Quaternary Extinctions: A Prehistoric Revolution, P. Martin and R. Klein, eds., pp. 223–49. Tucson: University of Arizona.

Gramly, R.M.
1982 The Vail site: a Palaeo-Indian encampment in Maine. Bulletin of the Buffalo Society of Natural Sciences, 30.

Gramly, R.M., and J. Lothrop
1982 Pièces esquillées from the Vail site. Archaeology of Eastern North America 10:1–22.

Gramly, R.M., and G. Summers
1986 Nobles Pond: a fluted point site in northeastern Ohio. Midcontinental Journal of Archaeology 11:97–123.

Green, F.E.
1963 The Clovis blades: an important addition to the Llano Complex. American Antiquity 29:145–65.

Greiser, S.T.
1977 Micro-analysis of wear-patterns on projectile points and knives from the Jurgens site, Kersey, Colorado. Plains Anthropologist 22:107–17.

Grimes, J.R.
1979 A new look at Bull Brook. Anthropology 3:109–30.

Grimes, J., W. Eldridge, B. Grimes, A. Vaccaro, J. Vaccaro, N. Vaccaro, and A. Orsini
1984 Bull Brook II. Archaeology of Eastern North America 12:159–83.

Grimes, J.R., and B.G. Grimes
1985 Flakeshavers: morphometric, functional and life-cycle analyses of a Paleoindian unifacial tool class. Archaeology of Eastern North America 13:35–57.

Gronnow, B, M. Meldgaard, and J.B. Nielsen
1983 Aasivissiut--The Great Summer Camp: Archaeological, Ethnographical and Zoo-Archaeological Studies of a Caribou-Hunting Site in West Greenland. Meddelelser on Greenland, Man and Society, 5. Copenhagen.

Hammatt, H.H.
1970 A Paleo-Indian butchering kit. American Antiquity 35:141–52.

Hart, J.A.
1978 From subsistence to market: a case study of the Mbuti net hunters. Human Ecology 6:325–53.

Hayden, B.
1978 Stone tool functions in the Western Desert. In: Stone Tools as Cultural Markers: Change, Evolution and Complexity, R. Wright, ed., pp. 178–88. Atlantic Highlands, N.J.: Humanities.
1979 Snap, shatter and superfractures: use-wear of stone skin scrapers. In: Lithic Use-Wear Analysis, B. Hayden, ed., pp. 207–29. New York: Academic.
1980 Confusion in the bipolar world: bashed pebbles and splintered pieces. Lithic Technology 9:2–7.
1982 Interaction parameters and the demise of Paleo-Indian craftmanship. Plains Anthropologist 27:109–23.
1986 Use and misuse: the analysis of endscrapers. Lithic Technology 15:65–70.

Haynes, C.V., D. Donahue, A. Hull, and T. Zabel
1984 Application of accelerator dating to fluted point Paleoindian sites. Archaeology of Eastern North America 12:184–91.

Headland, T., and L. Reid
1989 Hunter-gatherers and their neighbors from prehistory to the present. Current Anthropology 30:43–66.

Henry, D., C. Haynes, and B. Bradley
1976 Quantitative variations in flaked stone debitage. Plains Anthropologist 21:57–61.

Hester, J.J.
1972 Blackwater Locality No. 1: A Stratified Early Man Site in Eastern New Mexico. Fort Burgwin Research Center, Southern Methodist University.

Hester, J.J., and J. Grady
1977 Paleo-Indian social patterns on the Llano Estacado. The Museum Journal 17:78–96.

Holman, J., D. Fisher, and R. Kapp
1985 Recent discoveries of fossil vertebrates in the Lower Peninsula of Michigan. Paper presented at the Annual Meeting of the Michigan Academy of Science, Arts and Letters. Big Rapids.

Hough, J.L.
1958 Geology of the Great Lakes. Urbana: University of Illinois.

Hull, K.
1987 Identification of cultural site formation processes through microdebitage analysis. American Antiquity 52:772–83.

Ingold, T.
1980 Hunters, Pastoralists and Ranchers: Reindeer Economies and Their Transformations. Cambridge: Cambridge University Press.

Irwin, H.T., and H.M. Wormington
1970 Paleo-Indian tool types in the Great Plains. American Antiquity 35:24–34.

Jackson, L.J.
1983 Geochronology and settlement disposition in the Early Paleo-Indian occupations of southern Ontario, Canada. Quaternary Research 19:388–99.

Jackson, L.J., and H. McKillop
1991 Approaches to Palaeo-Indian economy: an Ontario and Great Lakes perspective. Midcontinental Journal of Archaeology 16:34–68.

Jacobson, G.L., T. Webb, and E.C. Grimm
1987 Patterns and rates of vegetarian change during the deglaciation of Eastern North America. In: North America and Adjacent Oceans During the Last Deglaciation, W.F. Ruddimain and H.E. Wright, eds., pp. 277–88. Geological Society of America. Boulder, Colorado.

Janes, R.R.
1983 Archaeologieal Ethnography among Mackenzie Basin, Dene, Canada. Arctic Institute of North America Technical Paper, 28. University of Calgary.

Jochim, M.A.
1979 Postglacial adaptations. In: Proceedings of the Conference on Northeastern Archaeology, pp. 49–79. Department of Anthropology Research Report, 19. University of Massachusetts. Amherst.

Judge, W.J.
1973 Paleoindian Occupation of the Central Rio Grande Valley in New Mexico. Albuquerque, New Mexico.

Kamminga, J.
1982 Over the Edge: Functional Analysis of Australian Stone Tools. Occasional Papers in Anthropology, 12. University of Queensland. St. Lucia, Australia.

Kapp, R.O.
1977 Late Pleistocene and postglacial plant communities of the Great Lakes region. In: Geobotany, R. Romans, ed., pp. 1–26. New York: Plenum.

Karrow, P., T. Anderson, A. Clarke, L. Delorme, and M. Sreenivasa
1975 Stratigraphy, paleontology and age of Lake Algonquin sediments in southwestern Ontario, Canada. Quaternary Research 5:49–87.

Kaszycki, C.
1985 History of glacial lake Algonquin in the Haliburton region, south central Ontario. In: Quaternary Evolution of the Great Lakes, P. Karrow and P. Calkin, eds., pp. 109–23. Geological Association of Canada Special Paper, 30.

Keeley, L.H.
1980 Experimental Determination of Stone Tool Uses: A Microwear Analysis. University of Chicago.
1982 Hafting and retooling: effects on the archaeological record. American Antiquity 40:798–809.

Kerfoot, C.W.
1974 Net accumulation rates and the history of cladoceran communities. Ecology 55:51–61.

Kintigh, K., and A. Ammerman
1982 Heuristic approaches to spatial analysis in archaeology. American Antiquity 47:31–63.

Knudson, R.A.
1983 Organizational Variability in Late Paleo-Indian Assemblages. Washington State University, Laboratory of Anthropology, Report of Investigation, 60. Pullman.

Kopper, J., R. Funk, and L. Dumont
1980 Additional Paleo-Indian and Archaic materials from the Dutchess Quarry Cave area, Orange County, New York. Archaeology of Eastern North America 8:125–37.

Kraft, H.C.
1973 The Plenge site: a Paleo-Indian occupation site in New Jersey. Archaeology of Eastern North America 1:56-117.

Krakker, J., M. Shott, D. Taggart, and P. Welch
1982 Report of Phase I Archaeological Investigation of US-23 in Arenac County, Michigan. Unpublished report on file, University of Michigan Museum of Anthropology. Ann Arbor.

Lahren, L., and R. Bonnichsen
1974 Bone foreshafts from a Clovis burial in southwestern Montana. Science 186:147–50.

Lane, A.C.
1900 Geological report on Huron County, Michigan. Geological Survey of Michigan 7(2):1–329.

Larsen, C.E.
1985 Geoarchaeological interpretations of Great Lakes coastal environments. In: Archaeological Sediments in Context, J. Stein and W. Farrand, eds., pp.91–110. Institute for Quarternary Studies. Orono.

Leacock, E.
1954 The Montagnais Hunting Territory and the Fur Trade. American Anthropological Association. Washington, D.C.
1982 Relations of production in band society. In: Politics and History in Band Societies, E. Leacock and R. Lee, eds., pp. 159–70. Cambridge: Cambridge University Press.

Lee, R.B.
1979 The !Kung San: Men, Women, and Work in a Foraging Society. Cambridge: Cambridge University Press.

Lewarch, D., and M. O'Brien
1981 Effects of short term tillage on aggregate provenience surface pattern. In: Plowzone Archaeology: Contributions to Theory and Technique, M. O'Brien and D. Lewarch, eds., pp. 7–49.

Vanderbilt University Publications in Anthropology, 27. Nashville.

Lieth, H.
1975 Modeling the primary productivity of the world. In: Primary Productivity of the Biosphere, H. Lieth and R. Whittaker, eds., pp.237–64. New York: Springer-Verlag.
1975 Primary production of the major vegetation units of the world. In: Primary Productivity of the Biosphere, H. Lieth and R.H. Whittaker, eds., pp. 203–15. New York: Springer-Verlag.

Lothrop, J.
1986 Activity structure on northeastern Paleo-Indian habitation sites. Paper delivered at the 52nd Annual Meeting of the Society for American Archaeology. New Orleans.
1988 The Organization of Paleoindian Lithic Technology at the Potts Site. Unpublished Ph.D. dissertation, State University of New York-Binghamton.

Luedtke, B.E.
1976 Lithic Material Distributions and Interaction Patterns during the Late Woodland Period in Michigan. Unpublished Ph.D. dissertation, University of Michigan. Ann Arbor.

Luke, J.T., and S. Beld
1977 The Steere Collection and a Preliminary Report on the Steere Site, 20ML27, Montcalm County, Michigan. Unpublished ms. on file, Michigan Bureau of History. Lansing.

MacDonald, G.F.
1968 Debert: A Paleo-Indian Site in Central Nova Scotia. National Museums of Canada, Anthropological Papers, 16. Ottawa.

Magne, M., and D. Pokotylo
1981 A pilot study in bifacial lithic reduction sequences. Lithic Technology 10:34–47.

Mallouf, R.J.
1982 An analysis of plow-damaged chert artifacts: the Brookeen Creek cache (41HI86), Hill County, Texas. Journal of Field Archaeology 9:79–98.

Manny, B., R. Wetzel, and R. Bailey
1978 Paleolimnological sedimentation of organic carbon, nitrogen, fossil pigments, pollen, and diatoms in a hypereutrophic, hardwater lake: a case history of eutrophication. Polskie Archiwum Hydrobiologii 25:243-67.

Mansur-Franchomme, M.
1987 Outils ethnographiques de Patagonie: Emmanchement et traces d'utilisation. In: La Main et L'Outil: Manches et Emmanchements Prehistoriques, D. Stordeur, ed., pp. 297–307. Paris: CNRS.

Marshall, S.B.
1985 Paleoindian artifact form and function at Shawnee Minisink. In: Shawnee Minisink: A Stratified Paleoindian-Archaic Site in the Upper Delaware Valley of Pennsylvania, C. McNett, ed., pp. 165–209. New York: Academic Press.

Martin, H.M.
1936 The Centennial Geological Map of the Southern Peninsula of Michigan. Department of Conservation. Lansing.

Mason, R.J.
1958 Late Pleistocene Geochronology and the Paleo-Indian Penetration into the Lower Michigan Peninsula. Anthropolological Papers, University of Michigan Museum of Anthropology, 11. Ann Arbor.
1962 The Paleo-Indian tradition in eastern North America. Current Anthropology 3:227–78.
1981 Great Lakes Archaeology. New York: Academic.

Mason, R.J., and C. Irwin
1960 An Eden-Scottsbluff burial in northeastern Wisconsin. American Antiquity 26:43–57.

McDonald, J.
1984 The reordered North American selection regime and Late Quaternary megafaunal extinctions. In: Quaternary Extinctions: A Prehistoric Revolution, P. Martin and R. Klein, eds., pp. 404–39. Tucson: University of Arizona Press.

McNett, C., B. McMillan, and S. Marshall
1977 The Shawnee-Minisink site. Annals of the New York Academy of Science 288:282–96.

Meltzer, D.J.
1985 On stone procurement and settlement mobility in eastern fluted point groups. North American Archaeologist 6:1-24.

Miller, P.A.
1980 Archaic lithics from the Coffey Site. University of Kansas Publications in Anthropology 12:107–11.

Moeller, R.W.
1980 6LF21: A Paleo-Indian Site in Western Connecticut. American Indian Archaeological Institute Occasional Paper, 2. Washington, Ct.

Morris, E.A., and R.C. Blakeslee
1987 Comment on the Paleoindian occurrence of spurred end scrapers as reported by Rogers. American Antiquity 52:830–31.

Morse, D.F.
1971 The Hawkins cache: a significant Dalton find in northeast Arkansas. Arkansas Archaeologist 12:9–20.

Mott, R., and L. Farley-Gill
1978 A Late-Quarternary pollen profile from Woodstock, Ontario. Canadian Journal of Earth Sciences 15:1101-11.

Munson, P.
1991 Early Paleoindian settlement of the Grand Prairie. Paper delivered at the 56th Annual Meeting of the Society for American Archaeology. New Orleans.

Murdoch, J.
1892 Ethnological Results of the Point Barrow Expedition. Bureau of American Ethnology, Annual Report, 9. Smithsonian Institution. Washington, D.C.

Murray, P.
1980 Discard location: the ethnographic data. American Antiquity 45:490–502.

Naze, B.
1986 The Folsom occupation of Middle Park, Colorado. Southwestern Lore 52(4):1–32.

Nissen, K., and M. Dittemore
1974 Ethnographic data and wear pattern analysis: a study of socketed Eskimo scrapers. Tebiwa 17:67–88.

Norusis, Marija. J.
1985 SPSSX Advanced Statistics Guide. New York: McGraw Hill.

O'Connell, J.
1987 Alyawara site structure and its archaeological implications. American Antiquity 52:74–108.

Odell, G.H.
1981 The morphological express at function junction: searching for meaning in lithic tool types. Journal of Anthropological Research 37:319–42.

Odell, G.H., and F. Cowan
1987 Estimating tillage effects on artifact distributions. American Antiquity 52:456–84.

Osgood, C.
1940 Ingalik Material Culture. Yale University Publications in Anthropology, 22. New Haven.

Oswalt, W.
1976 An Anthropological Analysis of Food-Getting Technology. New York: Wiley and Sons.

Ozker, D.B.
1982 An Early Woodland Community at the Schultz Site 20SA2 in the Saginaw Valley and the Nature of the Early Woodland Adaptation in the Great Lakes Region. University of Michigan Museum of Anthropology, Anthropological Paper, 70. Ann Arbor.

Palmer, H., and J.B. Stoltman
1976 The Boaz mastodon: a possible association of man and mastodon in Wisconsin. Midcontinental Journal of Archaeology 1:163–77.

Parry, W.
1987 Chipped Stone Tools in Formative Oaxaca, Mexico: Their Procurement, Production and Use. University of Michigan Museum of Anthropology, Memoir 20. Ann Arbor.

Payne, J.H.
1987 Windy City (154–16): A Paleoindian Lithic Workshop in Northern Maine. Unpublished M.A. thesis, University of Maine. Orono.

Peebles, C.S., and M. Shott
1981 The distribution and abundance of archaeological sites in the River Raisin Watershed, Michigan. Paper delivered at the 46th Annual Meeting of the Society for American Archaeology. San Diego.

Peru, D.V.
1965 The distribution of fluted points in the counties of Kent and Allegan, Michigan. Michigan Archaeologist 11:1–8.
1967 The distribution of fluted points in Cass County, Michigan. Michigan Archaeologist 13:137–46.

Plog, S., and J. Hantman
1990 Chronology construction and the study of prehistoric culture change. Journal of Field Archaeology 17:439-56.

Pregitzer, K.E.
1978 Soil Survey of Clinton County, Michigan. U.S. Department of Agriculture, Soil Conservation Service. Washington, D.C.

Price, T.D., and J.A. Brown
1985 Prehistoric Hunter-Gatherers: The Emergence of Cultural Complexity. New York: Academic.

Prufer, O.H., and N. Wright
1970 The Welling site (33 CO-2): a fluted point workshop in Coshocton County, Ohio. Ohio Archaeologist 20:259-68.

Purdy, B.A.
1975 Fractures for the archaeologist. In: Lithic Technology: Making and Using Stone Tools, E. Swanson, ed., pp. 133–41. The Hague: Mouton.

Quimby, G.I.
1958 Fluted points and geochronology of the Lake Michigan Basin. American Antiquity 23:247–54.

Raab, M., R. Cande, and D. Stahle
1979 Debitage graphs and Archaic settlement patterns in the Arkansas Ozarks. Midcontinental Journal of Archaeology 4:167–82.

Redman, C.L.
1974 Archaeological Sampling Strategies. Addison-Wesley Modules in Anthropology.

Ritchie, W.A., and R.E. Funk
1973 Aboriginal Settlement Patterns in New York State. New York State Museum, Memoir 20. Albany.

Ritzenhaler, R.
1967 A cache of Paleo-Indian gravers from the Kouba site. Wisconsin Archaeologist 48:261–62.

Roberts, A.
1984 Paleo-Indian on the north shore of Lake Ontario. Archaeology of Eastern North America 12:248–65.

Roberts, F.H.
1939 The Folsom problem in American archaeology. Smithsonian Institution Annual Report, 1938, pp. 531–46.

Rogers, R.A.
1986 Spurred end scrapers as diagnostic Paleoindian artifacts: a distributional analysis on stream terraces. American Antiquity 51:338–41.

Roosa, W.B.
1965 Some Great Lakes fluted point types. Michigan Archaeologist 11:85–88.
1977a Great Lakes Paleoindian: the Parkhill site, Ontario. Annals of the New York Academy of Science 288:349–54.
1977b Fluted points from the Parkhill, Ontario site. In: For the Director: Research Essays in Honor of James B. Griffin, C. Cleland, ed., pp. 87–122. Anthropological Papers, University of Michigan Museum of Anthropology, 61. Ann Arbor.

Roosa, W.B., and D.B. Deller
1982 The Parkhill Complex and eastern Great Lakes Paleo Indian. Ontario Archaeology 37:3–15.

Root, D.
1980 Tracking the archaeological record: interpretations of the Archaic periods in southern New England. Paper presented at the 45th Annual Meeting of the Society for American Archaeology. Philadelphia.
1983 Information exchange and the spatial configuration of egalitarian systems. In: Archaeological Hammers and Theories, J. Moore and A. Keene, eds. New York: Academic.

Roper, D.C.
1976 Lateral displacement of artifacts due to plowing. American Antiquity 41:372–75.

Rule, P., and J. Evans
1985 The relationship of morphological variation to hafting techniques among Paleoindian endscrapers at the Shawnee Minisink site. In: Shawnee Minisink: A Stratified Paleoindian-Archaic Site in the Upper Delaware Valley of Pennsylvania, C. McNett, ed., pp. 211–20. New York: Academic.

Sanders, T.
1983 The Manufacturing of Chipped Stone Tools at a Paleo-Indian Site in Western Kentucky. Unpublished M.A. Thesis, University of Kentucky. Lexington.

Savage, H.
1981 Post-glacial caribou in southern Ontario. Paper presented at the 8th Annual Meeting of the Ontario Archaeological Society. Midland.

Schiffer, M.B.
1975 The effects of occupation span on site content. In: The Cache River Project, M. Schiffer and J. House, eds., pp. 265–69. Arkansas Archaeological Survey. Fayetteville.
1976 Behavioral Archaeology . New York: Academic.

Schiffer, M.B., and J.M. Skibo
1987 Theory and experiment in the study of technological change. Current Anthropology 28:595–622.

Seeman, M.F.
1984 Craft specialization and tool kit structure: a systematic perspective on the midcontinental flint knapper. In: Lithic Resource Procurement: Proceedings from the Second Conference on Prehistoric Chert Exploitations, S. Vehik, ed., pp.7–36. Center for Archaeological Investigation. Carbondale, Illinois.
1991 Inter-cluster lithic patterning at Nobles Pond: a case for "disembedded" procurement among early Paleo-Indian societies. Paper delivered at the 56th Annual Meeting of the Society for American Archaeology. New Orleans.

Semonov, S. A.
1970 The forms and functions of the oldest tools. Quartar 21:1–20.

Shoshani, J., H. Wright, and A. Pilling
1990 Ecological context of two Early Archaic projectile points from Michigan: a LeCroy and a Kessel point recovered at 20OK394. Michigan Archaeologist 36:1-20.

Shott, M.J.
1986a Settlement Mobility and Technological Organization among Great Lakes Paleo-Indian Foragers. Unpublished Ph.D. dissertation, University of Michigan. Ann Arbor.
1986b Forager mobility and technological organization: an ethnographic examination. Journal of Anthropological Research 42:15–51.
1989a On tool class use-lives and the formation of archaeological assemblages. American Antiquity 54:9-30.
1989b Diversity, organization and behavior in the material record: ethnographic and archaeological examples. Current Anthropology 30:283–315.
1989c Bipolar industries: ethnographic evidence and archaeological implications. North American Archaeologist 10:1–24.
1989d Technological organization in Great Lakes Paleo-Indian assemblages. In: Eastern Paleoindian Lithic Resource Use, C.Ellis and J.Lothrop, eds., pp. 221–37. Boulder: Westview.
1990 Stone tools and economics: Great Lakes Paleoindian examples. In: Early Paleoindian Economies of Eastern North America, B. Isaac and K.Tankersley, eds., pp. 3–43. Research in Economic Anthropology, Supplement 5. Greenwich, Ct.: JAI Press.
n.d. Spears and Arrows: Late Woodland Hunting Techniques and Economic Trends in the Upper Ohio Valley. Unpublished ms. on file, Department of Sociology and Anthropology, University of Northern Iowa. Cedar Falls.

Shott, M.J., and H.T. Wright
in press The Paleo-Indian Period. In: Retrieving Michigan's Buried Past: Prehistoric and Historic Archaeology of the Great Lakes State, J. Halsey, ed. Cranbrook Institute of Science. Bloomfield Hills, Michigan.

Shott, M., and P. Welch
1984 Archaeological resources of the Thumb area of Michigan. Michigan Archaeologist 30:1–79.

Siegel, P.E.
1984 Functional variability within an assemblage of endscrapers. Lithic Technology 13:35–51.
1985 Edge angle as a functional indicator: a test. Lithic Technology 14:90–94.

Siegel, S.
1956 Nonparametric Statistics for the Behavioral Sciences. New York: McGraw-Hill.

Simons, D., M. Shott, and H. Wright
1984a The Gainey site: variability in a Great Lakes Paleo-Indian assemblage. Archaeology of Eastern North America 12:266–79.
1984b Paleoindian research in Michigan: the Gainey and Leavitt sites. Current Research in the Pleistocene 1:21–22.
1987 Paleoindian research in Michigan: current status of the Gainey and Leavitt projects. Current Research in the Pleistocene 4:27–30.

Simpson, G., A. Roe, and R. Lewontin
1960 Quantitative Zoology. New York: Harcourt, Brace.

Sokal, R.R., and P.H. Sneath
1973 Numerical Taxonomy: The Principles and Practice of Numerical Classification. San Francisco: W.H. Freeman.

Spiess, A., M. Curran, and J. Grimes
1985 Caribou (*Rangifer tarandus L.*) bones from New England Paleoindian sites. North American Archaeologist 6:145–60.

SPSS, Inc.
1986 SPSSX User's Guide. New York: McGraw Hill.

Statistical Research Laboratory
1976 Elementary Statistics Using MIDAS. University of Michigan. Ann Arbor.

Stewart, A.
1984 The Zander site: Paleo-Indian occupation of the southern Holland Marsh region of Ontario. Ontario Archaeology 41:45–79.

Storck, P.L.
1978 Some recent developments in the search for Early Man in Ontario. Ontario Archaeology 29:3–16.
1979 A report on the Banting and Hussey sites: two Paleo-Indian campsites in Simcoe County, southern Ontario. Archaeological Survey of Canada Paper, 93. National Museum of Man. Ottawa.
1981 A "behind the scenes" view of fieldwork or the coming of age of a research programme. Archaeological Newsletter, N.S. 188. Royal Ontario Museum. Toronto.
1982 Paleo-Indian settlement patterns associated with the strandline of glacial Lake Algonquin in southcentral Ontario. Canadian Journal of Archaeology 6:1–31.
1983 The Fisher site, fluting techniques, and early Paleo-Indian cultural relationships. Archaeology of Eastern North America 11:80–97.
1984 Research into the Paleo-Indian occupations of Ontario: a review. Ontario Archaeology 41:3–28.
1988 Recent excavations at the Udora site: a Gainey Clovis occupation site in southern Ontario. Current Research in the Pleistocene 5:23–24.

Storck, P.L., and P. Von Bitter
1981 The search changes direction: Ice Age man in Ontario. Rotunda 14:28–36.

Stout, W., and R. Schoenlaub
1945 The Occurrence of Flint in Ohio. Division of Geological Survey, 46. Ohio Deptartment of Natural Resources. Columbus.

Strelis, I., and R.W. Kennedy
1967 Identification of North American Commercial Pulpwoods and Pulp Fibres. Toronto: University of Toronto Press.

Sullivan, A.P., and K.C. Rozen
1985 Debitage analysis and archaeological interpretation. American Antiquity 50:755–79.

Taggart, D.W.
1981 Notes on the comparative study of fire-cracked rock. In: Report of Phase I and Phase II Archaeological Survey of the Proposed M-275 Right-of-Way in Western Oakland County, D. Ozker and D. Taggart, eds., pp. 142–52. University of Michigan Museum of Anthropology. Ann Arbor.

Tankersley, K.
1990 Late Pleistocene lithic exploitation in the Midwest and Midsouth: Indiana, Ohio and Kentucky. In: Early Paleoindian Economies of Eastern North America, K. Tankersley and B. Isaac, eds., pp. 259–99. Research in Economic Anthropology, Supplement 5. Greenwich, Ct.: JAI Press.

Thomas, D.H.
1978 Arrowheads and atlatl darts: how the stones got the shaft. American Antiquity 43:461–72.
1983 The Archaeology of Monitor Valley. Epistemology. Anthropological Papers of the American Museum of Natural History 58, Part 1.

Tunnell, C.
1977 Fluted projectile point production as revealed by lithic specimens from the Adair-Steadman site in northwest Texas. The Museum Journal 12:140–68.

Van Horn, D.
1988 Mechanized Archaeology. Calabasas, CA: Wormwood.

Verrey, R.A.
1983 Bifacial tool manufacture at the Thunderbird site irr northwestern Virginia. Paper presented at the 48th Annual Meeting of the Society for American Archaeology. Pittsburgh.

Voss, J.E.
1977 The Barnes site: functional and stylistic variability in a small Paleo-Indian assemblage. Midcontinental Journal of Archaeology 2:253–305.

Voss, J.E., and M. Shott
1981 Activity structure of Great Lakes Paleo-Indian sites. Paper delivered at the 46th Annual Meeting of the Society for American Archaeology. San Diego.

Walker, P.L.
1978 Butchering and stone tool function. American Antiquity 43:710–15.

Watt, W.A.
1973 Rates of change and stability in vegetation in the perspective

of long periods of time. In: Quarternary Plant Ecology, H.J. Birks and R.G. West, eds., pp. 195–206. New York: Wiley and Sons.

Webb, T.
1981 The past 11,000 years of vegetational change in eastern North America. Bioscience 31:501–6.

Webb, T., E. Cushing, and H.E. Wright
1983 Holocene changes in the vegetation of the Midwest. In: Late Quarternary Environments of the United States, Vol. 2, The Holocene, H.E. Wright, ed., pp. 142–65. University of Minnesota.

Wendorf, F.
1968 Site 117: a Nubian final Paleolithic graveyard near Jebel Sahaba, Sudan. In: The Prehistory of Nubia, F. Wendorf, ed., Vol. 2, pp. 954–55. Fort Burgwin Research Center Publication, 5.

Whallon, R.
1971 A Computer Program for Monothetic Subdivisive Classification in Archaeology. Technical Reports, University of Michigan Museum of Anthropology, 1. Ann Arbor.
1984 Unconstrained clustering for the analysis of spatial distributions in archaeology. In: Intrasite Spatial Analysis in Archaeology, H. Hietala, ed., pp. 242–77. Cambridge: Cambridge University Press.

Wheat, J.B.
1977 Technology, typology, and use patterns at the Jurgens site. The Museum Journal 12:126–39.

Whittaker, R.H.
1970 Communities and Ecosystems. London: MacMillan.

Wilmsen, E.N.
1968 Lithic analysis in paleoanthropology. Science 161:982-87.
1970 Lithic Analysis and Cultural Inference: A Paleo-Indian Case. University of Arizona Anthropological Papers, 16. Tucson.
1989 Land Filled with Flies: A Political Economy of the Kalahari. Chicago: University of Chicago Press.

Wilmsen, E.N., and J.R. Denbow
1990 Paradigmatic history of San-speaking peoples and current attempts at revision. Current Anthropology 31:489–524.

Wilmsen, E.N., and F. Roberts
1978 Lindenmeier, 1934–1974: Concluding Report on Investigations. Smithsonian Contributions to Anthropology, 24. Washington, D.C.

Winterhalder, B.
1977 Foraging Strategy Adaptations of the Boreal Forest Cree: An Evaluation of Theory and Models from Evolutionary Ecology. Unpublished Ph.D. dissertation, Cornell University. Ithaca, New York.
1980 Environmental analysis in human evolution and adaptation research. Human Ecology 8:135–70.

Witthoft, J.
1952 A Paleo-Indian site in eastern Pennsylvania: an early hunting culture. Proceedings of the American Philosophical Society 96:464–95.

Wobst, H.M.
1978 The archaeo-ethnology of hunter-gatherers, or the tyranny of the ethnographic record in archaeology. American Antiquity 43:303–9.
1983 Paleolithic archaeology: some problems with form, space and time. In: Hunter-Gatherer Economy in Prehistory: A European Perspective, G. Bailey, ed., pp. 220–25. Cambridge: Cambridge University Press.

Wright, H.T.
1981a Technology and economy: recent research on early hunters of the central Great Lakes. Paper presented at the Annual Meeting of the Society for American Archaeology. Eastern States Archaeological Federation. Ann Arbor.
1981b A fluted point from the Muskegon Valley. Michigan Archaeologist 27:87–91.

Wright, H.T., and W.B. Roosa
1966 The Barnes site: a fluted point assemblage from the Great Lakes region. American Antiquity 31:850–60.

Yellen, J.
1977 Archaeological Approaches to the Present: Models for Reconstructing the Past. New York: Academic.

Yesner, D.R.
1989 Moose hunters of the boreal forest? A re-examination of subsistence patterns in the western Subarctic. Arctic 42:97–108.

Yorston, R.M., V.L. Gaffney, and P.J. Reynolds
1990 Simulation of artifact movement due to cultivation. Journal of Archaeological Science 17:67–83.

Zurel, R.
1979 A Paleo-Indian site in Monroe County, Michigan. Paper presented at the Annual Meeting of the Eastern States Archaeological Foundation. Ann Arbor.